MP3!

I Didn't Know You Could Do That...™

Guy Hart-Davis ~~160101~~
Rhonda Holmes

SYBEX®

San Francisco • Paris • Düsseldorf • Soest • London

Associate Publisher: Roger Stewart
Contracts and Licensing Manager: Kristine O'Callaghan
Acquisitions & Developmental Editor: Diane Lowery
Editor: Laurie Stewart
Production Editor: Shannon Murphy
Book Designers: Franz Baumhackl and Kate Kaminski
Electronic Publishing Specialist: Maureen Forys, Happenstance Type-O-Rama
Proofreaders: Laurie O'Connell, Andrea Fox, and Laura Schattschneider
Indexer: Ted Laux
CD Technician: Ginger Warner
CD Coordinator: Kara Schwartz
Cover Designer: Daniel Ziegler
Cover Illustrator/Photographer: PhotoDisc

This book is dedicated to the people who made MP3 happen.

Acknowledgments

We'd like to thank the following people for their help with the second edition of this book:

- Gary Masters for deciding the first edition of the book was a good idea and asking us to write it—and maintaining equal enthusiasm for this edition

- Diane Lowery for developing the book

- Laurie Stewart for editing the book with patience and care and making the schedule work

- Shannon Murphy for coordinating the production of the book efficiently and good-naturedly

- Maureen Forys for typesetting the manuscript

- Laurie O'Connell, Andrea Fox, and Laura Schattschneider for proofreading the book

- Ted Laux for creating the index

- Ginger Warner for creating the CD

- Dan Mummert for rounding up the software that's on the CD

Contents

Introduction

MP3 is the coolest audio technology to hit the market in the last ten years. By packing high-quality audio into computer files small enough to store and transfer easily, MP3 has delighted tens of millions of music lovers, fueled the spread of independent artists, and annoyed major record companies into dancing with rage like toddlers suffering tantrums.

This book gets you up and running with MP3, adding you to the first of those groups—and perhaps to the second as well, but (we hope) not to the third.

What Can You Do with MP3?

With MP3, you can do the following—and much more:

◆ Play high-quality music on your computer using attractive, customizable players with full equalization capabilities

◆ Download hundreds of thousands of tracks—many of them free—from the Internet to your computer

◆ Listen to thousands of radio stations over the Internet

◆ Turn your computer into a jukebox that contains and plays only the music you like

◆ Play music on skip-proof portable players, such as the Diamond Rio, Samsung Yepp, and Sony VAIO Music Clip

◆ Create a digital jukebox in your car so that you'll never have to change CDs on mountain roads again

◆ E-mail music to your friends

◆ Record MP3 files of your own music and distribute them with minimal effort and cost

◆ Get your own music onto the Web for everyone to listen to

◆ Share your own music, and find the music you want, by using Napster

◆ Broadcast your music over the Internet from your computer

This book shows you how to do all these things. Whether you're a music lover or a musician, you'll find all the information you need to know to create and play MP3 files. You'll also learn how to get the right hardware and software to make and enjoy MP3 files.

Who Is This Book For?

This book is for anyone who has a computer and is interested in music, either as a fan or as a recording artist. MP3 is revolutionizing the music-distribution landscape in much the same way that the Web has revolution-ized the distribution of information. Here's what that means in practice:

◆ If you're a music enthusiast, MP3 provides you with not only a way of creating and managing the ultimate personalized jukebox on your computer, but also an inexhaustible source of new music to access via the Internet. And much of that music is free. Whatever your taste in music, chances are you'll find scores of Internet radio stations playing it around the clock. If there's no Internet radio sta-tion broadcasting what you like, you can even set one up yourself without much difficulty.

◆ If you're a recording artist, MP3 provides an exciting new distribution channel for your music, allowing you to bypass the bottleneck of the record companies once and for all. By using MP3, you can distribute your music over the Internet and Web within minutes of recording it, allowing you to reach current and potential listeners all over the world immediately—and get feedback from them.

What Does This Book Cover?

This book contains 11 parts that cover everything you need to know to use MP3 effectively:

MP3 Basics   This part discusses what you need to know about MP3 to get started with it. You'll learn how MP3 works, what its advantages and disadvantages are, and where digital music is heading. We show you how to get the right hardware for working with MP3. And we tell you what you need to know about MP3 and the law—because if you screw up, you can land yourself in jail and Fine City.

Find MP3 Files and Music Online   This part shows you how and where to find MP3 files online. You'll start by visiting some of the key MP3 sites on the Web and seeing what they contain. You'll then learn how to find MP3 files via newsgroups and how to search for MP3 files using search tools. Lastly, we show you how to tune into servers broadcasting music over the Internet.

Windows MP3 Players   This part shows you how to get, install, configure, and use the two leading MP3 players for Windows—Winamp and Sonique. Each of these players offers strong features to help you enjoy MP3 music, including trippy visualizations and an interface customizable with *skins* (different looks). And we'll show you how to slum it with the Windows Media Player if you're stuck using a computer on which you can't load any software.

Windows MP3 Rippers and Jukeboxes   This part describes how to work with two of the key MP3 ripper-jukeboxes for Windows—MusicMatch Jukebox and RealJukebox. You'll learn how to use the ripper features to create MP3 files and the jukebox features to store, categorize, and play them.

Mac MP3 Players and Rippers   This part shows you how to create, play, and listen to MP3 files on the Macintosh. We describe how to use the SoundApp and MACAST players to create playlists and listen to music, and how you can use QuickTime and RealPlayer to listen to MP3 files in a pinch. And finally we show you how to use SoundJam, the first full-featured ripper/player/jukebox for the Mac.

Linux MP3 Players and Rippers   This part describes how to use xmms (one of the best MP3 players for Linux, and a relative of Winamp) and Grip (a freeware ripper) to enjoy MP3 files on Linux.

Ten Cool MP3 Maneuvers   This part describes ten advanced maneuvers you'll want to try when you've gotten thoroughly into MP3. We start by showing you how to choose a default MP3 player out of the many you'll have installed by now under Windows, and how to turn Windows' annoying AutoPlay feature off (or back on, if you must). Then we discuss how to choose a CD recorder suitable for your computer and your wallet, and how to use it to create audio CDs from MP3 files and data CDs containing ten or more hours of music. We show you how to create executable MP3 files so that people too lame to have MP3 players can listen to MP3 as well. And we even show you how to enter information into the CDDB database for CDs that haven't yet been listed there.

Find and Share Music with Napster   In this part, we show you how to use the phenomenally popular—and equally controversial—Napster software to share your own MP3 files with other people and to search for the music you yourself want. Napster is popular because it lets you find and share music quickly and easily; it's controversial because some claim it encourages music piracy. This part shows you how to use Napster itself (the Windows client), Macster (c'mon, guess the platform), and Gnapster (for Linux).

Publish and SHOUTcast Your Music   In this part, you'll learn how to get MP3 files of your own music (or poetry, or whatever) onto the Web on distribution sites such as Riffage.com and MP3.com. The highlight of this part is a detailed section that shows you how to turn your PC into a SHOUTcast server and broadcast your own music over the Internet for anyone to hear.

MP3 Beyond the Computer   You *can* take it with you! This part tells you how to make the most of MP3 when you don't have your computer with you. You'll learn how to choose a portable MP3 player suitable for you; how to play MP3 files on a Palm-size PC or a hand-held PC; the different options for playing MP3 files in your car; and how to connect your PC to your stereo system so that you can rock out in style.

Top 11 MP3 Troubleshooting Tips   The title of this part says it all: We show you how to troubleshoot the top 11 problems with MP3 that people keep running into.

What You Need to Use MP3

To use MP3, you need a moderately powerful computer (PC or Macintosh) with a sound card and speakers or headphones. You'll want an Internet connection to download MP3 files and receive streamed audio from the Internet and to post MP3 files and stream audio of your own. To create MP3 files from CDs, you'll need a CD drive on your computer.

You'll also need some software, much of which this book provides on the companion CD.

What's on the CD?

The CD at the back of the book is packed with the tools you'll need to get started enjoying MP3 music, including rippers (programs for creating MP3 files), players, jukeboxes, and broadcasting software.

For details on what's on the CD, turn to the last page of the book.

Terminology and Conventions

To keep this book down to a manageable size, we've used a number of conventions to represent information concisely and accurately:

◆ The menu arrow, ➤, indicates selecting a choice from a menu or submenu. For example, "choose Edit ➤ Preferences" means that you should pull down the Edit menu and select the Preferences item from it.

◆ + signs indicate key combinations. For example, "press Ctrl+P" means that you should hold down the Ctrl key and press the P key; and "press Apple+Q" means that you should hold the Apple-symbol key and press the Q key. Likewise, "Ctrl+click" and "Shift+click" indicate that you should hold down the key involved and then click.

◆ *Italics* indicate new terms being introduced.

◆ **Boldface** indicates items that you may need to type letter for letter.

◆ Unless we're missing it, there's no really appropriate word in English for "chunk of audio." For example, a *song* is usually understood to have words, and a *track* is usually understood as meaning one piece of music (or speech) from a CD, a cassette, or one of those black-vinyl frisbees old people call "records." In the absence of a better word, we'll refer to a chunk of audio as a *track*, except where one of the applications chooses to refer to it as a *song*.

◆ While we're on the subject of words, the words *folder* and *directory* mean the same thing for Windows-based computers. We've used them interchangeably, trying to follow the terminology that the application being discussed uses.

MP3 Continues to Evolve Quickly...

You'll see the phrase *at this writing* appear frequently in this book. This book went to press in April 2000 and reflects the state of MP3 and its software at that time.

On the CD, we've put the latest versions of the players and rippers that were available when the book went to press. But it's highly likely that new versions of the software will be available by the time you read this, so you'll probably want to check the Web sites involved for new versions. The versions of the software on the CD are a great place to start, and (of course) they're the versions that the book describes. By using these descriptions, you should be able to get a good idea of how subsequent versions of the programs work; if they're not the same feature for feature, they should at least be similar in enough ways for you to figure them out easily.

Enjoy!

MP3 Basics

In this part of the book, we'll run through what you need to know about MP3. You'll learn what MP3 does, what you can do with it, and what hardware and software you'll need to take advantage of the possibilities it offers. We'll also make sure you understand the legalities of downloading, creating, and distributing MP3 files.

1 Understand What MP3 Is and What It Does

Put simply, MP3 is a highly compressed file format for storing digital audio in computer memory. MP3 takes up only a tenth of the space that was needed before to store high-quality audio. The audio can be anything from the spoken word to soothing ocean sounds to the latest speed metal. If you can hear it, you can create an MP3 version of it.

Once you've recorded an MP3 file, you can store it on a computer—a laptop, desktop, or server—and play it back whenever you want, using MP3 player software, such as the applications included on this book's CD. You can also download an MP3 file to a portable hardware MP3 player (like a digital Walkman) or a hand-held computer or a Palm-size PC and listen to it wherever you roam. In addition, you can get hardware MP3 jukeboxes, which function more like stereo components than computers, and MP3 players for your car—so with a little effort and a lot more money, you can have MP3 audio with you more or less wherever you go.

MP3 Turns Your Computer into a Jukebox

Computers have been able to record high-fidelity sound for many years now. But the resulting audio files have been far too large—from 35MB to 50MB for a typical music track of three to five minutes—to handle easily. So as recently as 1997, you could fit only a few hours of high-quality audio onto the largest hard drive the average wallet could provide, which meant that it wasn't worth using a computer to store music unless you had a compelling reason.

Many recording studios had been using computers to record, process, and enhance audio because computers let them record and manipulate the sound more easily, more accurately, and more cheaply than analog recording equipment. But once the engineers finished processing the files, they stored them on tape and then duplicated them onto noncomputer technologies—cassettes, records, and CDs—that could easily be distributed to, and played by, the target audience.

The development of the MP3 format has changed all that. Compressed as MP3 files, high-quality audio takes up much less space than it used to. And because hard drives have grown dramatically over the past few years, you can fit several months' worth of music—playing 24/7—on a single hard drive.

Using a computer to record, store, and play music has become not only feasible, but also advisable. With a little effort, you can put your entire CD collection on your computer and manage it effortlessly, turning your computer into an MP3 jukebox. From the computer, you can download MP3 tracks into your portable player or car player, burn them onto CDs, or simply pipe them to speakers strategically placed in various rooms of your house until your family or roommate has fled with their ears ringing…at which point you'll be able to crank the volume up a little further.

Why Is MP3 Such a Breakthrough?

MP3 is a major breakthrough because it retains high-quality audio while maintaining a small file size. MP3 works very well for both music and voice recordings, such as radio shows, speeches, or audio books.

Before the MP3 standard was developed, it took hours to download a single track of CD-quality audio over a modem. For example, in the early 1990s, Aerosmith broke new ground by releasing a single as a WAV file on CompuServe, which at the time was an influential online service rather than a struggling subdivision of America Online. Because the file was so huge (something like 35MB) and the highest modem speed being used then was 28.8kbps, it took the best part of four hours to download. Few people bothered to download the file; it simply wasn't worth the time or the money—in those days, CompuServe charged by the minute.

MP3 files are far more compressed than WAV or other sound files. They need only about 1MB per minute of music to retain great quality. Spoken-word audio, which typically doesn't need such high fidelity to sound okay, can fit several minutes into each megabyte of an MP3 file.

Not only have modem speeds increased, but an increasing number of people have better-than-modem access to the Internet. To start with, many homes in North America now have access to cable modems or digital subscriber lines (DSLs), which provide download speeds of several megabytes a minute—50 to 100 times faster than a modem. These high-speed connections give you the power to download an MP3-compressed song of average length in a minute or less. Some tech-heavy communities are now hooking up new residences with fiber-optic lines so fast that you'll be able to download a whole song in the time it takes to have a couple of good sneezes. Then there are the many colleges that are way ahead of those tech communities in the bandwidth stakes, with their dorms wired at blazingly fast speeds.

You can also play songs directly off the Web without downloading them to your hard drive. This can come in handy when you're sampling new music and don't want to commit drive space to music you aren't sure of. When you do find something you like, just download it, and it will be available to you until your music tastes change or your hard drive dies.

Where Did MP3 Come From?

The MP3 format gets its name from having been created under the auspices of the Motion Picture Expert's Group (MPEG for short, pronounced *em-peg*). Dr. Karlheinz Brandenburg at the Fraunhofer Institute for Integrated Circuits IIS-A in Germany developed the coding method, thus ensuring himself a listing in the digital-music hall of fame.

Why 3? MP3 is the third compression method Fraunhofer developed. As you'd imagine, the first two methods were MP1 and MP2, respectively. They offered less compression than MP3 and didn't catch on widely, though a number of people did get rather excited at the time.

How Does MP3 Work?

We mentioned that MP3 files are compressed, making them about ten times smaller than equivalent CD audio files or WAV files. Let's look quickly at how this works. We won't get too technical here, but there are a couple of points you need to understand so that you can create high-quality MP3 files that you'll enjoy listening to.

The key to the compression that MP3 uses is *sampling*. This isn't the same kind of sampling that techno artists use to achieve their musical effects—grabbing pieces of other artists' songs and inserting mutated forms of them in their own creations. As far as MP3 is concerned, sampling is the process of examining the patterns of a sound to determine its characteristics and to record it from an analog format into a digital format.

The *sampling rate* is the frequency with which the sound is examined, and the *sampling precision* (also called the *sampling resolution*) is the amount of information about the individual sample that is saved to the audio file.

NOTE   Tech moment: *Analog* is continuously variable, while *digital* is binary with two positions only—on or off. To create a digital version of an analog sound, you examine it at a sampling rate and a sampling precision and digitize the resulting data points. The higher the sampling rate and the sampling precision, the more accurate the sound is, the more data has to be stored, and the bigger the file is.

CDs sample audio at a sampling rate of 44.1 kilohertz (kHz)—44,100 times a second—with a sampling precision of 16 bits (2 bytes) per sample. This high sampling rate is considered perfect as far as the human ear goes—the sampling is frequent enough, and the sampling precision stores enough information about the sound, that the human ear can't detect anything missing.

Is CD-quality audio perfect? Not really, but it's more than good enough for most people. If you look around hard enough, you can find a few people who claim to hear defects in CD-quality sound. Such people can probably hear dog whistles and see in the dark, too.

Scientists call the study of what people can and can't hear *psychoacoustics*. In this case, *hear* doesn't refer to the ear's capacity to pick up the sound, but rather to the brain's capacity to identify it as a separate sound. You hear many things every day that your brain filters out, and there are whole sections of the spectrum of sound that you don't hear at all. (Ask dogs and bats.) An MP3 encoder trashes the frequencies and sounds that you won't be able to hear and saves only those that you will be able to hear. When a loud sound occurs at the same time as a quieter sound around the same frequencies, the encoder keeps only the loud sound because the loud sound masks the quieter sound.

Technically, MP3 is a *lossy* method of compression—it actually removes information from the source rather than just squashing the source down to its smallest possible size. (The opposite of lossy compression is *lossless* compression.) Because it's lossy, MP3 can compress audio to different degrees: the more you compress it, the more information is removed, and the worse the result sounds.

If you've ever listened to a CD on decent equipment, you know that CD-quality audio can—and should—sound great. But if you listen to CD-quality audio on poor equipment, you'll hear the defects in every measure.

So, CD-quality audio is basically excellent or at least good enough for 99.5 percent of the population. The only problem with it is that the files it produces are huge. If you sample at 44.1kHz and 16 bits, the files will run between 9MB and 11MB a minute. Because you can get about 650MB on a regular CD, most CDs can hold up to about 74 minutes of music. (Extended-capacity CDs, new at this writing, can hold 700MB and 80 minutes—a relatively trivial increase in capacity.) Not so coincidentally, most artists these days judge 50 to 70 minutes to be a CD's worth of music. (If you're old enough to have enjoyed vinyl before it became outmoded, you'll remember that most albums in those days were more like 30 to 45 minutes long—the amount that would comfortably fit on a vinyl LP.)

CD-quality audio is fine for CDs. But when a four-minute track weighs in at a hefty 40MB, you don't want to try to transfer it over the Internet. At that kind of size, you can put a couple of tracks on a 100MB Zip disk, but not enough music to entertain you for longer than a 40-oz. soda. Ten minutes of music isn't going to get you very far. These huge file sizes are great for the record companies because they amount to de facto copy protection—the files are too big for anyone to distribute easily. But for the audio fan, something smaller is needed.

Enter MP3. Providing almost CD-quality audio together with a decent rate of compression, MP3 solves both the quality problem and the file-size problem. Recorded at a decent sampling rate (as you'll see in a bit, you can use various sampling rates when recording MP3 files), MP3 provides the high-quality sound that audiophiles demand, but with enough compression that the resulting files can easily be transferred from one computer to another and from a computer onto Palm-size PCs and dedicated hardware MP3 players.

That's the key feature of MP3—quality with portability. But wait, there's more.

In addition to the audio information stored in an MP3 file, there's also a *tag*—a container with various slots to hold key pieces of information about the MP3 files. A typical tag would contain the artist's name, the title of the song or audio item, the title of the album (if applicable), the genre, the year, and an optional comment.

Tags are great because they give you the power to sort your MP3 files by any of the pieces of information in the tags. As you'll see later in this book, most of the MP3 jukeboxes let you sort your collection of MP3 files by the information in the tags. So you can easily pull up everything in your Techno-Industrial, Nippon Pop, or Christian Metal collection.

Compare that to WAV files. WAVs have a filename and nothing else. You can sort them by filename, but you haven't a hope in hell of sorting them by genre or artist. And WAV files of a quality comparable to MP3 files are the same size as CD tracks. MP3 wins hands down.

What Can You Do with MP3?

Briefly put, you can easily create MP3 files from already-recorded music or audio (for example, from CDs) or audio you create yourself. You can save the files on your computer; play them back either on the computer or on portable players; sort them into collections or databases; and distribute them easily via the Internet (or other computer networks) or on conventional portable media, such as CDs or removable disks (Zip, Jaz, Orb, and others). In essence, you can become a music creator *and* publisher. David Geffen, move over.

What Are the Advantages of MP3?

MP3 has massive advantages over conventional methods of distributing and listening to music. (Most of these advantages apply to other audio as well—for example, poetry or other spoken-word audio—but in this section, we'll assume you're mostly interested in music.)

For the Music Lover

The advantages of MP3 are clearest for the music lover. Now you can do the following:

Bring your music with you   MP3 provides portable audio that you can play back on small players that don't skip, don't break, and are small enough to hide from view.

Store files on your electronic pal   You can store the files on computers.

Download and upload files easily   You can download or upload files without difficulty, even over a lame modem connection.

Create your own customized CDs   You can convert MP3 files to WAV format and burn them onto CDs. Better yet, if you use the MP3 format, you can fit between *100 and 200 tracks* onto one CD—up to a full night's worth of music, from seduction to regrets.

For the Artist

MP3 offers compelling advantages to artists, too. Here's what you can do:

Publish and distribute your own music over the Internet   You no longer need to find a record company prepared to spend many thousands of dollars signing, packaging, and promoting you and your music. You can simply record the music, convert some tracks to MP3 format, and post them on the Web so that people can download them instantly and listen to them.

Promote your work by releasing samples of it   You can do this in any or all of several ways, including placing MP3 files on Web sites for distribution, posting them to MP3 newsgroups, distributing them as e-mail attachments, or sharing them via Napster (which provides instant sharing of tracks by all members logged into a loose online community).

Easily release different versions of a track rather than agonizing over which version to include on an album   You can even release work in progress and have your fans vote on which direction you should pursue.

Keep control of your destiny   No record company need be involved, whether you're releasing one track every decade or a couple of albums' worth of music every year.

As you might imagine, the point about the record company is where friction starts to set in. Until the mid-1990s, record companies decided which artists would be unleashed on the public, when the music would appear, and how it would be produced, packaged, presented, and priced.

Recording and producing an album took weeks or months—even years, if you were The Human League. The album then had to be manufactured (at great expense) and distributed in quantity to radio stations and record stores, preferably accompanied by an expensive promotional campaign and Bolivian Marching Powder to persuade the DJs to play the record and the stores to carry it.

Now an artist or a band can record high-fidelity sound with an affordable computer, mix it to professional quality, and then distribute it immediately and painlessly using MP3 files. If anyone likes the music, they can pay to download further songs or buy a CD directly from you.

You can see why the record companies weren't pleased when MP3 took off.

For the Record Company

MP3 seemed to pose a severe threat to record companies by bypassing first their control of the selection and recording process and then their expensively built production and distribution systems.

But MP3 cuts both ways: If it wants to, a record company can use MP3 to promote its songs and artists to customers—just as independent artists can, only more so. By using cross-promotion and the economies of scale, a record company can reap great benefits from MP3.

Here are the basic advantages for a record company using MP3:

Reduced production and distribution costs—*way* reduced   If the record company no longer needs to manufacture a hundred thousand CDs by its great new hope, print a hundred thousand inlay cards, buy a hundred thousand jewel cases, assemble them, and truck them around the world, it will save a huge amount of money.

Simple promotion   By offering a good selection of freely downloadable MP3 files, a record company can make its Web site a major destination for music fans. They can then move on to the next advantage—direct sales.

Direct sales to customers via the Web   What could be sweeter? The record company produces the music as usual and then sells it direct via the Web to the customer. Better yet, the record company can sell dozens of different mixes of any track. (Who knew that people would pay for the Ultra Boonga-Chonka Techno remix as well as the Extended Boonga remix and the Techno remix?) As a distribution mechanism, the Web allows far greater customer choice than physical stores can. The record company can also sell CDs—regular CDs and custom-made CDs—via mail order.

Simple cross-promotion   The record company can present information about related bands to customers, offering them free tracks to try. Customers can sign up for news (via, say, e-mail newsletters) on bands they're interested in, upcoming releases, concerts, and so on.

Seeding the market with low-fi tracks   The music company can release low-fidelity MP3 files of music they want to promote and then wait for people to buy the high-fidelity versions.

The advantages of MP3 for record companies are almost enough to make you want to start a record company yourself. And with MP3, there's little to stop you.

What Are the Disadvantages of MP3?

To go with its advantages, MP3 also has several disadvantages. For most people, they're not too severe.

For the Music Lover

For the music lover, MP3 has only a few disadvantages. First of all, in most cases you have to have a computer to download, record, and play MP3 files. You can now get portable MP3 players and MP3 players for cars, but you still need a computer to get and store the files. (There *are* hardware MP3 players that resemble stereo components, but inside, they're computers.)

Second, the music quality isn't quite as high as CD quality. Most people find the music quality good enough, and for most spoken-word recordings, quality isn't an issue. You can adjust the quality of MP3 files by choosing a higher or lower sampling rate when you create them.

And third, you may receive illegal MP3 recordings unwittingly. We'll examine the legal issues in *4. Go to Jail for Distributing MP3 Files,* but you need to know from the beginning that it's illegal to distribute someone else's MP3 files without permission, and it's illegal to have illegally distributed MP3 files in your possession.

For the Artist

For the artist, the main disadvantage of MP3 is that any CDs they have released can be *ripped* (extracted and compressed) to MP3 files and distributed illegally, either directly (on CDs or other removable media) or via the Internet. Because MP3 files are digital, each copy retains the same quality of the original—unlike, say, audio tapes, for which each generation of duplication loses sound quality. In this way, an artist can lose money through piracy. Using software such as Napster, people can achieve savage levels of piracy within a period of hours.

At this writing, various artists groups, from the Recording Industry Association of America (RIAA) and downward, are working on ways to keep MP3 piracy down to a tolerable level. *Tolerable* is hard to define in this context, but you'd think a good target would be a level analogous to the level of piracy tacitly accepted when people taped LPs and duped cassettes for their friends. Suggested "solutions" range from banning the MP3 format (which, even if it were not stupid and impractical, would be ineffective) to vigorously policing Web sites and newsgroups for illegal content, which is already happening to some extent.

For the Record Company

For the record company, the main disadvantage of MP3 is the same as that for the artist: The record company can lose money through piracy of released material.

When it comes to MP3, some record companies are in a more peculiar situation than others. For example, Sony is a top record label with big-name artists, such as Celine Dion and Fiona Apple, but it's also a major manufacturer of audio equipment. Sony's hardware division spent late 1998 and most of 1999 chomping at the bit to release a killer MP3 player in the hopes of locking up the market—a market that could be even more lucrative than the Walkman market it created in the 1970s. But Sony's music side has been scared spitless that a cataclysmic showdown with MP3 hardware would leave its massive revenue stream from music limping maimed into the desert to die.

Toward the end of 1999, Sony finally released the VAIO Music Clip—externally exactly the kind of innovative MP3 player that you'd have expected to see from it about a year earlier. Longer and much thinner than most portable hardware MP3 players, the VAIO Music Clip handles MP3 and ATRAC3 formats, is SDMI compliant, and is designed to be hung on a strap around the user's neck rather than being clipped to a belt like most portable players. Unfortunately, the stringencies presumably exercised by Sony's music side have resulted in a truly grotesque software implementation that forces you to convert each MP3 file into a secure format before you can upload it to the Music Clip—a severe pain in the anatomy.

Where Is MP3 Heading?

MP4—of course. An MP4 Structured Audio format is currently under development, but it's far from mainstream deployment.

At this point, it's hard to say with any certainty what's going to happen with MP3 in the long term. The dramatic spread of MP3 has already started a tectonic shift in how music is distributed, at least among people who have computers. The three key groups involved with music—fans, artists, and record companies—can benefit greatly from MP3. Artists and record companies can also benefit from other audio-compression technologies that are less friendly to the consumer than MP3.

It should be no surprise to learn that—after a couple of years of denial—the music business and technology companies are working hard to neutralize the threats that MP3 presents to them. Initial efforts included a suit by the RIAA to prevent the release of the Diamond Rio hardware MP3 player. (It failed.) There has also been talk of trying to "ban" the MP3 format. Subsequent efforts have—more realistically—centered on securing the files so that you cannot play them at all or play them more than a few sample times without paying for them. And copying them without paying (more) is out of the question.

At this writing, several technologies have been developed for distributing music securely online, including a2b, ATRAC3, Liquid Audio, MS Audio, Mjuice, and VQF. We'll give you a short overview of each in the following sections, but first, these prefatory words of wisdom.

Reduced to the essentials, there are two problems for music formats competing with MP3. Neither problem is insurmountable, but each is huge, and together they make a formidable roadblock. They are as follows:

◆ The first problem is that, from the consumer's point of view, none of the wannabe music formats has any compelling appeal. Each format is designed for secure distribution of music, which almost invariably means that consumers (*a*) get to pay for the music, preferably through the nose and (*b*) are restricted from using the music as they want. (For example, some technologies can lock a particular track to the computer on which you first play it, so that you cannot play it on another computer without paying more. Imagine how you'd react if your portable CD player prevented you from playing a CD on your car CD player.) The only advantages the wannabe music formats can claim for the consumer are a smaller file size (which is nice, but MP3 files are already plenty portable) and better audio quality (which is even nicer, but MP3 quality is more than good enough for most people).

◆ The second problem is that MP3 has such a massive lock on the market right now—because it's free, easy to use, and delivers more than acceptable audio quality—that it's hard for any other format to build any momentum behind it.

The wannabe formats are essentially aimed at commercializing the online distribution of music (or, to put it another way, enabling commercial online distribution of music). Because MP3 has such a head start over the other formats; is widespread, if not rampant, at this time; is open to everyone; is essentially free; and is easy to use, it's likely that MP3 will remain the dominant audio-compression technology for several years.

Okay, enough general blather. Let's get into the formats.

a2b

The a2b format from AT&T stores audio in compressed and encrypted files. a2b claims better compression (2.25MB for a three-minute song) and sound quality than MP3 and has the advantage of being able to store text and art with the audio. With this feature, a track can bring with it its lyrics, its credits, a brief plea to save the whales, and a picture of the CD cover (or of a friendly whale). But these advantages are more than offset by a2b's minimal distribution so far; at this writing, a2b is more of a curiosity than a valuable way of playing digital audio.

On installation the a2b music Player creates a digital ID that's used to encrypt the music you download, but apart from that, installation is straightforward.

At this writing, a2b music Players are available for Windows (95, 98, NT 4, and 2000) and the Macintosh (PowerPC). To download a player, go to the a2b Web site (`http://www.a2bmusic.com`). The illustration below shows the a2b music Player for Windows cranking out a Love and Rockets remix.

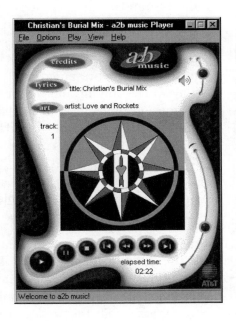

ATRAC3

ATRAC3 is a sound compression format developed by Sony for use with its OpenMG copyright-protection technology. Together, ATRAC3 and OpenMG enable secure distribution of digital music. At this writing, ATRAC3 has been implemented only in Sony hardware and software, making it a marginal player so far. ATRAC3's presence in the market may change, though, now that RealNetworks is integrating ATRAC3 into its RealJukebox ripper/player/jukebox, which will help bring ATRAC3 into the mainstream.

Liquid Audio

Liquid Audio makes a player that can play secured files and can also burn CDs. Liquid Audio has been used for several years on the Internet Underground Musical Archive (IUMA), which describes itself as "the granddaddy of all music Web sites." Liquid Audio is almost a major player in the digital music market, but it has yet to achieve truly widespread distribution. Not that it isn't trying; Liquid Audio made a splash in late 1999 by persuading Alanis Morissette to use Liquid Audio in the Internet marketing campaign for her CD *MTV Unplugged*.

Liquid Audio's player is called Liquid Player and is available for Windows and the Mac. You can download it from the Liquid Audio Web site, `http://www`
`.liquidaudio.com`, or from various MP3 software sites. Installation is straightforward, involving a tedious reboot under Windows, and you'll need to register the software before you can use it to download and play files. You can register it either for use with just one computer (limiting your use of that music to that computer) or for multiple computers; the latter requires a credit card.

The illustration below shows the Liquid Audio player for Windows grinding out a Smashing Pumpkins track. Liquid Player can also play MP3 files, so it's more flexible than some of its competition.

MS Audio

Microsoft's Windows Media Technologies 4 has a secure compression scheme called MS Audio that claims to surpass MP3 in both compression and music quality. The problem is that Microsoft has been struggling to get enough music available in the MS Audio format for consumers to start taking them seriously. Several MP3 players, including Winamp and Sonique, can play MS Audio files, as can later versions of the Windows Media Player.

Mjuice

Mjuice (http://www.mjuice.com) is a secure digital format that includes features, such as an expiration date, that allow artists and record companies to release promotional files that will expire at a suitable point. For example, an artist promoting her forthcoming CD might release Mjuice versions of several tracks online, using an expiration date that coincides with the CD's release, a tactic used recently by bands such as Third Eye Blind (or, to be more precise, their record company, Elektra). A number of MP3 players (including Winamp) and jukeboxes (including RealJukebox) can play Mjuice files, so if you get them, you'll have no problem listening to them.

VQF

The VQF format (Transform-domain Weighted Interleave Vector Quantization, if you must know) boasts better compression and higher sound quality than MP3, but almost nobody's using it at this writing. If you do decide to try VQF, you can download a Winamp plug-in to play the tracks or use the MP3 player K-jofol. For information on the VQF format, visit http://www.vqf.com.

2 Get the Right Hardware

To record and play MP3 files, you need to have a moderately powerful computer. It doesn't matter if it's a PC, a Mac, or a Unix or Linux box—even a Be box is fine. What does matter is that it needs enough horsepower to process the MP3 files and play them back without faltering.

What does *moderately powerful* mean? Well, the computer doesn't have to be the latest screamer, though the faster chips with multimedia features will rip songs faster than older chips. For example, Pentium II–, Pentium III–, Celeron-, K6-2–, and Athlon-based computers rip at a goodly speed, as do PowerPC-based Macs. A 486 won't cut it (unless you've added one of the more serious hamster-on-methedrine chip-enhancers). But if you're currently using your computer to play games involving sound and motion, and you haven't yet put a brick through your monitor in frustration at the lack of speed, you're probably in pretty good shape for playing MP3 music. If you have a CD-ROM as well, you'll also be able to rip MP3 files from CDs you own.

Let's look at the specifics of what you need in a computer to play, rip, and enjoy MP3 music.

> **N O T E**   If your computer is generally underpowered, you'll probably do better to buy a new one rather than upgrade multiple components. Because computer prices have fallen dramatically in the last two years, and continue to fall, you can now buy a reasonably full-featured PC for around $500—only a little more than it would cost to upgrade the processor, RAM, and hard drive of an older computer. Weigh your options carefully before putting any money down. Use shopbots (shopping robots) such as the Excite Shopping bot at `http://www.jango.com` to search for the lowest price available. The least you should do is cruise major online computer-hardware sites, such as **Computer Discount Warehouse** (CDW; `http://www.cdw.com`), **PC Connection** (`http://www.pcconnection.com`), and **Outpost.com** (`http://www.outpost.com`) to make sure that you're not overpaying savagely for a common piece of hardware.

The Chip: Pentium 200MMX or Better; Mac G3

For most ripping programs, you need at least a Pentium 200MMX, though for older rippers you may be able to get by with an ancient Pentium 133 (that's the "classic" Pentium without the MMX extensions). But as you'd imagine, a faster chip will give you better performance.

For playing back MP3 files, you may be able to stagger along with a Pentium 75 or so (or even a 486DX4 with a high clock speed), depending on the program you're using. Be warned that if the computer is around this level, you may hear interruptions in the audio as it struggles to keep up, and you may not be able to run other applications without interrupting playback.

For the Macintosh, you'll want a PowerPC chip—preferably a G3. 233MHz or above will give you plenty of performance.

RAM: 32MB or More (Preferably Much More)

For ripping, you need 32MB of RAM—absolute minimum. For playback, you need 16MB of RAM—absolute, absolute minimum. As with almost any program, more RAM will make rippers and players run better. At this writing, RAM is once again nearing the historic low price it reached in mid-1999 (before an earthquake in Taiwan temporarily doubled prices). An extra 32MB or 64MB of RAM is a bargain that will give your computer a decent boost in performance. If you're buying a new PC, get 128MB to start with; you won't regret it.

CD or DVD Drive

For ripping CDs, you need a CD drive or a DVD drive. Most any CD speed above 2× will work, but a modern drive (say 40× or better) will give far better performance. A SCSI drive minimizes the load on the processor, whereas ripping with an IDE drive imposes a significant load. If your chip is lame, a SCSI drive might help you out, but it'll be more expensive than an IDE drive.

The CD drive needs to support digital audio extraction in order to rip tracks digitally. (Most rippers offer an analog ripping option for CD drives that don't support digital audio extraction, but the results typically aren't as good as digital ripping.) If your CD drive isn't up to ripping, get another; it'll cost you anything from $35 and up.

WARNING DVD speeds refer to the speed at which the DVD drive works with DVDs, not with CDs, which they read at a faster rate. For example, a 6× DVD drive typically delivers more like 24× performance for CDs—enough to rip at a decent speed.

Sound Card

To produce any sound worth hearing, you need a decent sound card. All other things being equal, the better your sound card, the better the music will sound. Most rippers use the sound card, though some (such as the Linux ripper cdparanoia) grab audio directly from the CD drive. Usually, all playback uses the sound card.

Choosing a sound card is about as personal as choosing underwear. But we'll give you a few pointers to help you avoid buying the digital equivalent of nylon briefs that are one size too small:

◆ Make sure the sound card will work with your computer and operating system. If your PC doesn't have a PCI slot free, a PCI sound card won't do you much good. If you *do* have PCI slots free, you probably don't want to get an ISA sound card. ISA cards draw much more heavily on the computer's processor than PCI cards do, so go with PCI if it's an option. Many modern ATX motherboards have 16-bit Sound Blaster chips built into the motherboard, which may be enough to get you started with MP3. But if you find yourself listening to a lot of music, you'll probably want to get something better pretty soon.

◆ Choose the number of *voices*—individually mixed tracks—that you'll need the sound card to produce. You'll need at least 64 voices to make music sound good because most music is mixed with 64 separate tracks. Advanced sound cards support several hundred voices. That'll probably be overkill—until you get seriously into MP3 and want your music to sound as good as it possibly can.

◆ Make sure you have the appropriate connectors for connecting your sound card to your speakers or your stereo. You'll think this is dumb advice until you find that you don't have the right connectors. If you want to connect your PC to your stereo, you'll usually need different connectors than if you're just going to plug a pair of speakers into the sound card. If you're buying connectors, make sure they're of an appropriate quality for your sound card. There's no sense in using RadioShack's cheapest connectors with an advanced and expensive sound card because, chances are, they'll lower the quality of the output.

◆ If you're making your own music, make sure that the sound card provides the MIDI (musical instrument digital interface) connections you need.

The following list mentions some sound cards you may want to consider, with approximate prices as of this writing. But because hardware companies are constantly bringing out new models, you'll probably want to do some research on your own.

◆ The Sound Blaster Live! from Creative Labs is a PCI card that can play up to 512 voices at the same time—enough for professional-quality music playback. The Sound Blaster Live! MP3+ costs $99, comes with a bundle of MP3-oriented software, and is a good value. If you want bells and whistles, the Sound Blaster Live! Platinum costs $199 and includes a Live! Drive—a drive bay that fits into the front of your computer like a CD-ROM drive and provides input and output jacks for S/PDIF, headphones, line or microphone, and MIDI. Having the jacks right there is much handier than having them at the back of the PC, but you may not need to spend the extra money.

◆ The Sound Blaster AWE64 from Creative Labs is a 64-voice ISA card that costs about $199. It's also available in a Value Edition that costs $99.

◆ The Turtle Beach Montego II Quadzilla, which costs $79, is a 320-voice card that supports four-speaker output for quadraphonic audio. If you want digital I/O, Voyetra Turtle Beach Inc. also makes the Montego II Plus, a $149 board that provides lossless digital signal transfer and four-channel positional audio.

◆ The Diamond Monster Sound MX400 supports up to 1,024 voices and costs around $79.

WARNING Before you buy a sound card for a Linux box, make sure that drivers are available for it; otherwise its voices will be silent. A good place to start looking for information on drivers is the sound card vendor's Web site, followed by the Linux distributor's site. For example, Red Hat Software keeps a list of supported hardware on its Web site at http://www.redhat.com. At this writing, leading sound cards such as the Sound Blaster Live! and Montego II Quadzilla do not have solid Linux drivers—though the folks at Creative are working hard to deliver them for the Sound Blaster Live! sound card.

Now you need speakers (discussed in the next section) or headphones (discussed in the section after that). Alternatively you can direct the output from your computer into your stereo system and use its speakers instead; we'll discuss how to do this in *105. Connect Your PC to Your Stereo System.*

Speakers

Speakers come in a wide range of sizes, prices, and capabilities. This section discusses the key points that you need to keep in mind before opening your wallet.

Good Speakers Don't Come Free

Most PCs sold these days proudly advertise that they come with "multimedia speakers." Most of these speakers aren't worth their weight in landfill. You can listen to spoken audio or to low-fi radio through them without annoyance, but music will suffer, along with your ears and your brain. Plan to invest some money in better speakers right from the start. Anywhere from $60 to $400 will get you what you need, though you can easily spend more than that if you feel the need.

Tweeters, Woofers, and Subwoofers

Each speaker contains two or more *cones* or *drivers*. In a two-cone speaker, the *tweeter* plays the treble (high-frequency) sounds, and the *woofer* plays bass sounds. In a subwoofer system, the *subwoofer* plays the bass and very low-frequency sounds—those bass rumbles you feel reverberate in your body more than you hear in your ears. A subwoofer typically provides more bass sounds than a non-subwoofer setup and is considered a must by most gamers and many audiophiles. (Bear in mind that subwoofers have also been considered grounds for arrest, divorce, and eviction—not necessarily in that sequence.)

Passive or Amplified?

You need to choose between passive speakers—unpowered speakers—and amplified speakers. *Passive speakers* are typically used with an amplifier (which is often integrated into a receiver), as in a "normal" stereo system: The output from the CD, cassette deck, and radio goes into the amplifier, into which you plug the speakers. The amplifier runs on AC and provides the heavy-duty lifting; the speakers just reproduce the sound. When you plug passive speakers into a sound card that's designed to work with amplified speakers, you get minimal volume.

Amplified speakers, as their name suggests, contain their own amplifier or amplifiers. Usually there's one amplifier in one of the speakers, which makes it much heavier than the other one. That speaker is the one that receives the power—usually from AC because batteries won't get you far— and provides the boosting. In a subwoofer set, the subwoofer typically contains the amplifier and lives on the floor so that it doesn't break your furniture.

How Loud Are They?

Speaker volume is measured in watts, but the way manufacturers measure the wattage of speakers varies wildly. You'll see measurements in RMS watts (*root mean square* watts), which measures the wattage that the amplifier or speaker can deliver continuously rather than the wattage volume at which it maxes out. The peak wattage is sometimes referred to as *peak output* or *peak power*. The peak is basically the point beyond which the speaker blows up.

Unless you live for distortion and feedback or are the reincarnation of Jimi Hendrix, you'll seldom want to listen to music anywhere near your speakers' peak power because it'll sound horrible. But many manufacturers of, uh, less expensive speakers list the peak wattage rather than RMS wattage so that the figure looks more impressive. So if you see inexpensive speakers advertised as delivering 100 watts, be on your guard: they probably can't sustain that volume, and if they can, you won't want to listen to it. 100 watts RMS is enough to shake your house on its foundations and make the neighbors call the cops. Believe us, we *know*.

5-watt or 10-watt passive speakers may be about right for discretion in an office cubicle; amplified speakers of the same power will give the feeling of a bit more punch, even if you keep the volume turned down.

If you want to rock out, you'll need a speaker system that delivers more like 20 to 50 watts. For example, the Altec Lansing ADA880R subwoofer system ($299) delivers 40 watts RMS through its satellites and 40 watts RMS through the subwoofer, giving a total of 80 watts RMS. The Creative Labs Micro-Works subwoofer system (built by Cambridge SoundWorks), which was one of the systems we used for everything from Morphine to The Chemical Brothers while writing this book, delivers 13 watts per channel on the satellites and 45 watts on the subwoofers. This is enough to disturb the rest of the household. A nice feature of the MicroWorks system is that it accepts twin inputs, so you can hook in two computers at the same time and play them simultaneously for bizarre mixing effects when the urge strikes you.

Choose Your Poison

Different speakers are designed for different types of uses. Some speakers are specifically designed for gamers, so they're better at reproducing shotgun blasts and roars of monstrous rage than delivering delicate violin passages. Other speakers are built for rock music and others for classical music. Make sure the speakers you get are suited to your needs.

Some speakers succeed in being, if not all-purpose, at least multipurpose. For example, the MidiLand S2/4030 subwoofer set (around $200—you don't pay more for the catchy and memorable name) can comfortably both detonate the earth on *Armageddon* and deliver the details of your favorite Van Halen guitar solo. (We won't vouch for their fidelity on Chopin, though—our ears are still ringing.) The 4030s provide 30 watts. There's also a S4/4060 set that delivers 60 watts (30 from the subwoofer and 15 from each of the twin satellites).

Surround Sound and Home Theater

Surround sound uses four or five speakers to produce the effect of you being surrounded by the sound source. For example, when a car zips by in the background, you'll hear it go from left to right as you would with a normal stereo system, but you'll also hear that it's behind you rather than in front of you (or going straight through your head). Surround sound systems typically cost more than regular subwoofer systems, but if you like the effect, you may well find the expense justified.

If you have a DVD drive or a sound card that supports positional audio, you may want to consider a *home theater system*. Home theater systems typically use *5.1* setups—five satellite speakers with a powered subwoofer—to deliver realistic sound effects; some even use 7.1 setups. One example of a 5.1 setup is the DeskTop Theater 5.1 from Cambridge SoundWorks, which costs $299. DeskTop Theater is rated at 5 watts RMS to the main speakers and the surround speakers, 15 watts RMS to the center speaker, and 15 watts RMS to the subwoofer. The numbers may not seem impressive, but the sound is room filling. Other home theater systems cost upwards of $1000 and are designed to hook into your TV and stereo system—into which you can hook your PC, as we'll discuss in *105. Connect Your PC to Your Stereo System*.

Listen to Them

It's an obvious suggestion—but if you can, listen to speakers before you buy them. Many stores display demonstration sets of speakers pulling from a common control panel that delivers samples of different types of audio so that you can test-drive the speakers with rock, classical, soothing sounds, or games to see if they meet your needs.

Take along a short stack of variegated CDs or a portable MP3 player loaded with tracks that span the breadth of your listening interests, and see if you can twist the store's arm into letting you pipe your own sounds through the system. That'll give you a better lock on the speakers' suitability than the store's default Counting Crows/Indigo Girls/Engelbert Humperdinck compilation.

Known Brands

We've mentioned a couple of PC speaker brands: Altec Lansing and Creative Labs, who also distributes speakers made by Cambridge Sound-Works. Other well-known speaker brands include Bose (stunningly good, shatteringly expensive), Boston Acoustics, JBL, Yamaha, and Philips. Even Microsoft is getting in on the act, offering a speaker/subwoofer set that plugs into your computer's USB port.

Headphones

If anything, headphones are even harder to choose than speakers: One person's dream set is another person's instrument of torture. So it's hard to give specific recommendations. But we can tell you this much: Rather than buying headphones as an accessory to your stereo based largely on looks and price, you need to establish what you need in a pair of headphones and then find it.

There are several different styles of headphones:

Circumaural headphones or over-the-ear headphones   These are the headphones that completely enclose your ears. You can get either *open headphones,* which expose the back of the diaphragm to the air, providing better sound, or *sealed headphones* that look and act more like a pair of ear defenders, insulating you somewhat from outside sound. As you'd guess, sealed headphones are good for noisy environments such as music studios or busy family rooms. If you've worn them, you'll know they're heavy enough for Ah-nold to use for neck presses. If you're looking for a recommendation, we can give you a couple to try. The Beyerdynamic DT831 headphones (about $200) deliver music pure enough to fry your brains if your ears don't melt from being clamped in. The Sennheiser HD 565 Ovation headphones (about $220 street) are super-comfortable, open circumaural headphones that give a very civilized feel to all but the most raucous music while delivering exceptional punch and clarity.

Supra-aural headphones or on-the-ear headphones   These are the ones that sit on your ears. They're lighter and smaller than circumaural head-phones, so they can be more comfortable to wear, provided they don't press too hard against your ears. Like circumaural headphones, most supra-aural headphones use a headband to keep them in place, but Koss makes a style of supra-aural headphones that use ear clips (they call them "sportclips") to attach to your ears. This style frees you from a headband but makes you look like you're Spock using two old-fashioned hearing aids. A recommendation for standard supra-aurals? Check out the Grado 225s (about $200), which provide a good kick throughout rock ranges and whose leather headband snuggles sexily against your shaven skull.

Ear-bud headphones   These come in two styles: with a headband (buds that poke into your ears but don't wedge there) and without a headband (buds designed to wedge into your ear and stay there). Ear buds deliver an intense music experience but typically lower music quality and serve up less bass than circumaural or supra-aural headphones. They're considered by some to carry a higher threat of hearing damage than circumaural headphones or supra-aural headphones. No recommendation here because a good fit depends on the shape of your ears and the state of your brain—but anything real cheap is probably a bad idea. Because ear-bud headphones actually sit in your ear, you need to be especially alert for discomfort—it can indicate imminent damage.

You don't have to pay a huge amount for headphones. A $20 set of ear buds can sound great, and a $75 set of supra-aural or circumaural headphones can sound better than a $300 set of speakers. But if you want to, you can drop the best part of a grand on headphones.

When buying headphones, don't overlook mundane concerns in your quest for the perfect sound for you. First, make sure that the headphone cord is long enough for your needs so that you can bop your head to the music without yanking the player off your belt or the stereo stand. (If the cord's not long enough, get an extension.) Second, make sure the headphones come with the right kind of plug for the output jack you're planning to use. Many headphones use the ¼-inch plug that slides into the ¼-inch jacks on stereo equipment rather than the mini-plug that most portable audio items use. You may need to get a ¼-inch plug–to–mini-plug adapter. (The better headphones usually come with one.)

Big names in headphones include AKG, Beyerdynamic, Grado, Koss, and Sennheiser. (That's alphabetical order, not an order of recommendation.)

NOTE If you'll always be using headphones rather than speakers, you may want to invest in a headphone amplifier to help power your headphones. For home use, you may also want to get wireless headphones that will let you roam further from your sound source. *Try these out before you buy them.* Cheaper sets can seriously clip the top and bottom end of the frequencies, and even better sets tend to suffer in comparison to wired headphones.

As with speakers, you'll want to listen to headphones before buying them. Besides the obvious—to hear the sound quality—you should make sure they fit your ears and are comfortable enough to wear for your typical listening session.

Plenty of Storage

If you're going to store MP3 files (and we'll bet you are), you'll need plenty of storage space. Typically, this means space on your hard drive or drives, though you may also choose to use removable media as well. We'll discuss each in turn.

Hard Drive Storage

With MP3 providing roughly a 10:1 compression rate at almost CD quality, each minute of music takes up about 1MB. So a four-minute song runs around 4MB in MP3 format, and each gigabyte (GB) of disk space can store around 250 songs. At this writing, the biggest affordable hard drives are in the 40GB range and cost around $300. (The biggest *unaffordable* hard drives are in the 73GB range and cost more like $1700.) You don't even need to do the math to know that this translates to a serious boatload of songs.

All IDE-controlled motherboards can take at least two drives; many can hold four; and if you have SCSI, you can chain a small horde of devices. Consult your friendly computer store for upgrade possibilities. And if you're prepared to roll up your shirt sleeves and get your hands dirty, grab *Complete PC Upgrade and Maintenance Guide* or *PC Upgrading and Maintenance: No Experience Required*. (Both books are from Sybex; both are good; and the former is three times the size of the latter.)

Removable Media Storage

If you're all maxed out for hard disk storage space, or you need portable storage, you may want to fall back on removable media. These are the main candidates at this writing:

Zip drive Made by Iomega Corporation, Zip drives should need no introduction, as they've been around a number of years. Zip drives come in IDE, SCSI, parallel port, and USB versions. The basic Zip—the Zip Classic, if you think in marketing-speak—holds a marketer's 100MB, which translates to 95.7MB in the real world. (You'll recall that a megabyte is 1024×1024 bytes—1,048,576 bytes—rather than a million bytes clean.) The Zip 250 holds two-and-a-half times as much—250 marketing megabytes.

Jaz drive As you probably know, this is the bigger brother of the Zip, with the original Jaz holding 1GB and the Jaz 2GB packing twice that. (Again, these measurements are in millions—make that *billions*—of bytes rather than true gigabytes.)

Orb drive From Castlewood Technologies, the Orb is a 2.2GB drive—a little bigger than the Jaz and at a better price.

CD-R and CD-RW drives The media for these drives hold 650MB each (or 700MB for extended-capacity CDs).

DVD-RAM drive   Disks for these drives hold 2.3GB a side. You can get single-sided or double-sided disks; as you'd guess, double-sided are more expensive. At this writing, DVD-RAM is too expensive for most people to use as a regular storage medium—but if you've got the bucks, it sure is fast and convenient.

Lastly, if you're hurting for disk space, consider external hard drives such as those made by LaCie. Various sizes of drive are available, from parallel port to USB, SCSI, FireWire, and PC Card.

Port City

If you'll be using a portable hardware MP3 player, you'll want to make sure that your computer has the right port or ports for it.

The first generation of hardware MP3 players relied on the parallel port, whereas the second generation tends toward USB. The main advantage of the humble parallel port is that it is almost as ubiquitous as the even more humble serial port (though not quite as slow). Almost every computer built since about 1990 has a parallel port.

The main disadvantage of the parallel port (apart from its lack of speed) is that the parallel port on many computers is already in use. It's either being used for a printer (the main beneficiary of the parallel port) or for one of the several technologies that have glommed onto the parallel port as the easiest way of connecting to a computer without adding hardware and expense, such as scanners, removable drives (such as external Zip drives, CD drives, and DVD drives), the occasional bizarre network adapter, and even some cameras. If you've got a device using your parallel port, you'd do well to look for an MP3 player with a better connection.

NOTE   Some MP3 players come with pass-through ports that theoretically pass through any data intended for devices other than the MP3 player. In practice, pass-through ports make many printers and scanners unhappy. Another possibility for attaching an MP3 player via a parallel port that's already in use is to add a PCI card that provides one or more additional parallel ports.

More recent MP3 players use the USB port to provide decent speed; USB can (and should) provide much faster throughput than the parallel port. If your computer already has USB and an operating system that can handle it, you're all set; if your computer doesn't have USB but your OS is okay, you can add USB with a PCI card easily enough. It'll cost a few bucks, but the installation procedure is straightforward.

For a desktop computer, get a PCI card with two or more USB ports. Siig makes an interesting PCI card that has five USB ports, but it's hard to find at this writing. In general, you'll probably do better to get a two-port USB card and plug into it a hub that has the number of ports you require. Unless you keep your computer front and center on your desk, a hub will usually be easier to plug USB devices into than the computer itself.

What lies in the future for hardware MP3 devices? For the larger players, conventional internal hard drives are the obvious way to go, with the HanGo Personal Jukebox blazing the trail at this writing. For smaller players, CompactFlash and Memory Card technology provide convenient and flexible but painfully expensive storage; some players, such as the eGo, can even use the IBM Microdrive, which uses the CompactFlash form factor and connections but sucks power like nobody's business. For ultraportable players, internal flash memory is small, effective—and expensive. Other players use alternative storage media to store MP3 files—for example, the Sharp MD-MT15(S) uses MiniDiscs—at the cost of some severe compromises.

On the port side: FireWire connections will provide savagely fast download speeds. FireWire—or IE1394, if you go for the technical number; or iLink, if you have a Sony machine—looks to be the wave of the future, offering bandwidth almost enough to meet the dreams of Croesus.

Also in the near future is USB 2.0, which promises far higher speeds than the 12Mbps of current USB devices. USB 2.0 will provide either 400Mbps or 800Mbps, depending on whom you listen to, and will be *totally free* of all the problems that have dogged the first generation of USB. (Quick chorus of "Yeah, right!")

Will USB beat out FireWire for dominance of the next generation of local-machine connectivity, or will FireWire manage an end-around and take the prize? The contest will be academically interesting, but as a consumer, you don't have to worry too much about the result of this battle at this point. If you're one of the minority who now has FireWire available, you'll probably want to use it—at least until USB 2.0 makes its presence felt. And if you don't have FireWire, make the most of USB—it's your best bet.

Internet Connection: As Fast As Possible

Lastly, you'll want an Internet connection in order to be able to download MP3 files—and possibly to publish your own MP3 files as well.

Many books have been written about how and why to get on the Internet, so you probably know the basics. We'll confine ourselves to the key points:

- If cable modem access is available where you live, go for it. Cable provides the fastest affordable residential access—up to several megabits (millions of bits) a second—with some drawbacks, such as upload speed caps and some security concerns that you can deal with.

- If digital subscriber line (DSL) access is available and affordable where you live, get that. DSL typically offers between 384kbps and 1.5Mbps downstream (to the consumer) and slower upstream (to the ISP) speeds. At this writing, the Baby Bells are vying with the cable companies for high-speed customers, so the cost of DSL is reasonable—from $35 to $50 per month for good service, including an account with their ISP.

- If you can't get cable or a DSL, try for ISDN (Integrated Services Digital Network)—a digital line that's not as fast as a DSL but is more widely available, especially for people outside major metropolitan areas. ISDN's *basic rate interface* or *BRI* provides two bearer channels that deliver 64kbps each, plus a 16kbps signaling channel, so it delivers decent speeds when both bearer channels are open. Check the prices before you order ISDN: It's traditionally been a business service, and it can be expensive (can you say *per-minute charges*?).

- If you're too rural to get ISDN, or if ISDN is too slow for you, consider one of the satellite solutions available, such as DirecPC. Satellite solutions have one major drawback: The satellite provides only downlink capabilities, so you have to use your phone line to send data to your ISP to tell them which information to deliver by satellite. But given that your only alternative is likely to be a modem connection, you may find this flaw quite sufferable. DirecPC currently offers plans starting at $19.99 a month for a truly miserable number of hours; make sure the plan you choose provides enough hours each month so that you don't start incurring expensive extra hours every month.

- If you're stuck with modem access, try to get 56K modem access—the fastest possible. Consider getting a *dual-line modem* that bonds together two conventional modems (on two separate phone lines) to increase your speed. (A dual-line modem is also known as a *shotgun modem*, after the old-style shotguns with two barrels side by side—before the shotgun became an urban-combat weapon.) You need an ISP that supports modem bonding for this to succeed—and two phone lines, of course.

◆ Whatever speed modem you have, make sure you're getting maximum performance out of it. Use a utility such as TweakDUN (DUN is the acronym for *dial-up networking*) or MTU Speed Pro (MTU is the abbreviation for *maximum transfer unit*). Both TweakDUN and MTU Speed Pro tune your TCP/IP settings to make sure that your connection is as efficient as possible. TweakDUN and MTU Speed are shareware and are available from many shareware archives. They're not infallible, but they're worth a try.

◆ If your connection is less speedy than you'd like, get a download-scheduling utility such as GetRight from Headlight Software (`http://www.getright.com`) or AutoFTP from PrimaSoft (`http://www.primasoft.com`) that will let you line up your downloads to perform at a time when you don't need to do other things on your computer. For example, you can arrange to download a hundred megs of music at an antisocial hour in the early morning, when your corner of the Internet is likely to be less busy.

3 Get the Right Software

To record and play MP3 files, you need two different types of applications: a *ripper* to record MP3 files from existing sound sources and a *player* to play them back. As you'll see, some applications combine rippers and players.

This book's companion CD contains several of the most popular rippers and players—plenty to get you started with MP3. But because MP3 is such a fast-changing technology, you'll want to check for the latest versions of the players and rippers online. You'll probably also find newly released rippers and players that weren't available when this book went to press.

To organize your collection of MP3 files, you may want some form of jukebox software that enables you to catalog the tracks, arrange them by category, and so on. Some applications combine a jukebox with a ripper.

Some of the main MP3 players have add-on features, including plug-ins that create special audio and visual effects, and *skins* (not drums but alternative graphical interfaces for the player) that change the player's appearance.

4 Go to Jail for Distributing MP3 Files

You need to read this section. It could save your ass. We'll keep it brief.

There's a lot of confusion about what's legal and what's illegal about creating, playing, and distributing MP3 files. The truth is really very simple, but you need to know what you're doing before you start creating and distributing MP3 files.

There's nothing inherently legal or illegal in MP3. It's just a file format for compressed audio. MP3 is an ISO (International Organization for Standardization) standard, so it's not controlled by any one company in the way Microsoft controls, say, the Word document file format.

For an MP3 file to be distributed legally, the copyright holder for the music or other material in question needs to have granted permission for the music or material to be downloaded or played. The copyright holder might be the artist, their record company, or a distributor.

The Politically Correct Version

If you're downloading MP3 files from the Internet, make sure that the files you're downloading are being distributed legally. If you spend more than even a few minutes looking for MP3 files, you'll start running into pirated files.

Sites such as Riffage.com, MP3.com, and EMusic.com post only MP3 files that they have permission to distribute. Other sites, including many of those that blast you with porn banners and most all of those that use the words *pirate* and *warez*, are (how shall we put this?) less discriminating about the provenance of the files they make available for download.

The only way you'll be able to tell if a file is legal or not is from the source supplying it. You'll find plenty of files that look like someone has ripped them illegally but that are fully legal, though incompetently labeled and delivered. (Some of the worst perpetrators of badly labeled MP3 files are the garage bands who stand to benefit most immediately from MP3.)

Most people agree that you can rip MP3 copies of music (or other material) for your personal use. That's legal, much the same way recording a CD onto a cassette tape for personal use is legal. What's not legal is distributing MP3 files that you make from your CD collection, records, or whatever—or selling MP3 files created from such sources. In other words, you can't distribute or sell MP3 files without the explicit written permission of the copyright holder.

That's the theory—the politically correct version. But we'd be doing you a disservice—read: *lying*—if we pretended that legal MP3 distribution is the only thing that's going on in the real world.

The Politically Incorrect Version

So what's *really* happening? *Weeeelll,* some people are ripping everything in sight to MP3 tracks, permission or no (that'd be mostly no), and either posting them to pirate MP3 sites on the Web for the world to download or just sharing them on-the-fly via Napster. Other people are chopping MP3 files up into manageable segments that can be sewn together again easily and posting them to MP3 newsgroups on the Internet for the world to download. Other people are e-mailing MP3 files directly to one another, much to the distress of their ISPs and of AOL, whose servers don't appreciate 5MB files piling through like semis ganging the carpool lane of the New Jersey turnpike.

So—where do *you* come into this? Are you a decent, moral, upstanding citizen, or are you going to be bending the copyright laws into a pretzel the moment you pick up your mouse?

Don't answer that—but know that the penalties for copyright infringement are savage. Under the No Electronic Theft Act (NET Act for short—a nice acronym) passed in 1997, you're committing a felony when you infringe copyright by creating or distributing unauthorized copies of copyrighted work, *even if you're not doing it for commercial advantage or private financial gain*. The penalties include up to three years in jail for the first offense and six for the second—and fines, of course.

If you *are* infringing a copyright for commercial advantage or private financial gain, the penalties include up to five years in jail for the first offense. Financial gain is defined as including you receiving anything "of value" in return, specifically including other copyrighted works. So trading or swapping MP3 files is not a good idea from a legal point of view.

If you're feeling cynical, the copyright laws are a bit like the speeding laws. The highway patrol tends to tolerate most people cruising a few miles per hour above the speed limit, only pulling over vehicles that blow past them at grossly illegal speeds, weave, or whose drivers flip them the bird. They're also only looking at a tiny minority of cars on the road at any given time.

Similarly, the forces of the law seem seldom to bother swinging the heavy hammer of copyright infringement law at relatively discreet individuals. In practical terms, the copyright police expend most of their effort on the gross violators, shutting down as soon as they can such pirate MP3 sites as they find. But Jane and Joe Sixpack with their 40GB hard drive stuffed with MP3 files, some legal and some perhaps not, are unlikely to find the feds busting down their front door. (Still, it could happen.)

Morally, the situation is clear: Ripping off music is theft, and you know the seventh commandment (yeah, the one about not stealing). But because morality bends with the wind these days (ask Linda Tripp), you may be motivated more by practical concerns than morality.

The reason you shouldn't steal too much music is that if everyone steals music, nobody will be able to make a living creating it. All the artists (debate the word if you must) will be reduced to assembling Grande Meals and Big Macs for a living, and your only sources of music will be advertising jingles and such recycled '90s riffs as you can cobble together yourself.

Frightened enough to abide by most of the laws? Okay, good. Let's move into the Twilight Zone of Temptation and look at how you can find MP3 files—legal and illegal—online. Turn the page.

Find MP3 Files
and Music Online

In this part of the book, we'll discuss how and where to find MP3 files online. This being 2000, we'll assume that you're a member of Generation X or Generation Y and that you know your way around Web browsers and the Internet, but that you could use a few quick pointers. (If you're not up to speed on the Internet, try *Internet! I Didn't Know You Could Do That…*, also from Sybex and with a cover picture almost as sharp as this book's.)

As you'd imagine, you can find MP3 files on many Web sites. We'll start by pointing you to a few specific sites and indicating where you can find others. Most of these sites are based on HTTP, the hypertext transfer protocol, but some use FTP, the file transfer protocol that has long been the workhorse for transferring information over the Internet. You can access most FTP sites seamlessly from your browser; the main difference in practical terms is that instead of pretty Web pages, you'll see an ugly, minimalist interface with little more than a directory listing. Even though FTP sites have Lyle Lovett–style looks, FTP transfers tend to be as fast as speed-metal guitar solos, and they're easier for people to maintain than Web sites. So there are a lot of them around.

You'll also find MP3 files in MP3 newsgroups (not to mention a whole lot of *really* strange people). We'll show you how to do that next. We won't spend a lot of time on the newsgroups because many of the MP3 files you'll find in them are illegal—and we're *sure* you won't want any of those.

We'll then look at how you can use search engines and the MP3 Star Search utility to find specific MP3 files.

Lastly, we'll look at how to find SHOUTcast streams. SHOUTcast is a technology for broadcasting music over the Internet, enabling you to create Internet radio stations. As you'll see, you can find a good variety of SHOUTcast stations to keep the music—ambient, industro-goth, trance, whatever your local DJs haven't heard of—coming at you.

One means of finding MP3 files that we *don't* discuss in this section is Napster, the music-sharing phenomenon of the new millennium (or at least of late 1999 and the year 2000). Napster is a huge topic, so we discuss it in depth in its own section, *Find and Share Music with Napster,* later in the book.

N O T E As you'd guess, the other major source of MP3 files is creating them yourself. We'll look at how to create MP3 files in the parts of the book that discuss MP3 recording software, starting with *Windows MP3 Rippers and Jukeboxes*.

5 Find MP3 Sites on the Web

The first place to start looking for MP3 files online is on the Web. (The second is via Napster, which we discuss later in the book.) As you'll see, there are hundreds (if not thousands) of Web sites that provide MP3 files for download.

Because Web sites change so frequently, we won't fill this section with endless lists of MP3 sites. By the time you read this, they may have moved, merged, or started moldering. Instead, we'll point you to a few of the more enduring destinations (enduring so far, anyway). We'll also discuss general principles for finding MP3 files on the Web so that you'll be able to find music even if all the sites we mention have mysteriously gone under.

Before we start, one general point. You can either download MP3 files to your computer and then play them from the computer, or you can play them directly from the Web—from sites that stream them to you. Sites such as Riffage.com and MP3.com typically provide separate links for playing MP3 files from the Web and downloading them. Other sites, including FTP sites, are set up only for downloading and do not have streaming capabilities.

Playing MP3 files directly from Web sites requires a fast Internet connection—preferably a cable connection or a digital subscriber line (DSL). Playing MP3 files over a modem link delivers choppy sound and usually isn't worth doing unless you're big into recreating the AM-radio-of-the-'70s-in-the-mountains feeling.

Riffage.com

One of your first stops when looking for music on the Web should be Riffage .com (`http://www.riffage.com`), which has one of the best collections of authorized files of cutting-edge music. Riffage.com focuses not only on having a boatload of music but enabling you to find it easily. The site has both a large number of free tracks and tracks that you have to pay for.

Riffage.com lets listeners post ratings and reviews of tracks, using these to maintain an average rating for the track so that you have some idea of how popular it's proved with the people who have listened to it so far. You can also put together playlists that Riffage.com can then share with other people who appear to have similar tastes.

Riffage.com is a very full-featured site. In the next few pages, we'll get you started with it—but you'll find there are many more features for you to explore on your own.

Navigating Riffage.com

Finding artists and tracks on Riffage.com is mostly intuitive, but we'll give you a few pointers to get you started:

◆ From the Riffage.com home page (shown below), you can quickly access the main areas of Riffage.com by using the column of navigation buttons on the left. As you can see, in the middle of the page, Riffage.com presents the current featured artist; as you can't see, below that is a list of new arrivals, giving you immediate access to some of the latest music, a calendar of today's music releases, and a list of today's live events.

◆ Click the Get Music Now! link to get to the Bands & Music page, from which you can follow links to bands arranged from A to Z, songs arranged from A to Z, labels arranged from A to Z, and featured artists in each of the genres.

◆ To search for an artist or a track, enter your search terms in the Search Riffage text box, and click the Go button.

◆ Once you reach the page of a band you're interested in, you can click the Band Details button to display the Band Details page, click the Add to My Bands button to add the band to your list of bands, or investigate one of the tracks or albums that the band has available. You can then access this band from the Bands tab of your My Riffage page, which we'll discuss in a moment.

◆ To investigate the current Top 40 list for a genre, click the Top Songs link near the top of that genre's page.

Registering for Riffage.com

Before you can do anything on Riffage.com, you need to register as a user (or "open an account," as Riffage.com terms it). You might want to register right away, but we think you'll probably want to wander around Riffage.com for a little while first to see what you find. The moment you try to download something, Riffage.com will hit you with the Riffage: My Riffage Login window, shown below. (You can access this page directly by clicking the My Riffage item in the left-hand column on the Riffage.com home page.)

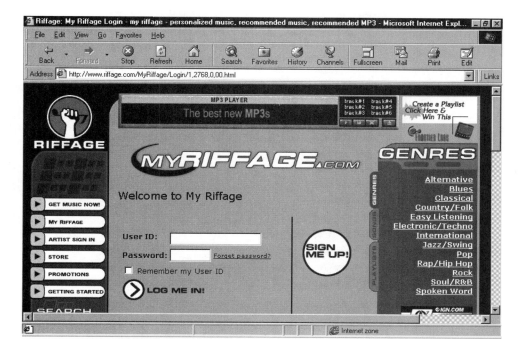

Click the Sign Me Up! link, and Riffage.com will display the MyRiffage: My Riffage Policy window, shown below.

Read through the My Riffage Agreement, which basically says that anything you post to Riffage.com becomes the property of Riffage.com and enjoins you not to swear or advertise in your reviews, on penalty of expulsion. Then click the Agree button at the bottom of the window if you can live with these terms. (Otherwise, click the Disagree button and git the hell outta town.)

You'll then see the Riffage: Register New User screen, shown below.

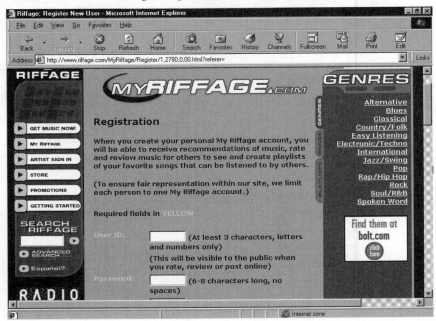

Fill in the registration information—the user ID and password you want, your name, e-mail, login name, password, a hint for the password, types of music you like, and so on—and click the Save button to save it. Registration is straightforward, but keep the following in mind:

- The Type of Connection drop-down list controls the rate at which Riffage.com tries to stream music to you when you hit a streaming link, so don't choose T1 if you only have a modem.

- You have to complete only the fields in yellow. You may want to think twice before giving out the details of your education—they're not required. And you might want to lie about your age—that field is required.

- The How Experimental Are You with Regards to Your Music Listening? an option button controls the accuracy or wildness of the recommendations that Riffage.com makes for music it thinks you might like. Selecting the Only in My Favorite Genres option button is too limiting for most people, but selecting the I Want to Hear Something New All the Time option button can produce absurd suggestions—so you might want to choose the An Even Mix of My Favorite and New Music option button.

Rating Tracks

Once you've registered, Riffage.com will drop you in your My Riffage area, with five tracks for you to rate, as shown in the first illustration on the next page, and five playlists to rate, as shown in the second illustration on the next page (further down the Web page, so you can't see them in the illustration). If you have time, go ahead and rate the tracks and playlists—doing so will help Riffage.com learn your taste in music and make solid recommendations in the future.

Click the link for a track to display the listing for the track, as shown on the next page (bottom). Click the Download It! link to download the track or the Play It! button to play the track. (To play a track at a decent quality, you'll need a fast Internet connection.)

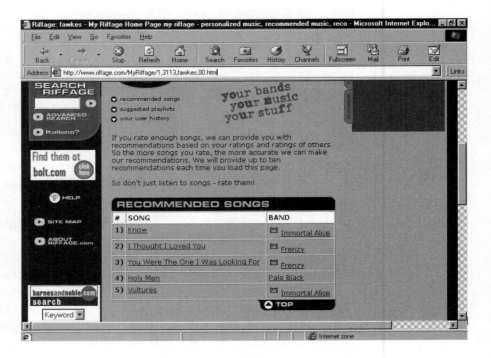

To rate the track, click the Rate/Review It! button, which you'll find lower down the page for the track. Riffage.com will open a MyRiffage: New Review window for the track, as shown below.

Select the rating for the song (from 1 - pathetic to 5 - fantastic), enter your comments in the Review area, and click the Save button. Click the OK button in the following window, and your review will be posted.

Confirming Your E-Mail Address

When you register as described above, your account is functional for only five days unless Riffage.com is able to confirm your e-mail address. If you don't perform the confirmation process, the account expires.

Here's how the process works: Riffage.com sends you an e-mail to confirm that the e-mail address you gave is correct and functional. When you receive this e-mail, click (or double-click, depending on your e-mail application) the hyperlink in it. Your e-mail application will start (or awaken) your Web browser, which will display the Riffage: My Riffage Login screen. Enter your user ID and password, select the Remember My User ID check box if you want your computer to store the ID and password, and click the Log Me In! button. This process confirms your e-mail address and makes your account permanent.

Using Riffage.com Playlists

Riffage.com lets you build playlists of music that you want to be able to access easily. To create a playlist, click the Add to My Playlist button for a track. Riffage.com will display the MyRiffage: Add Song to Play List window, shown below. Either select one of your existing playlists in the drop-down list (until you create your first playlist, this option won't be available) or enter the name for a new playlist in the Create New Play List Name text box. Then click the Save button. Riffage.com will display a window telling you that the track has been added to the playlist; click the OK button to dismiss this window.

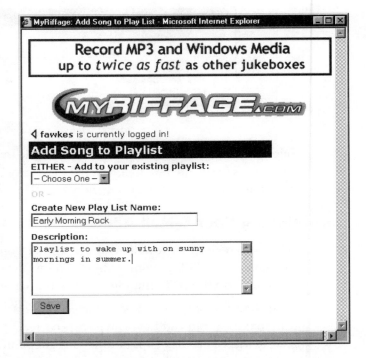

To access one of your playlists, click the Playlists tab on the right-hand side of your My Riffage page. To change one of your playlists, click the Modify My Playlists button, and use the resulting pages to work on the playlist.

Wave Goodbye and Say Hello

At the end of a Riffage.com session, click the Logout link near the top of your My Riffage page to log out.

To get back into your My Riffage area when you return to Riffage.com, click the My Riffage button on the Riffage.com home page. Make sure Riffage.com has identified you correctly on the Login page, enter your password, and click the Login button.

MP3.com

One of the granddaddies of the Web MP3 scene is MP3.com (`http://www
.mp3.com`), whose home page (shown below) contains links to its various genres of music, to the main areas of MP3.com, to stories, and to news items.

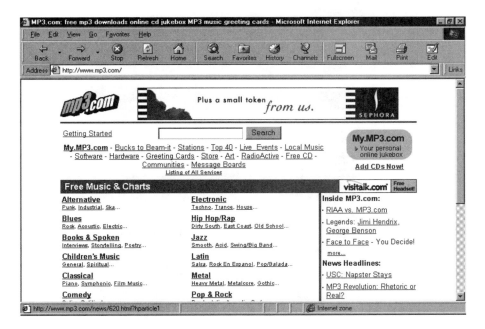

MP3.com focuses on providing access to both known and unknown artists and provides a huge number of MP3 files for free download. Most artists who supply MP3 files to MP3.com supply at least two or three tracks, and

many supply two or three tracks from each album. As a result, you may find up to 20 or more songs for some bands.

MP3.com sells CDs, both conventional ones and ones in its own DAM format. A DAM CD includes tracks in both CD-DA format (the regular format for CD tracks) and MP3 format, saving you the modest labor of ripping the tracks yourself. MP3.com sells DAM CDs off its own secure site. For sales of conventional CDs, MP3.com redirects you to online music vendors such as CDnow.com and Amazon.com.

Searching for an Artist or a Song

Once you get beyond the first page in MP3.com, pretty much every page displays a Search button and text box, as shown here:

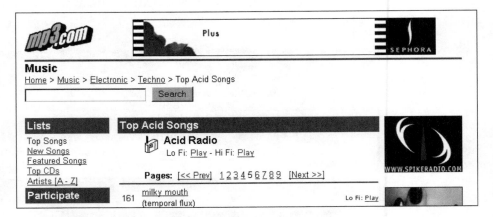

To search for an artist or a song by name, enter the name into the text box and click the Search button. The search engine will return artist, song, region, station, and similar matches. From there, click a link to jump to whichever category attracts you.

In the illustration at the top of the next page, we've searched for *dog* and found 73 artist matches, 316 song matches, 2 region matches, 25 station matches, and 113 similar matches—plenty to snoop around with.

Clicking the link for Kick The Dog takes us to the Kick The Dog page, shown below. From here, we can download a song, read information about the artist, e-mail the artist, go to the artist's Web site (if they have one), learn about CDs they have for sale, and so on.

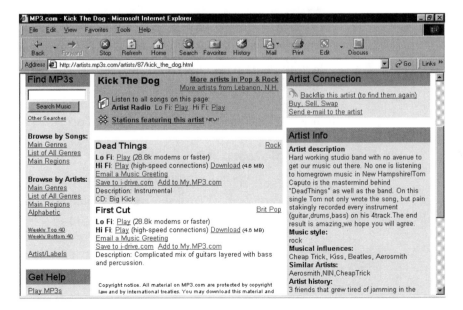

Investigating a Genre

If you're interested in a particular genre of music, follow the genre link from the home page to the genre page, the subgenre links from there to the subgenre pages, and so on. For example, if you're interested in gothic metal, follow the Metal link to get to the Metal page, and then choose the Gothic Metal link to reach the Gothic Metal page, as shown here:

From a subgenre page, you can browse any of the following lists by clicking its link in the Lists column at the left-hand side of the page: the Top Songs list (which is displayed by default), the New Songs list, the Featured Songs list, the Top CDs list, or the complete A–Z list of artists in the subgenre.

Top 40 and Bottom 40

If your tastes are eclectic, or you'd like them to be, check out MP3.com's Top 40 list for a variety of what's currently most popular. (To get to the Top 40, click the Top 40 link on the MP3.com home page.) Don't just download the Top 40—if everyone did that, it'd never change. Try following links from the Top 40 page to subgenres, artists, or bizarre track titles that grab your fancy. Doing so will often lead to spelunking through depths of MP3.com that you'd never imagined existed.

If you're feeling more adventurous, MP3.com also maintains a Bottom 40 list of what's currently least popular. Given the number of people hitting MP3.com for free music 24 hours a day, any track that ends up in the Bottom 40 is getting a serious lack of attention. But of course, if enough people check out one of the Bottom 40 tracks, it moves out of the Bottom 40. You'll find many of the tracks that appear in the Bottom 40 richly deserve their listing there, but others are undiscovered gems, so a visit may be worth your while. To get to the Bottom 40, choose the Weekly Bottom 40 link from the Top 40 page.

Creating a My.MP3.com Area

MP3.com offers a feature named My.MP3.com that lets you corral the type of music you like into one convenient virtual area. You can add to My.MP3.com tracks you find online, the contents of CDs you buy online, and the contents of CDs that you have at home.

To try My.MP3.com, click the My.MP3.com link at the upper-right corner of MP3.com's home page, and then click the Sign Up button. On the My.MP3 .com Membership Signup page, enter your e-mail address and a password, read the terms and conditions and the privacy policy, and then click the Done button. MP3.com will display your My.MP3.com area, which will look something like the illustration below (shown in Netscape Navigator for a change).

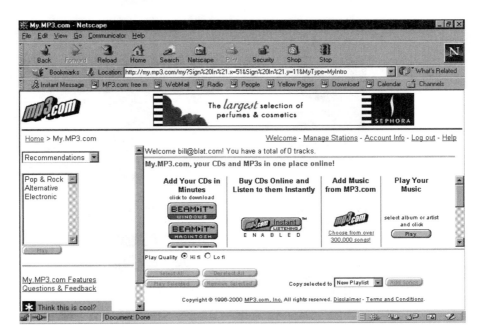

Once you're signed up, you can do the following with My.MP3.com:

◆ Store your own MP3 tracks on MP3.com quickly by using its Beam-it technology, and then access the tracks from whichever computer you happen to be using. We'll discuss Beam-it in *74. Store MP3 Files Online with MP3.com's Beam-it.*

◆ Buy CDs online and listen to them straightaway, with no waiting for delivery.

◆ Add tracks from MP3.com by clicking the Add to My.MP3.com link on any artist's page. (Clicking this link adds to your My.MP3.com a link to the track—it doesn't copy the whole track to your area.)

◆ Create playlists and play the music you've uploaded, bought, or linked to.

EMusic.com (Formerly goodnoise.com)

EMusic.com, which used to be goodnoise.com until it took its name commercial, is another great site for finding MP3 files. The illustration below shows the EMusic.com home page.

EMusic.com takes a very different approach from MP3.com and Riffage .com, selling individual MP3 files and whole albums for download. As a result, EMusic.com has more big (or at least medium-sized) names than MP3.com, but fewer artists overall and even fewer free songs. EMusic.com does have a number of bargains, though, including compilation CDs that give you a good introduction to a number of artists.

Use the Browse By Genre list on the left-hand side of the home page to navigate to the type of music you want, or use the links in the EMusic.com navigation bar at the top of the screen to access free tracks, the artist index, or the label index.

Finding the Few Free Tracks

To get to the Free Tracks area (shown below), click the Free Tracks link in the EMusic.com navigation bar. Click a link to start downloading one of the free tracks.

You'll also see free tracks listed for most artists along with the tracks for which you have to pay, as shown here. Click the Free item to download the track.

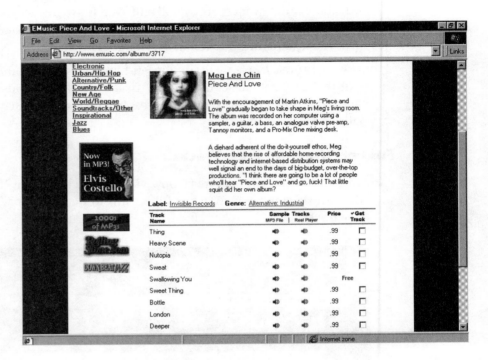

Buying Music from EMusic.com

To buy music from EMusic.com, you first need to create an account. Start by clicking the My Account link in the upper-right corner of the home page to get to the Log in to EMusic.com page. Then click the Create New Account button to display the New Personal Information form.

Fill in the resulting New Personal Information form and click the Update Our Records button to submit it. You'll then be able to click the My Account link in the upper-left corner of most EMusic.com pages to access your account, where you can enter (or remove) your credit card information and generally manage your account.

You can then add tracks to your cart by selecting the check box for the track in the album listing and then clicking the Add to Cart button.

NOTE Before you buy a track from EMusic.com, listen to any snippet available in the Sample Tracks column. For most tracks, EMusic.com provides snippets between 20 and 30 seconds long—enough to let you make sure that the track rocks and that you haven't confused hip-hop with trip-hop.

Click the Shopping Cart item in the EMusic.com navigation bar to access your cart. When you've selected all the music you'd currently like to pay for, use the Proceed to Checkout link from your shopping cart to get to the pages that surgically remove your hard-won dollars from your favorite wedge of magic plastic.

songs.com

songs.com claims the largest group of successful (note the qualifier) independent artists on the Web, with more than 350 listed at this writing. The illustration below shows the songs.com home page.

Click the mp3 link at the top of the songs.com home page to get to the MP3 section of the site, mp3.songs.com (shown below). You'll find that songs.com typically provides fewer tracks per artist for download than MP3.com, but the samples will give you an idea of each artist's music.

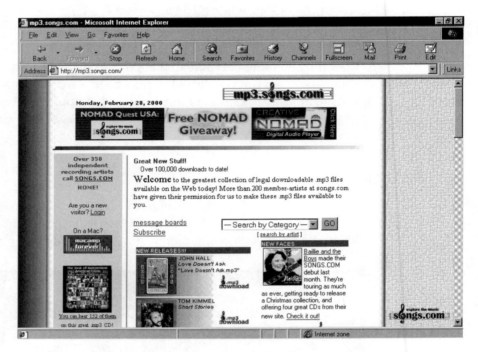

Click one of the mp3 Download buttons to display the download form for a track. On songs.com, you need to supply your e-mail address (real or otherwise) for each track you download.

Scour.net

Scour.net is a gateway site that includes an MP3 search engine and an überdirectory of downloadable music. Scour.net is a tool for finding the music you want. Most of the music is actually stored on other sites, including MP3.com, EMusic.com, songs.com, and musicmatch.com. Scour.net is great for getting an overview of what's out there for download, but if you find yourself constantly hitting the same site (say, MP3.com) when following links from Scour.net, take the hint and go straight to that site in the future.

From the Scour.net home page, click the Downloads link under the Music link on the left side of the screen to reach the search area for downloadable music. In the Search For text box, enter the name of the artist or song you're looking for, then click the Go button, as shown below. Use the resulting links to access the music.

Crunch

Crunch bills itself as "essential UK music online," which you should be able to interpret easily enough. From the Crunch home page (http://www.crunch.co.uk—*not* http://www.crunch.com, which is a fitness site), shown on the next page, you can access a wide variety of music. Most of the tracks have samples that you can play or download, but most of the full tracks you have to pay for.

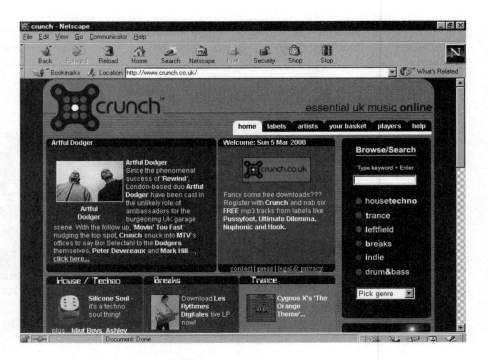

Listen.com

Listen.com is a gateway site that provides access to a wide variety of music and audio, which it sorts into categories ranging from alternative and electronica to comedy and self-help. Using Listen.com, you drill down to find the music or audio you want, and then choose a link to direct you to the site on which it is stored. For example, if you follow Listen.com's links for 10,000 Maniacs, you'll be directed to sites such as MP3.com, LAUNCH, and the Microsoft Network (MSN).

The illustration on the next page shows Listen.com's home page.

Record Company Sites

As we mentioned in *1. Understand What MP3 Is and What It Does*, the record companies are now—finally—starting to get up to speed with MP3. (Do they really have a choice?)

At this writing, a number of record companies, including big ones such as Columbia Records, offer RealAudio tracks that you can play. We expect—and hope—that even major record companies will soon offer some MP3 files for download in the hope of spreading their gospels further. These will likely be low-fi versions that let you begin to like the tracks without giving you the quality to enjoy them fully. At that point the record company hopes to hook you so that you'll plunk down the cash for a higher-fi version, perhaps in one of its preferred secure digital-music formats rather than as an MP3 file.

Still, free music can't be wholly bad, can it? Well, a few exceptions come to mind, such as that 30-minute rap on "Rawhide" by Country Nell and the Pig-Hollerers at the New Wilmington County Fair last year.

Other Sites Worth Mentioning

At this writing, there are a huge number of MP3 sites on the Web—and by the time you're reading this book, it's a safe bet that many more have sprung up. Given the rate of change, it'd be futile for us to try to list the sites for you—but here, as a start, are six other sites worth mentioning:

amp3.com (http://www.amp3.com)   This site has MP3 files from a wide variety of independent artists, categorized into genres from Alternative to Zydeco.

eatsleepmusic.com (http://www.eatsleepmusic.com)   This site provides a number of MP3 files, concentrating on alternative, dance and techno, metal and punk, rock and pop, and rap and hip-hop. eatsleepmusic.com requires you to register, after which they promise not to bug you.

The Free Music Archive (http://www.free-music.com)   This site provides a ton of free MP3 files, though little information about most of the artists. Make sure you enter the hyphen in the URL, because freemusic.com is a different site that concentrates on music in mod format.

The MP3 Place (http://www.mp3place.com)   This site specializes in alternative, techno and dance, hip-hop, and punk and ska music. If these interest you, browse the site for music that appeals to you. If not, you may still want to stop by for the news, skins, and forums it also provides.

RioPort (http://www.rioport.com)   This site provides enough MP3 files to make it worth visiting—and to make you ignore the relentless ads for the Rio MP3 player.

WorldWideBands (http://www.worldwidebands.com)   This site provides an eclectic selection of MP3 files from a wide variety of bands. You won't find bands from *every* corner of the earth, but WorldWideBands appears to be working toward that goal.

Pirate Sites

If you search for even a few seconds, you'll also find plenty of sites offering pirated MP3 files—often accompanied by *warez* (pirated software) and pornography, making up the three most sought clandestine categories on the Internet. Some pirates refer to pirated MP3 files as *MP3z*.

Should you choose to download pirated files, keep the following in the front of your skull:

It's illegal to have pirated MP3 files. The odds against the FBI conducting a house-to-house search of your neighborhood for pirated MP3 files seem high, but the penalties can be severe. (Quick—how long has that panel van been outside your place?)

Anyone supplying pirated (or ostensibly pirated) MP3 files doesn't have much respect for the law. Do you think they respect your computer—or your wallet? Be very careful what buttons you click when exploring or downloading files from these sites. In particular, *don't* run any EXE files. Use an up-to-date virus scanner to check the files you download before you try to use them, however harmless they may sound. Tiny reminder: File extensions under Windows are *not* an accurate indication of the file's contents. A file with an MP3 extension could be an executable file waiting to nuke your virtual existence off the face of the planet. And that's not all. DOC files and XLS files can contain macro viruses that'll eat your music as an entrée and chew up your hard drive if they disagree with your taste.

Watch out for any suspicious signs on your computer. If the hard drive starts thrashing unexpectedly or the processor gets stuck in overdrive when you're putting minimal demands on it, you may have a problem. If you suspect that someone is trying to access your computer—or has succeeded in doing so—drop the connection immediately. If dial-up networking is locked, disconnect the phone line from the modem. If you're using a network connection to connect to the Internet, pull the cable out of the back of the computer. Got the picture?

Escape from Pirates and Porn Sites

Because of the popularity of MP3 music, it's become an even more favored decoy of Web predators than top-name stars such as Jennifer Lopez, Ricky Martin, or Calista Flockhart. If you click on the wrong link after searching for MP3 files (or for Ricky, Jennifer, or Calista), you may find yourself caught surfing a porn site rather than an MP3 site (or star site). Caught? Yes—by using a number of HTML and scripting tricks, a Web site can effectively capture your PC: Every time you close a browser window, it automatically opens another one; and every time you give it a moment, it opens another window to tempt you with more of its wares.

The illustration below shows us in the type of site from which you may get in trouble. Here, 40best.com is offering us links to "25000 illegal MP3 downloads" and "100% illegal fast MP3 downloads." At this point, we would advise you to back out before you hit anything unpleasant.

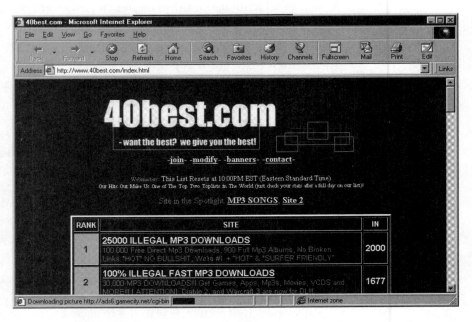

If you get caught by a porn site (or indeed any other site—anybody can do this, though in our experience nobody but porn merchants, pirates, and angry teenagers seems to think this is a good idea), these are your best shots at escape, in order of preference:

◆ Use the Alt+F4 key combination to try to kill all the browser windows. Using the keyboard like this is usually faster than trying to click the Close button on a multitude of windows of varying sizes.

◆ If you have work open in any other application, switch to it (by using the Taskbar or by Alt+Tabbing to it), save the work, and close the application. Doing so may well seem like preparation for craven surrender—but believe us, you'll regret it if you don't. Close any other applications you can, even if they're not doing anything useful.

◆ Unplug your modem line (if you're using a modem) or your network connection (if you're connecting to the Internet via a network, via a cable modem, or via a digital subscriber line). If you're using an external modem, you can just switch it off instead (or unplug its power supply if it has no on/off switch).

◆ Press Ctrl+Alt+Delete to display the Close Program dialog box (in Windows 95 or 98), the Windows NT Security dialog box (in Windows NT 4), or the Windows Security dialog box (in Windows 2000). Then:

   ◆ From the Close Program dialog box (shown below), select the offending instance of the browser and click the End Task button. Repeat as necessary. If that doesn't do the trick, click the Shut Down button to shut down your computer.

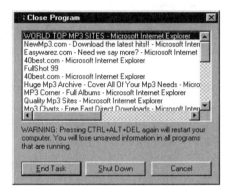

   ◆ From the Windows NT Security dialog box in Windows NT 4, or from the Windows Security dialog box in Windows 2000, click the Task Manager button to display the Task Manager dialog box. Display the Applications page if it's not already displayed, then select the offending instance of Internet Explorer in the Tasks list box, and click the End Task button. If NT or Windows 2000 displays the Ending Task dialog box, click the End Now button. Repeat until each instance of Internet Explorer controlled by the site is closed.

◆ If all else fails, press the Reboot button on your PC to reboot your computer. You may lose any configuration changes you've made in this Windows session, but if you suspect that the porn site is raiding your hard drive for information or attempting to damage it, the pain of a hard reboot pales in comparison.

NOTE   If you're desperate not to run into porn (or want to keep your children away from it), you may want to start at the Pure MP3 site (http://www .puremp3.org), which guarantees that the sites it's linked to (*a*) do not have porn themselves and (*b*) do not link to any sites that have porn.

6 Find MP3 Files via MP3 Newsgroups

Internet newsgroups provide another possible source of MP3 files, but you'll need lots of patience to get through the high levels of noise (extraneous information, cluelessness, and invective) that most newsgroups inflict on you at the same time.

Current versions of the three main browsers—Netscape Communicator, Microsoft Internet Explorer, and Opera from Opera Software—each provides a full-featured newsreader application, so chances are you already have one available to you. If not, consider getting a specialized newsreader, such as Forté's Free Agent (http://www.forteinc.com).

Here's an example of finding MP3 files via MP3 newsgroups. We'll use Internet Explorer's Outlook Express newsreader, but you can follow similar techniques with the other newsreaders.

1. Start your newsreader.

2. Display the Newsgroup Subscriptions dialog box by clicking the Newsgroups button or choosing Tools ➤ Newsgroups.

3. Enter **mp3** in the Display Newsgroups Which Contain text box in Internet Explorer.

4. Select the Also Search Descriptions check box to have Outlook Express search the descriptions of the newsgroups as well as the names. As you can see, there's a fair smorgasbord of newsgroups devoted to MP3 files.

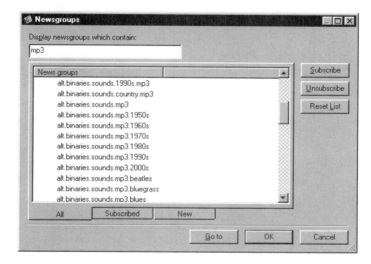

5. To subscribe to a newsgroup, you can double-click it or select it and click the Subscribe button. But first you'll probably want to examine it by selecting it and clicking the Go to button. If you find it useful, then subscribe to it.

When you visit one of the newsgroups, you'll find all sorts of files, as you see in the illustration on the next page, which shows the alt.binaries .sounds.mp3.1980s newsgroup we visited. Because we're feeling charitable and don't want to cast any nasturtiums on the participants identified here as *Regrind* and *Willem*, we'll describe these files as being of questionable legality. (Files from people named Bluebeard and Kaptain Kidd, however, should be assumed to be as clean as Dubya's conscience on death-row executions.)

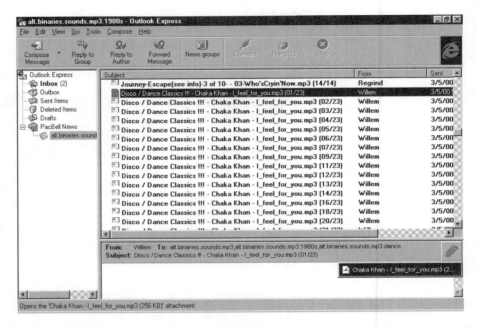

In the illustration, the first part of Chaka Khan's classic track "I Feel for You" is attached to the message. You can easily download it by clicking the Attachment button in Outlook Express.

As you can see, there are 22 other parts to the track. To get the whole thing, you'd download all 23 parts and then sew them back together with editing software. (Other posts contain the text of binary files that you need to sew together and then decode to get the MP3 file. A program like WinCode will walk you through the decoding process.) The deed done, you'd then be a miserable sinner, ripping with your bare hands at the fabric of society as we know it and helping push honest artists into penury. And, uh, if you'd used Napster, you could probably have committed twice the crime in half the time. (Napster provides a fast way of searching for MP3 files, both legal ones and pirated ones. We discuss it in detail later in the book.)

7 Search for MP3 Files

In this section, we'll look at a couple of ways to search for MP3 files on the Internet: by using a search engine, Oth.Net, and by using a meta-search utility, MP3 Star Search.

We chose Oth.Net for this section because at this writing it delivers some of the most accurate results and is one of the easiest to use. Other search engines you may want to try for MP3 files include the following:

Lycos MP3 Search (`http://mp3.lycos.com`)   This engine provides easy searching for MP3 files and claims to have more than 1 million files indexed. But in our testing, it turned up distressingly large numbers of dead links. Your mileage may vary.

MusicSeek (`http://www.musicseek.net`)   This lets you search for files in MP3, VQF, AAC, and RA (RealAudio) formats. It allows you to specify a minimum reliability rating for the results so that you avoid lame and flaky sites.

AudioGalaxy (`http://www.audiogalaxy.com`)   This search engine provides a rich searching environment and makes downloading very easy for users of GlobalScape's CuteFTP FTP client application.

Oth.Net

When you're searching for MP3 files, your first port of call should be the search engine at Oth.Net (`http://www.oth.net`). Oth.Net's search engine is minimalist yet fast and accurate, and you can download directly from its results page.

To search for MP3 files on Oth.Net:

1. Point your browser at `http://www.oth.net`.

2. Enter the terms of your search in the Search For text box, as shown on the next page, and click the Search button.

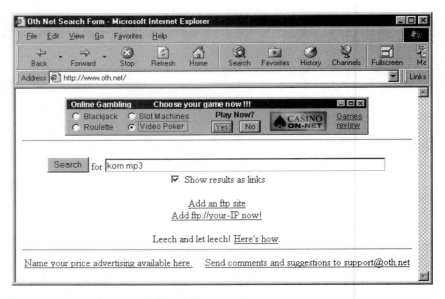

3. The search engine will return search results, as in the illustration below. Here we're looking at the first 20 links to Korn MP3 files; above the list, there are links to the other 180 results the search engine returned.

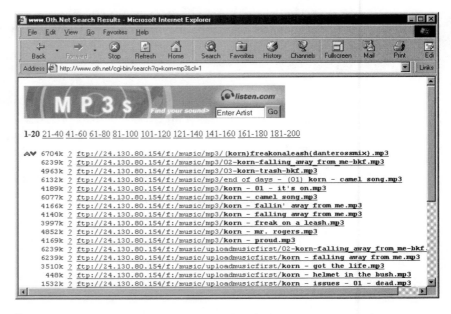

4. To start downloading, click a result. It's that easy—sometimes.

Some FTP sites make you upload music to them before they allow you to download any music. If you're using an FTP client such as CuteFTP, you may see a message such as the one shown in the Login Messages dialog box below, in which the site is demanding music with menace.

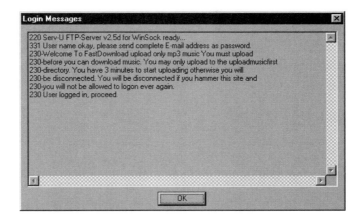

If you're trying to download from a Web browser, you may see messages such as the one shown below in Internet Explorer, saying that *the server returned extended information*. This doesn't necessarily mean that the site is demanding an upload, but when you're trying to access an MP3 FTP site, it's very likely.

Netscape gives a different message when it runs into this problem, as shown in the message box below. The message is perhaps a little misleading in that we know the file is there—we're just not allowed to get at it.

If you have music that you can legally distribute, feel free to go ahead and upload some. But keep in mind that because most people do not have music that they can legally distribute, these sites are pushing many people into uploading music illegally so that they can download music—which too might be illegal.

MP3 Star Search

If you're looking for MP3 files off the beaten path, consider trying MP3 Star Search, a wicked freeware utility that dredges through a multitude of search engines and integrates the results into an easy-to-use interface.

MP3 Star Search is designed to integrate with CuteFTP, an easy-to-use shareware FTP utility from GlobalScape. If you have CuteFTP (you can get it from `http://www.cuteftp.com`), you can download files directly from the MP3 Star Search interface.

At this writing, you can download MP3 Star Search from `http://www`
`.pcworld.com/r/shw/1%2C2087%2C6403%2C00.html`. Unzip the contents of the distribution file to a temporary folder and run `setup.exe`. MP3 Star Searcher has a standardized installation routine in which you select the folder in which to install MP3 Star Search and designate a Start menu group to which to add its items.

Here's how to use MP3 Star Search:

1. Run MP3 Star Search from the Start menu (wherever you put it).

2. Select the Get Queued Pages check box to make sure that MP3 Star Search returns all pages of search results from each server it checks.

3. In the Search box, enter the name of the artist or track for which to search and click the Let the Search Begin button. MP3 Star Search will build a list of results in the Search Results box, showing the number of results for each search engine contacted.

4. Double-click a non-zero result to display the results for that search engine.

5. Click the + signs to expand a list. In the illustration on the next page, you'll see that our search for **Rollins Band** has returned hits from the 2LOOK4, search.mp3.de, and MP3.BOX search engines. Most of the results we're looking at are on target. A check mark means that MP3 Star Search has tested the FTP server as being active; a cross in a red

circle means it's not active; a question mark in a green circle means that MP3 Star Search is still testing it.

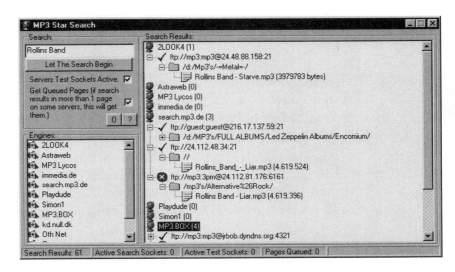

6. Download the MP3 file that appeals to you by doing one of the following:

◆ If you have CuteFTP and it's running, right-click the listing for the file you want and choose Get File from the context menu. CuteFTP will log into the FTP server and download the file.

◆ If you don't have CuteFTP, right-click the listing and choose Copy Location from the context menu. Switch to your Web browser, right-click in the address box, choose Paste from the context menu, and then press Enter to access the site. From there, you should be able to download the file as usual.

NOTE Another MP3 metasearch utility you might want to try is MP3 Fiend, which you can download from `http://www.mp3fiend.com`.

8 Search for MP3 Files Using Napster

At this writing, one of the most popular tools for searching for MP3 files is Napster. Napster is an application that creates MP3 communities on the fly from the users who log in to a server, enabling them to share MP3 files with one another.

Napster is such a hit that it has been, or is being, implemented on most of the operating systems currently known to computers—so it's a big topic to cover. We discuss Napster for Windows, Linux, and the Macintosh in depth in the section titled *Find and Share Music with Napster*.

9 Use RadioSpy to Find SHOUTcast Servers

As we mentioned earlier, SHOUTcast is a streaming technology for delivering compressed audio over the Internet. If you're going to tune into SHOUTcast broadcasts—and you should—your starting point should be RadioSpy from GameSpy Industries (`http://www.radiospy.com`).

RadioSpy is a tool for finding SHOUTcast broadcasts of MP3 music. At the risk of oversimplifying, RadioSpy is like a smart radio tuner for the Web, searching out signals and listing them for you so that you can play them back.

Getting, Installing, and Configuring RadioSpy

To get the latest version of RadioSpy browse on over to `http://www` `.radiospy.com`.

Here's how to install and configure RadioSpy:

1. Run the RadioSpy distribution file by double-clicking it in Explorer. You'll see the Please Select Your Language dialog box.

2. Select the language you want, and then click the OK button. Read and click your way through the Welcome dialog box and the License Agreement dialog box.

3. Specify the installation folder in the Choose Destination Location dialog box. Use the Browse button and the resulting Select Destination Directory dialog box if necessary to select a different folder.

4. Click the Next button. You'll see the Select Components dialog box.

5. Select the components to install—you'll probably want both the Winamp Skin and the RadioSpy QuickStart—and click the Next button to display the Select Program Manager Group dialog box.

6. Select the name of the Start menu group to which you want to add the RadioSpy icons. Click the Next button to display the Start Installation dialog box.

7. Click the Next button to run the installation. When the RadioSpy installation is finished, you'll see the Installation Complete dialog box.

8. Select options for what to launch, and then click the Finish button. RadioSpy will display the Configuration dialog box, shown below, with its General page displayed.

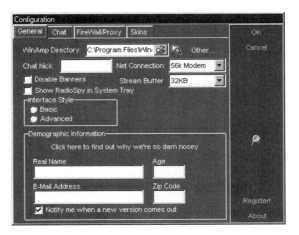

9. Choose from the plethora of options on the General page:

WinAmp Directory text box   Make sure RadioSpy has identified your Winamp directory. (If not, click the folder button to the right of the WinAmp Directory text box and use the Browse for Folder dialog box to identify the directory.) To use a different MP3 player, click the Other button and use the Select an Alternate MP3 Player dialog box to identify the player.

Chat Nick text box   In this text box, enter your handle for chat rooms. (MotorCity Madman and Snoop Doggy are already taken.)

Net Connection drop-down list   In this drop-down list, select the speed and type of your Internet connection. RadioSpy uses this setting to deliver the appropriate quality of music to you, so give it the correct speed.

Stream Buffer drop-down list   Set the size of buffer you want to use for RadioSpy broadcasts—the amount of information you want to hold in memory to smooth out unevennesses in the sound stream. The bigger the buffer, the smoother the sound, but the longer it will take for the sound to start.

Disable Banners check box   This check box is disabled until you register your copy of RadioSpy.

Show RadioSpy in System Tray check box   Select this check box if you want RadioSpy to display an icon in the system tray on the Taskbar rather than an item in the Taskbar. The icon in the tray usually provides the most convenient access to RadioSpy.

Interface Style group box   In this group box, choose Basic or Advanced. Basic style provides a little less information than Advanced, but it's easier to use. We recommend starting with Basic; you can switch to Advanced easily later if you want.

Demographic Information group box   Enter information in this group box as you see appropriate. If you want to be on RadioSpy's mailing list, make sure the Notify Me When a New Version Comes Out check box is selected; if not, make sure it's cleared. The Click Here to Find Out Why We're So Darn Nosey button displays a message box with a humorous explanation of why RadioSpy wants your demographic information (or an approximation of it).

10. Click the Chat tab to display the Chat page (the top part of which is shown on the next page), and select options as appropriate:

Connect to Chat on Startup check box   Select this check box if you want to connect to the chat group when you start RadioSpy.

Hide Join/Parts in Chat check box   Select this check box if you want to suppress messages about your leaving and joining chat rooms (often a good idea).

Don't Set Auto-Away check box   Select this check box if you want to suppress messages indicating you've left a chat room when you change to the News or Server pages in RadioSpy.

Home Channel text box   In this text box, enter the name of the channel you want RadioSpy to use as your home channel.

11. If you use a firewall or a proxy server, click the Firewall/Proxy tab to display that page, and enter your firewall or proxy server settings. (You might need to ask your system administrator for these settings; if you do, be sure to explain to him or her about all of the business and technical broadcasts that are available on the Web.)

12. To change the skin that RadioSpy uses, click the Skins tab to display the Skins page. Click the Get Skins Here link to download skins for RadioSpy, then select the skin in the Skin Name drop-down list.

13. Click the OK button to apply your configuration settings and launch RadioSpy.

14. Read the information in the RadioSpy Tips dialog box dialog box that RadioSpy displays, then clear the Show Tips on Startup check box and click the Close button.

Understanding the RadioSpy Interface

It takes a minute or two to grasp the complexity of the RadioSpy interface. In fact, the RadioSpy screen (shown at the top of the next page) is too complex to label all at once in this book, so we've broken it up into three parts to show it to you more effectively. Power has its price.

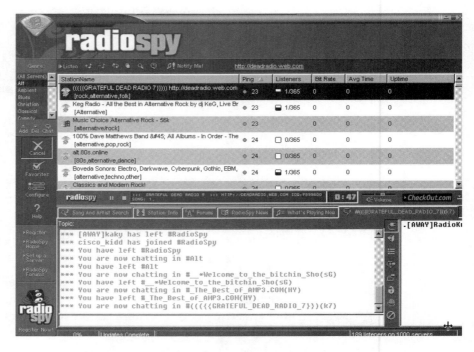

The illustration below shows the top part of the RadioSpy screen.

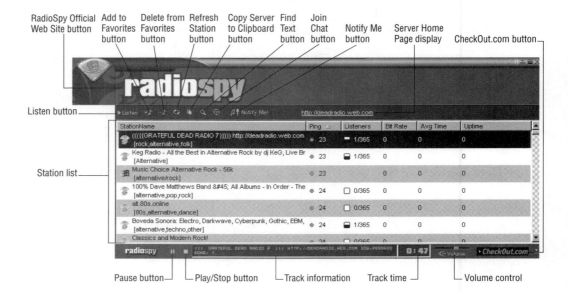

The illustration below shows the controls on the left-hand side of the RadioSpy screen.

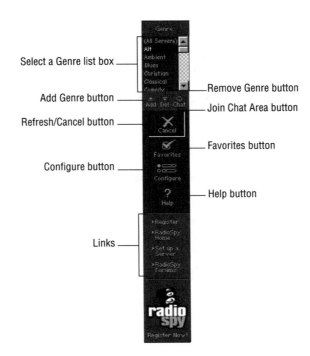

The illustration below shows the bottom portion of the RadioSpy screen.

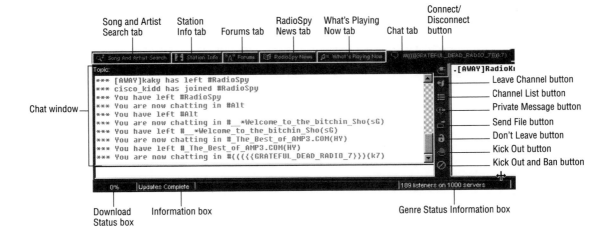

Here's what the components of the RadioSpy interface do:

RadioSpy Official Web Site button   Click this button to fire up your Web browser and access the RadioSpy Web site.

Listen button   Click this button to start listening to the currently selected station. (Alternatively, double-click the station to start listening to it without troubling the Listen button.)

Add to Favorites button   Click this button to add the selected station to your list of favorite stations.

Delete from Favorites button   Click this button to strike an existing favorite from the list.

Refresh Station button   Click this button to refresh the selected station (without refreshing the other stations the way the Refresh button does).

Copy Server to Clipboard button   Click this button to copy the IP address of the current station to the Clipboard. You can then paste it into a player (such as Winamp) or into a playlist.

Find Text button   Click this button to display the Find dialog box, in which you can enter a word and locate stations that include that word.

Join Chat button   Click this button to join the chat channel for the current station.

Notify Me button   Click this button to display the RadioSpy Song Notification dialog box, in which you can build a list of songs or artists. When one of these songs or artists is being played, RadioSpy will send you a notification.

Server Home Page display   The Server Home Page display shows the URL of the home page for the current station.

Station list   Click an entry in the station list to select that station, or double-click the entry to start the station playing.

Play/Stop and Pause buttons   Click the Play button to start the current station streaming. While the station is playing, clicking the same button—now the Stop button—will end the stream. Click the Pause button to pause the station.

CheckOut.com button   Click this button when it's available to be taken to an online music vendor to buy the CD from which the current track is playing. This button can be handy when you want to find out more about a CD or a band but have no intention of buying.

Select a Genre list box   Use this list box to select a genre of SHOUTcast station to display.

Add Genre button   Click this button to display the Add a Genre dialog box, in which you can add a genre to the list.

Remove Genre button   Click this button to remove the selected genre from the list.

Join Chat Area button   Click this button to join the chat area for the current genre.

Refresh/Cancel button   Click this button to refresh the server list displayed. While the refresh is taking place, the Cancel button is displayed in place of the Refresh button; you can click the Cancel button to cancel the refresh if it's taking too long for your temperament.

Favorites button   Click this button to display in place of the station list a list of the stations you've designated as your favorites. Click the button again to return to the station list.

Configure button   Click this button if you've screwed up your configuration and need to unscrew it.

Help button   Click this button if you feel a pressing need to see the Tips dialog box again. (If you've read them already, they won't do you much good.)

Status Bar (containing the Download Status, Information, and Genre Status Information boxes)   This status bar provides updates on what's happening in the RadioSpy window.

Connect/Disconnect button   Click this button to connect to or disconnect from the current chat channel.

Leave Channel button   Click this button to leave the current chat channel.

Channel List button   Click this button to display the Channel List dialog box, which contains a list of channels that you can join.

Private Message button   Select a chat participant, then click this button to start a private message to him or her.

Send File box   Select a chat participant, then click this button to begin the process of sending a file to him or her via DCC connection.

Don't Leave button   Click this button to prevent RadioSpy from leaving this channel automatically when you join another channel. When this button is selected, it appears pushed in.

Kick Out and Kick Out and Ban buttons   Click the Kick Out button to kick the selected user out of the channel. Click the Kick Out and Ban button to kick them out *and* prevent them from rejoining. In our experience, kicking out works well, but kicking out and banning tends to, uh, kick up errors.

The six tabs on the lower part of the RadioSpy window give you quick access to the six pages of information that RadioSpy supports:

Song and Artist Search page   Use this page to search for a particular artist or a song title in the stations' playlists.

Station Info page   This page displays information about the current station.

Forums page   This page provides quick access to any forums associated with the stations you're listening to.

RadioSpy News page   This page displays headlines with links to the current news on RadioSpy's Web site.

What's Playing Now page   This page displays a list of the tracks currently being played by the stations.

Chat page   This page provides a chat area that you can navigate by using the buttons on its right-hand side.

Connecting to a Station

To connect to a station, make sure your Internet connection is fired up. Then choose the genre of music in the Select a Genre list box to display the list of SHOUTcast stations available in that genre, as shown in the illustration on the next page.

Here's what you see in the station list:

StationName column   This column displays the name of the server and station.

Speed bar or Ping dot   The Speed bar (in the Basic interface) or the Ping dot (in the Advanced interface) shows the health of the server signal. A long green bar or a green dot represents a strong signal; a shorter orange bar or an orange dot shows a server that's getting a lot of traffic; and a short red bar or a red dot indicates that the server is either down or having problems with the signal skipping.

Listeners column   This column shows the number of people listening to the SHOUTcast station, from Empty to a few people to many people to Full. If a station is listed as Full, you won't be able to access that station. Click the Listeners column once to rank the stations in ascending order of number of listeners; click it again to rank the stations in descending order of number of listeners.

Quality or Bit Rate column   The Quality column (in the Basic interface) or the Bit Rate column (in the Advanced interface) shows the speed of the signal, from 16kbps (which sounds horrible even for spoken audio) to 128kbps (which is near CD quality). Pick a high-quality or high-bitrate station over a low-quality or low-bitrate station any day.

Uptime column   This column, which appears only in the Advanced interface, shows how long the station has been on the air this session. This information isn't usually relevant to the listening experience, though you've got to figure that any station with long airtime is more technically competent than a station that seldom breaks a couple of hours.

Once you've connected to a server and got it playing to your liking, you can minimize RadioSpy by clicking its minimize button. If you chose to display the system tray icon during configuration, RadioSpy won't appear in the Taskbar; click the RadioSpy button in the system tray to restore RadioSpy.

Using Favorites

RadioSpy makes it easy to maintain a list of your favorite stations for quick access. Here's how:

- ◆ When you decide a station rocks, add it to your list of Favorites by right-clicking it and choosing Add to Favorites from the context menu or pressing Ctrl+A.

- ◆ Toggle your list of favorites on and off by clicking the Favorites button.

- ◆ When you decide a station has started to suck, remove it from your Favorites list by right-clicking it and choosing Remove from Favorites on the context menu. If your fingers are glued to the keyboard, press Ctrl+D to nuke the station.

I Gotta SHOUTcast Myself!

Now that you've seen the possibilities, you must be drooling at the thought of setting up your own SHOUTcast server and inflicting 24/7 broadcasts of your guitar solos and teenage poetry on an unsuspecting Internet. Turn to *89. Build a SHOUTcast Server and Get on the Air* for instructions on how to set up KILZ Rebel Radio in the basement and cause your parents to evict you again.

Windows MP3 Players

In this part, we'll look at the two most popular and versatile MP3 players for Windows—Winamp and Sonique. We'll also look at one of the least versatile and least popular players but probably the most widespread one—the Windows Media Player—which comes free with Windows 95, Windows 98, Windows Millennium, and Windows 2000.

The Windows Media Player has MP3 features so basic as to make you wince, but it's effective in a pinch. By contrast, Winamp and Sonique both provide a terrific set of features for playing MP3 files, including playlists for organizing your music, graphical equalizers for adjusting its sound, skins for changing the looks of the players, and visualizations for spacing your mind out while listening to the music.

At this writing, all these players are free. Well, to get the Windows Media Player working, you have to buy a copy of Windows...but let's leave that quibble aside. If you don't have a copy of Windows, none of these players is going to be of more than academic interest to you anyway—with the possible exception of Winamp, which has assorted Linux/Unix implementations, most of which are named xmms.

The Windows Media Player is distributed with Windows. Winamp is distributed as part of Netscape Communicator. You have to seek Sonique out on your own (hint: Check the CD in the back of the book).

NOTE Another player you may want to check out is XingMP3 Player from Xing Technologies (http://www.xingtech.com). XingMP3 Player provides good playback and playlist features but has no graphical equalizer, no support for skins, and no visualizations. You'll find coverage of XingMP3 Player in the XingMP3 Player Web supplement to this book on the Sybex Web site (http://www.sybex.com).

10 Choose the Right Stand-Alone MP3 Player for You

Before we get into the details of the players, let's take a moment to answer a couple of questions that may have surfaced in your mind like a pair of predatory pike in a murky pool:

◆ First, given that you know from the *Introduction* and *Table of Contents* of this book (if not from your own research) that there are all-in-one ripper/player/jukeboxes (discussed in the next part of the book), do you need to have a stand-alone MP3 player?

◆ Second, assuming that you do decide that you need a stand-alone player, how do you decide between the many available?

It's true that a good ripper/player/jukebox (and there are several good ones) can take care of just about all of your MP3 needs. But in addition to a ripper/player/jukebox, many people like to have a stand-alone MP3 player as well—one that doesn't do the ripping and encoding, but instead concentrates on playing the music. The first reason for having a stand-alone MP3 player is that the best stand-alone MP3 players have more play features and tend to be cooler looking and easier to manipulate than most ripper/player/jukeboxes. Second, because most stand-alone MP3 players are smaller and more maneuverable pieces of software—smaller both in the requirements they impose on your computer's drive and memory and the amount of screen real estate they claim.

As you'll see in the next few sections of this book, there are a good number of stand-alone MP3 players available at this writing—and by the time you're reading this, chances are good that several more will have become available. How should you choose between them?

Which criteria you use to pick your favorite MP3 player (or players—there's no reason to stick with one if you feel promiscuous) depends on you, but here are a few things that you'll probably want to consider:

How much load does the player impose on your computer?　Any player that monopolizes your processor cycles is going to cause a problem if you run it regularly and expect to do anything constructive at the same time. Particularly if your computer is underpowered—say a Pentium MMX rather than a Celeron, Pentium II, Pentium III, or Athlon—you'll want to make sure that your player is modest in its CPU requirements.

Does it have the features you need?　*Duh*—but at a minimum, you'll need a comprehensible interface that lets you control the play easily, preferably including a volume control. For conventional use, you'll want a readout of the song and artist, plus playlist capabilities and a playlist editor (for creating the playlists).

Is it stable?　There are enough good, mature players out there that you'll have little reason to use buggy, underdeveloped players—unless they're wickedly cool, either in looks or in features (or both). Which brings us to the next point.

Does it look good?　If you need to choose between two feature-similar players, you'll probably want to go with the one that looks cooler. (Who wouldn't?)

Is the price right?　Many MP3 players cost only a few bucks, but others are free. We'll leave you to decide how important saving the price of a couple of burrito dinners is to you.

Does it automatically inform you about upgrades and add-ons?
If you're frequently online looking for new versions, or if you don't always want to keep your software absolutely up to date, you may not be too worried about having the MP3 player automatically inform you that a later and greater version has become available. But for most people, this feature can be useful.

Enough already. If you keep these half-dozen points in mind, you should have little difficulty finding a stand-alone MP3 player that meets your needs. In the following sections, we'll introduce you to some of the key contenders for your playing time.

11 Play MP3 Files with the Windows Media Player

If you want to play MP3 tracks on a work computer that you're not allowed (or able) to install software on, you may already have a solution—the Windows Media Player that comes with Windows. Most recent versions of the Windows Media Player can play MP3 tracks well enough for casual listening. And though the Windows Media Player only lets you open one file at a time, that file can be a playlist, so that you can keep the music rolling without constantly having to reach for your mouse to load another track.

Here's how to play MP3 tracks with the Windows Media Player:

1. Open the Windows Media Player by choosing Start ➢ Programs ➢ Accessories ➢ Multimedia ➢ Windows Media Player. (In some versions of Windows, you may need to choose Entertainment instead of Multimedia, but who's keeping score?)

2. Choose File ➢ Open or press Ctrl+O to display the first Open dialog box, which lets you type in a path and filename, if you feel so bold, but doesn't provide browsing capabilities. (We don't know why Microsoft makes things difficult this way, but we sure wish they wouldn't.)

3. Click the Browse button to display the second Open dialog box, which does provide browsing capabilities.

4. Select MP3 File in the Files of Type drop-down list, and then navigate to and select the MP3 file or playlist you want to open.

5. Click the Open button in the second Open dialog box, and then the OK button in the first Open dialog box. After this little rigmarole, the Windows Media Player will condescend to open the MP3 file or playlist.

The next illustration shows the Windows Media Player playing a playlist. As you can see, the Windows Media Player provides basic controls: buttons for Play, Pause, Stop, Skip Back, Rewind, Fast Forward, and Skip Forward, a volume control, a Mute button (the one with the speaker icon), and a progress slider. The remaining button shown (the one with the three double-headed horizontal arrows) is the Preview button, which plays the first ten seconds of each file in a playlist—a great feature for finding the track whose name and number were on the tip of your tongue.

NOTE If you use the Windows Media Player regularly, you'll probably want to optimize the view so that it shows you what you want but doesn't take up more screen real estate than it must. Choose View ➢ Compact to switch to Compact view (which saves a goodly amount of space) or View ➢ Minimal to switch to Minimal view (which saves even more but omits features such as the progress slider). You can customize the items displayed for Compact view and Minimal view by choosing Tools ➢ Options to display the Options dialog box, selecting and clearing the check boxes as appropriate in the Compact group box and Minimal group box, and then clicking the OK button.

12 Create Playlists for the Windows Media Player

Most MP3 players let you build and save playlists—but the Windows Media Player doesn't. So if you're stuck with the Windows Media Player, you may need to create your own playlists manually. All it takes is a little finger exercise as follows:

1. Choose Start ➢ Programs ➢ Accessories ➢ Notepad to open the Notepad text editor with a new empty document. (If you have another text editor that you prefer using, feel free to use that instead.)

2. Enter the path and filename of each track in the playlist on a new line. (Copy and paste the path if you're entering multiple files from the same folder.) The illustration below shows a short playlist under way in Notepad.

```
Untitled - Notepad
File   Edit   Search   Help
G:\Metallica\S & M\Metallica - S&M - One.mp3
G:\Metallica\S & M\Metallica - S&M - Fuel.mp3
G:\Metallica\S & M\Metallica - S&M - Intro (The Ecstasy of Gold).mp3
G:\Lloyd Cole and the Commotions\Speedboat.mp3
G:\Lloyd Cole and the Commotions\Perfect Skin.mp3
G:\Metallica\S & M\Metallica - S&M - Battery.mp3
G:\Metallica\S & M\Metallica - S&M - The Call of the Ktulu.mp3
```

3. Choose File ➢ Save to display the Save As dialog box.

4. In the File Name text box, enter the name for the playlist *in double quotation marks and with the extension M3U*. For example, to create a playlist named **Metal Morning**, you would enter this in the File Name text box:

```
"Metal Morning.m3u"
```

5. Click the Save button to save the playlist. Then open it up in the Windows Media Player as described in the previous section and see how it sounds.

13 Get and Install Winamp

We've included version 2.61 of Winamp on the CD. To be even more up to date, visit http://www.winamp.com and download the latest version. To install Winamp, double-click the Winamp distribution file. This is an executable file, so double-clicking it runs it. You'll see the Winamp Setup: License Agreement dialog box. Read the license and click the Next button if you can handle the terms. You'll see the Winamp Setup: Installation Options dialog box shown on the next page.

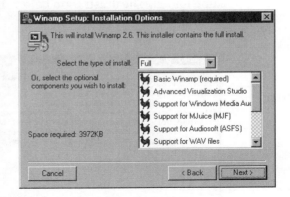

In the Select the Type of Install drop-down list, choose Full, Lite, Minimal, or Custom to select a predefined package of the options shown in the list box:

Full   Selects all options. We recommend this option unless you're severely short of disk space (at this writing, the full package takes around 4MB), sure you won't want advanced visualizations, or prejudiced against certain sound formats.

Minimal   Selects only the Basic Winamp option.

Lite   Adds to Basic Winamp support for the key music file types.

Custom   Lets you select whatever you want by clicking its entry in the list box. When you select an item, the llama to its left turns from gray to black and dons a check mark.

NOTE   You can also choose a custom setup by selecting and clearing llamas as you see fit—the Select the Type of Install drop-down list will select Custom automatically when you select any group of options other than Minimal, Lite, or Full.

Click the Next button to proceed. Setup will display the Winamp Setup: Installation Directory dialog box. If you don't like the directory that Winamp has chosen to install itself into, select a different directory. You can either type the directory's name into the text box or click the Browse button and use the resulting Select Install Directory dialog box to navigate to and select the folder you want to use.

Click the Next button when you're ready to proceed. Winamp will go ahead and install itself in the specified directory. You'll then see the Winamp Setup: Settings dialog box shown below.

Here's what the items in this dialog box do. (If you've got a later version of Winamp, there may be additional features.) Again, select and clear the llamas as you see fit.

Associate with Files   Selecting this check box makes Winamp the default audio player for all files in formats that Winamp considers to be audio. This list of formats includes MP3 (of course) and most audio file formats. If you prefer to play some forms of audio through a different player, you can deselect them later. Alternatively, you can specify Winamp as the default audio player for specific formats after installation.

Associate with Audio CDs   Selecting this check box causes Winamp to spring to life when you insert an audio CD into your computer's CD drive. If you don't like autoplay, clear this check box. Note that this setting does not change the Auto Insert Notification setting on your PC. If Auto Insert Notification is off (in the CD drive's Properties dialog box), Winamp will not automatically play CDs even if you select the Autoplay Audio CDs option.

Add Start Menu Icons   Selecting this check box adds a Winamp group to the Start menu. Unless you prefer to have a Winamp icon on the Desktop or the Quick Launch bar and nowhere else, keep this check box selected.

Add Desktop Icon   Selecting this check box adds a Winamp icon to the desktop. Having the icon there is often handy.

Add Quicklaunch Icon　This option is available only if your computer is running Windows 98 or Internet Explorer 4 or 5. Because the Quick Launch bar is always accessible, it's usually the quickest way to get to Winamp.

System Tray Icon　This option adds a Winamp icon to the system tray, so that you can quickly access Winamp and its bookmarks.

Preserve File Associations　This option instructs Winamp to defend its file associations when another application tries to steal them. Leave this llama selected unless you're sure you want to let other applications grab Winamp's file associations.

How Should Winamp Connect to the Internet drop-down list　This drop-down list lets you choose the way that Winamp will use the Internet. If the computer you're using doesn't have an Internet connection, or you don't want to use Winamp's Internet features, choose No Internet Connection Available. If your computer has a modem connection, choose Using Dial-Up Modem Internet Connection. If your computer connects to the Internet through a network (for example, a company's local area network or a home network, or a cable modem or DSL), choose Using LAN Internet Connection.

Click the Next button to proceed with the installation. Winamp will install the icons and groups you chose and will display the Winamp Setup: User Information dialog box. Enter information here if you want to—there's no obligation; if you don't want to be invited to register again, select the Stop Bugging Me check box. If you want to have Winamp announcements mailed to you, select the Please Send Me Winamp Announcements check box. You may find it easier to visit the Winamp Web site periodically at your convenience to scan for new information rather than having it pushed out to you. If you don't want Winamp to send back to Winamp.com anonymous statistics on how much you're using Winamp, clear the Allow Winamp to Report Simple, Anonymous Usage Statistics check box.

If you fill in the user information, click the Next button to send it. Winamp will connect to the Internet using the connection you specified in the previous dialog box and will send the information to Winamp.com. If you don't fill in the user information, click the Later button.

You'll then see the Winamp Setup: Winamp Successfully Installed dialog box. Click the Run Winamp button to run Winamp.

14 Use the Winamp Interface

In this section, we'll examine the Winamp interface. If you're feeling impatient and have some MP3 files already, click the Open button, select a track or three, and listen to some tunes while you're playing with the interface.

Exploring the Winamp Windows

The next illustration shows Winamp's basic look. As you can see, it consists of four windows: the Main window, the Playlist Editor window, the Graphical Equalizer window, and the Browser window. Here's a brief overview of each window:

Main window   This window displays information about the track that's currently playing and provides CD-player–style controls. The Main window also provides quick access to the Playlist Editor window and the Graphical Equalizer window.

Playlist Editor window   This window contains the current playlist, buttons for creating and manipulating playlists, and a minimal set of play controls (so that you can dispense with the Main window if you want).

Graphical Equalizer window   This window provides a software graphical equalizer that you can use to tweak the sound that Winamp produces.

Browser window   This window provides a quick way of inputting information into your main Browser window for searching Amazon.com for music by the current artist. Whether you find the Browser window useful depends on your interests. We tend to find it annoying and recommend turning it off straightaway.

Menu box   Main window   Toggle Windowshade Mode buttons   Browser window   Close button

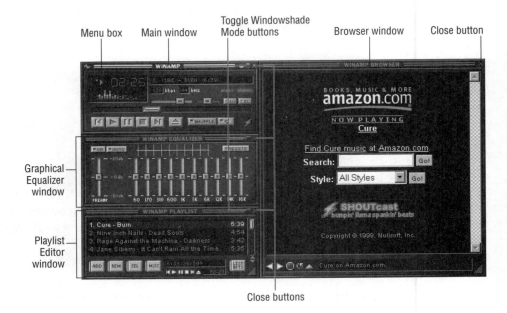

Graphical Equalizer window

Playlist Editor window

Close buttons

Arranging the Winamp Windows

Here's what you need to know about arranging the Winamp windows on screen. You can do the following:

◆ Close any of the Winamp windows by clicking its Close button—the × button in its upper-right corner. Clicking the Close button on the Main window closes Winamp.

◆ Rearrange the Winamp windows any way you want by clicking the title bar of a window and dragging it to where you want it to appear.

◆ Move each Winamp window independently. When you move the edge of one of the satellite windows so that it touches any edge of the Main window, the satellite window sticks to the Main window. When you then move the Main window, any windows stuck to it will move along with it.

◆ Minimize all displayed Winamp windows by clicking the Minimize button on the Main window.

◆ Reduce any of the windows, except the Browser window, to a window-shade strip by clicking its Toggle Windowshade Mode button. In Windowshade mode (shown below), Winamp takes up very little space and provides only key information and controls. You can keep Winamp on top of other applications (as described next) and keep it out of the way by positioning it in another application's title bar.

◆ Keep Winamp on top of all other running applications so that it's always at hand. Press Ctrl+A to toggle the Always on Top feature for all Winamp windows except the Playlist Editor. Press Ctrl+Alt+A to toggle the Always on Top feature for the Playlist Editor.

◆ Toggle the display of the Winamp windows with keyboard shortcuts: Press Alt+W to toggle the main Winamp window; press Alt+E to toggle the Playlist Editor window; press Alt+G to toggle the Graphical Equalizer window; and press Alt+T to toggle the Browser window. Alternatively, click the menu box in the upper-left corner of the Main window and select the entry for the window from the menu to toggle it on and off, as shown below.

NOTE When you've hidden all the Winamp windows, make sure that the Winamp item is selected in the Taskbar when you try to restore a Winamp window by using the keyboard shortcut. If another application is selected, you can press these keyboard shortcuts all you want, but Winamp won't react. You may find it easier to right-click the Winamp item in the Taskbar, select the Winamp Menu item from the context menu, and choose the window you want to restore from the submenu that appears.

◆ Display Winamp at double size by pressing Ctrl+D to make it easier to see what you're doing. When you need to reclaim your screen real estate, press Ctrl+D again to restore Winamp to its usual discreet size.

To exit Winamp, click the control menu on the Main window (or press Alt+F) and choose Exit from the menu. Alternatively, click the Close button (the × button) on the Main window.

NOTE If you chose during installation to add the Winamp icon to your system tray, you can also control Winamp from there when it's minimized. For example, right-click the system tray icon and choose Exit from the context menu to close Winamp.

15 Play Tracks and SHOUTcast Streams with the Winamp Main Window

The Main window is dead easy to operate with the mouse, but it has many keyboard access features that you'll want to know as well. The next illustration shows the components of the Main window.

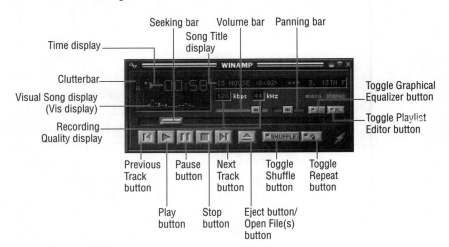

To open one or more tracks, click the Open File(s) button to display the Open File(s) dialog box. Navigate to the track or tracks you want and select them. To select a contiguous list of tracks, click the first track, then hold down Shift and click the last track. To select multiple individual tracks or to add them to a Shift-click–selected list, hold down Ctrl and click each track in succession. Click the Open button to open the files in Winamp. Winamp will add them to the current playlist and will start playing the first track. Usually Winamp decides that the last track you selected is the first track, so you may want to try selecting the tracks in reverse order.

Most of the buttons and displays in the Main window are easy to recognize because they look like those on a CD player or a cassette player. You click the Play button to play the current track, the Stop button to stop play, and so on. But there are a couple of mouse techniques you should know for the Main window:

- ◆ Click the time in the Time display to toggle it between time elapsed and time remaining on the track.

- ◆ Click the Visual Song display (the Vis display) to switch between visualization modes.

- ◆ Click the letters in the Clutterbar at the left side of the Time display window to perform common maneuvers. O displays the Options menu; I displays the File Info dialog box; A toggles the Always on Top feature; D toggles the double-size feature; and V displays the Visualization menu, which contains options for the visualization feature below the Time display.

- ◆ Right-click the Song Title display to pop up a context menu for moving around the current track and current playlist. (More on these in a moment.)

- ◆ Click the lightning-flash logo in the lower-right corner to display the About Winamp dialog box.

As well as listening to music you've downloaded, you can play music straight off the Web with Winamp—either MP3 files from a server or a SHOUTcast server stream. SHOUTcast is streaming software created by Nullsoft (the makers of Winamp) that allows you to broadcast music over the Web.

To play music straight off the Web, follow these steps:

1. Press Ctrl+L, or choose Play Location from the main Winamp menu (accessed by clicking the menu box in the upper-left corner of the Main window), to display the Open Location dialog box, as shown below.

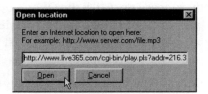

2. Enter the URL of a file or of a SHOUTcast stream. (*9. Use RadioSpy to Find SHOUTcast Servers* discusses how to find SHOUTcast streams.)

3. Click the Open button. Winamp will start playing the file or the stream.

You can also add Web tracks or SHOUTcast streams to the Playlist Editor as follows:

1. Display the Playlist Editor if it's not already displayed.

2. Click the Add button to display the menu of buttons, then choose the Add URL button to display the Open Location dialog box.

3. Enter the URL of a file or of a SHOUTcast stream.

4. Click the Open button. Winamp will add the file or stream to the playlist. You can then play the file or stream by using the Winamp controls as usual.

NOTE You won't always need to use this technique to play music directly off the Web because sites such as MP3.com include links that automatically start your MP3 player or browser plug-in playing the track.

16 Create and Use Winamp Playlists

Like most MP3 players, Winamp lets you build playlists—lists of tracks in the order in which you want to play them.

To work with playlists, you use the Playlist Editor. To display the Playlist Editor, click the Toggle Playlist Editor button in the Main window or press Alt+E. The illustration below shows the Playlist Editor with a playlist loaded in it.

NOTE Because you can control play by using the controls in the Playlist Editor, you may want to close the Main window to save space on screen. To toggle the Main window on and off, press Alt+W.

Creating a Playlist

To create a playlist, add tracks to it and arrange them in the order you want. You can add tracks to the playlist in several ways:

◆ Drag tracks from an Explorer window to the Playlist Editor.

◆ Double-click the Add button in the Playlist Editor to display the Add File(s) to Playlist dialog box, select the tracks, and click the Open button. (The first click of the Add button displays the menu of buttons, and the second selects the Add File button, which appears in place of the Add button—but you can perform the action as a double-click.)

◆ To add a whole directory to the playlist, click the Add button to display the menu of buttons, then choose the Add Dir button. Winamp will display the Open Directory dialog box shown below. Navigate to and select the directory you want to add. If you want to add all the subdirectories under the directory you're selecting, make sure the Recurse Subdirectories check box is selected; if you don't, make sure it's cleared. Then click the OK button.

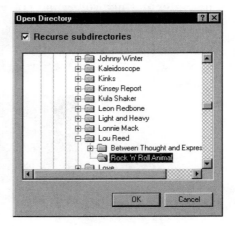

NOTE To play a track more than once in a playlist, add two or more instances of it to the playlist.

Arranging and Sorting a Playlist

You can then rearrange or remove the tracks as follows:

◆ To remove a track from the playlist, select it and press the Delete key or double-click the Rem button. (The first click displays the button menu, and the second selects the Rem Sel button—Remove Selection—that replaces the Rem button.)

◆ To rearrange the tracks in the playlist easily, select tracks with the mouse and drag them up or down to where you want it or them to appear.

◆ To sort the playlist, click the Misc button and choose Sort List from the menu of buttons, as shown below. You can sort a list by title, by filename, or by path and filename. You can also reverse the current order of the playlist—which can be good for variety—or randomize the playlist to produce something unexpected. There's nothing quite like the mind-jarring juxtaposition of Bach and Nine Inch Nails.

◆ To select all the tracks in the playlist, double-click the Sel button. (The first click displays the menu of buttons, and the second click selects the Sel All button that replaces the Sel button.) To deselect all tracks, click the Sel button and choose Sel Zero from the menu of buttons. To invert the selection (deselecting all selected tracks and selecting all unselected tracks), click the Sel button and choose Inv Sel from the menu of buttons.

Saving a Playlist

To save a playlist, click the List Opts button and choose Save List from the menu of buttons. Winamp will display the Save Playlist dialog box. Enter a name for the playlist—**Full Metal Morning**, **Dance into Bed**, whatever—and specify a different location if necessary. Then click the Save button to save the list. The default file format is M3U Playlist, but you can choose PLS Playlist in the Save As Type drop-down list if you want to save your playlists in the PLS format.

Opening a Saved Playlist

To open a playlist you've previously saved, double-click the List Opts button to display the Load Playlist dialog box. (The first click will display the menu of buttons, and the second will select the Load List button that replaces the List Opts button.) Navigate to the playlist, select it, and click the Open button.

Tips for Working with Playlists

Here's how to get around the current track and playlist quickly:

◆ To jump to a specific time in the track that is currently playing, press Ctrl+J or right-click the Song Title display and choose Jump to Time from the context menu to display the Jump to Time dialog box. Enter the time to which to jump in the Jump To text box in Minutes:Seconds format (for example, **2:15**) and click the Jump button. This is the precise way of skipping lame intros.

◆ To move less precisely through a track, drag the Seeking bar to the left or right.

◆ To jump to another track in the current playlist, press J or right-click the Song Title display and choose Jump to File from the context menu to display the Jump to File dialog box (shown next). The Jump to File dialog box lists the tracks in alphabetical order. Double-click the track to which you want to jump. To search for text in a track's name, you can enter the letters in the Search for Text text box. As you type, Winamp will reduce the list to tracks that have that sequence of letters in the title.

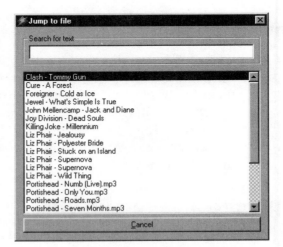

◆ You can also navigate around the playlist by using the Playback submenu on the main Winamp menu. This submenu offers navigation items including Stop w/Fadeout, Back 5 Seconds, Fwd 5 Seconds, Start of List, 10 Tracks Back, and 10 Tracks Fwd.

◆ You can control play by using the keyboard shortcuts listed below. These shortcuts aren't mnemonically obvious (though you can certainly make up some innovative mnemonics for them), but you'll notice that they're all on the left-hand bottom row of the keyboard, just where you can reach them most easily when you're lying wasted on the floor. (That's assuming you're using the QWERTY keyboard layout—if you're using a Dvorak keyboard layout, you'll need to get up off the floor to use the shortcuts.)

Keyboard Shortcut	Action
Z	Previous track
X	Play
C	Pause
V	Stop
B	Next

17 Use Winamp Bookmarks to Access Tracks Quickly

To enable you to quickly access a track or a SHOUTcast stream in your current playlist, Winamp provides bookmarks, virtual markers that you can use to tag a track or stream.

To bookmark the current track or stream, press Alt+I or choose Bookmarks ➢ Add Current As Bookmark from the main menu. You can also add a bookmark to one or more selected tracks or streams in the Playlist Editor window by right-clicking and choosing Bookmark Item(s) from the context menu.

Once you've added a bookmark, you can go to it by choosing its name from the Bookmarks submenu from the main menu, as shown below.

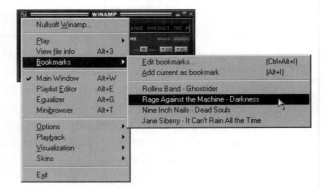

To edit a bookmark, press Ctrl+Alt+I with the Main window active or choose Bookmarks ➤ Edit Bookmarks from the main menu. Winamp will display the Winamp Preferences dialog box with the Bookmarks page displayed, as shown next.

Select the bookmark you want to affect in the Bookmarks list box, then take one of the following actions:

◆ Click the Edit button to display the Edit Bookmark dialog box, shown next. Change either the title of the bookmark or the file to which it refers, then click the OK button to close the dialog box and apply the change.

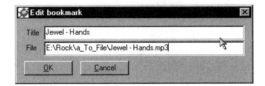

- ◆ Click the Remove button to remove the bookmark. Winamp doesn't ask you to confirm the deletion, so make sure you have the right bookmark selected before clicking the button.
- ◆ Click the Open button to open the bookmarked track in Winamp and start playing it.
- ◆ Click the Enqueue button to add the bookmarked track to your current playlist.

NOTE To go quickly to a bookmark, right-click the Winamp icon in the system tray, then choose the bookmark from the Bookmarks context menu.

18 Make Music Sound Good with the Winamp Graphical Equalizer

Winamp provides a full-featured graphical equalizer for adjusting the balance of the music. The graphical equalizer lets you increase or decrease ten different frequencies in the sound spectrum to boost the parts of the music you want to hear more of and reduce those you don't.

Graphical Equalizer Basics

To display the Graphical Equalizer window (shown below), click the Toggle Graphical Equalizer button in the Main window or press Alt+G. The frequencies are measured in hertz (Hz) and kilohertz (kHz)—the number of cycles per second. As you can see, the left-hand end of the graphical equalizer controls the lower frequencies—from 60Hz booms and rumbles upwards—and the right-hand end controls the higher frequencies—up to 16kHz. You can increase or decrease each frequency up to 20 decibels (dB), enough to make a huge difference in the sound. (For example, boost all the bass frequencies and crank up Hole to knock all the ice off your bedroom window on snowy winter mornings.)

First, make sure the graphical equalizer is on. (It's off by default.) Click the On button to toggle the graphical equalizer on and off. When it's on, the On button will display a bright green light; when it's off, the light is a darker green. Guess it's lucky the Winamp guys didn't design traffic signals.

The PreAmp slider on the left side of the Graphical Equalizer window raises or lowers the preamplification of the graphical equalizer all at once. Usually you won't need to mess with the PreAmp slider because you can control the Winamp volume output either through the Main window, through the Windows Volume Control (usually in the Taskbar's tray), or through the volume control on your amplifier or speakers. If you do adjust the PreAmp level, don't set it too high because that will distort the sound.

To adjust the sound, drag the sliders up and down. Winamp takes a second or two to implement the changes, so be patient. You'll notice that the equalizer display at the top of the Graphical Equalizer window changes shape to match the slider settings, as shown below with settings you might try for playing rap in a '65 Impala. This display helps you see when you've got a setting out of whack with the others.

Keep in mind that the graphical equalizer works with (or in some cases against) your sound card and your speakers. If your speakers are tinny and deliver too much treble, you can reduce the high frequencies on the graphical equalizer to help balance the music. And if your speakers are bass heavy, you can use the graphical equalizer to minimize the bass late at night when the folks next door start complaining—or crank it up if they tick you off.

NOTE Don't expect the graphical equalizer to act as a panacea for a poor stereo system. If your audio hardware sucks, clever use of the graphical equalizer may make it suck less. But it won't make it sound like a five thousand–dollar Bang & Olufsen system.

Saving and Loading Preset Equalizations

The graphical equalizer's killer feature is its ability to save and auto-load preset equalizations. This means that you can create a custom equalization profile for any particular track and have Winamp automatically use it each time you play the track.

To create an auto-load preset equalization for a track, play the track and set the graphical equalizer sliders appropriately. Then click the Presets button to display its menu, highlight the Save menu to display its submenu, and choose Auto-Load Preset to display the Save Auto-Load Preset dialog box (shown below). The dialog box will suggest the title of the song as the name for the equalization; edit the name if necessary, and click the Save button to save the preset.

Then enable the auto-load presets by clicking the Auto button in the Graphical Equalizer window so that it displays a light-green light. (It's off by default.) From here on, Winamp will use your customized equalization whenever you play the song.

NOTE When auto-load preset equalizations are enabled and Winamp finishes playing a track with a preset equalization, it will continue to use that equalization for the following track if that track does not have its own equalization.

Winamp comes with a set of preset equalizations that you can load at will by clicking the Presets button, highlighting Load to display its submenu, and choosing Preset to display the Load EQ Preset dialog box, as shown below. Drag the dialog box so that you can see the Graphical Equalizer window.

Select the equalization you want from the list box. Wait a couple of seconds and see how it sounds. To apply it, click the Load button. For example, you might select the Large Hall equalization to make Winamp sound as if it's playing in a large hall. Winamp's preset equalizations are well put together and demonstrate how different a graphical equalizer can make music sound. When you look at the slider positions for some of the equalizations, you may expect minimal changes in the sound—but your ears will tell you otherwise.

To add to the list of preset equalizations, set the sliders for the equalization, click the Presets button and choose Save ➢ Preset to display the Save EQ Preset dialog box. Enter the name for the new preset and click the Save button.

To delete a preset, click the Presets button and choose Delete ➢ Preset or Delete ➢ Auto-Load Preset to display the Delete Preset dialog box or Delete Auto-Load Preset dialog box. Select the preset and click the Delete button to delete it.

19 Check and Set Track Information with Winamp

Winamp lets you quickly view and change the track information, called tag information, that each MP3 file can store.

In the Playlist Editor, right-click a track and choose File Info from the context menu to display the MPEG File Info Box + ID3 Tag Editor dialog box (shown below) with the information for the track. (From the Main window, you can display this dialog box by double-clicking the track title.) Change the information as appropriate and then click the Save button to save it to the MP3 file. You can also click the Remove ID3 button to remove the tag information from the MP3 file.

![MPEG file info box + ID3 tag editor dialog box showing track information for mind_with_noise.mp3 with fields: Title "Mind With Noise!", Artist "Tommy and the Stompers", Album (blank), Year 1999, Genre "Instrumental Ro", Comment "http://mp3.com/TommyandtheSto". MPEG info: Size: 3823610 bytes, Length: 238 seconds, MPEG 1.0 layer 3, 128kbit, 9169 frames, 44100hz Stereo, Private: No, CRCs: No, Copyrighted: No, Original: Yes, Emphasis: None. Buttons: Save, Cancel, Remove ID3.]

20 Choose Visualizations for Winamp

Winamp's Vis display provides *visual entertainment* (read: graphics that look way cool when you're totally spaced) keyed to the frequencies of the music you're playing. In this section, we'll look quickly at the main options the Vis display provides.

Right-click the Vis display and choose Visualization Options from the context menu, or choose Visualization ➢ Visualization Options from the main menu, or press Alt+O to display the Winamp Preferences dialog box with the Visualization page displayed, as shown below.

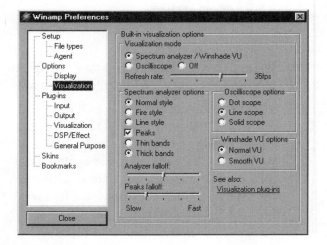

The bulleted list below describes what the options on the Visualization page of the Winamp Preferences dialog box do. Because Winamp implements the choices in the Winamp Preferences dialog box when you choose them, you can move the dialog box off the Winamp window and watch the effects of the changes you're making.

Visualization Mode group box In this group box, choose the visualization mode you want: Spectrum Analyzer/Winshade VU (rising and falling columns in regular mode, a rising and falling bar in Windowshade mode), Oscilliscope (an oscilloscope waveform), or Off (nada).

NOTE You can toggle visualization mode between Analyzer, Scope, and off by clicking the Vis display.

Spectrum Analyzer Options group box In this group box, select options to use when you're running the spectrum analyzer. Select the Normal Style option button, the Fire Style option button, or Line Style option button to determine the style; select the Peaks check box if you want the spectrum analyzer to mark the peaks momentarily; and select the Thin Bands option button or the Thick Bands option button to specify the width of the bands. Finally, adjust the Analyzer Falloff slider and the Peaks Falloff slider to give you the effect you want.

Oscilliscope Options group box In this group box, select the option button for the oscilloscope effect you want: Dot Scope, Line Scope, or Solid Scope.

Winshade VU Options group box In this group box, select the Normal VU option button for "normal" jerky movement on the windowshade meter or the Smooth VU option button for a smoother effect.

The illustration below shows the Vis display using Fire with Thin Bands and Peaks.

21 Change Winamp's Look with Skins

Winamp supports different skins—different looks that you can apply with the click of a couple of buttons. By applying different skins to Winamp, you can change its looks completely, while the functionality of each control remains the same—sort of like *Face Off* goes audio.

The illustration below shows the Sketchamp skin.

You can get skins from skin archives online, or you can create your own skins.

Getting Winamp Skins

You can download huge numbers of Winamp skins from the Internet. At this writing, key sites include the Winamp site (`http://www.winamp.com/winamp/skins/index.phtml`), the Winamp Skins Warehouse (`http://start.at/skins`), and the 1001 Winamp Skins site (`http://www.1001winampskins.com/`).

To try out a new skin, download it from the site and unzip it to a folder within your `\Winamp\Skins\` folder. You can then apply the skin as described in the next section.

Applying a Skin

To apply a skin quickly, choose the skin from the Skins submenu off the main menu. To apply a skin more slowly and thoughtfully, follow these steps:

1. Press Alt+S to display the Skins page of the Winamp Preferences dialog box with a list of the folders containing the skins in your designated skins directory.

   The first time you use the Skin Browser, you'll need to set your skins directory. Click the Set Skins Directory button to display the Select Winamp Skin Directory dialog box. In the tree list box, select the directory and click the OK button.

2. Select the folder for the skin you want. Winamp will apply it automatically.

3. Click the Close button to close the Winamp Preferences dialog box.

NOTE Once you've downloaded a variety of skins, you may want to introduce a little random variety into your life. Check the Select Random Skin on Play check box on the Skins page of the Preferences dialog box, and each time you set a track or playlist going, Winamp will take on a new look.

Creating Your Own Skins for Winamp

As you'll have guessed if you've looked at more than a few of the plethora of Winamp skins available on the Web, you can create your own skins for Winamp. We don't have space to cover this topic in this book (to cover it, we'd have to jettison some more vital information), but we do cover it in some depth in *Mastering MP3 and Digital Audio*, also published by Sybex and available as of August 2000 in all good bookstores known to sentient bipeds.

22 Add Functionality to Winamp with Plug-Ins

Winamp supports a variety of *plug-ins*—add-in components that enhance Winamp's capabilities and functionality. Here are a few examples of what plug-ins can do:

◆ Let you play RealAudio and RealMedia files, so that you can use Winamp instead of RealPlayer, or a plug-in that enables you to broadcast in the SHOUTcast format.

◆ Provide dreamy or intense visualizations to enhance the music you're playing.

◆ Let you control Winamp from an infrared remote control unit.

◆ Display the lyrics associated with an MP3 file.

◆ Add reverb and other effects to the audio you're playing.

◆ Start Winamp playing at a given time, so that you can use it as an alarm.

Winamp divides plug-ins into five categories: Input, Output, Visualization, DSP/Effect, and General Purpose. (DSP is the abbreviation for *digital signal processor*, a category of chip for creating sound effects.)

At this writing, most plug-ins are free, but there are some that you have to pay for. In this section, we'll show you three of our favorite free plug-ins.

Getting Plug-Ins

The first step in working with plug-ins is to download the ones you need. Your first stop should be the main Winamp site, `http://www.winamp.com`, which includes a large collection of plug-ins sorted into categories.

Navigate to the plug-in that you want and download it as usual. Then unzip the plug-in's files to your `\Winamp\Plugins\` folder.

NOTE You can use different folders for plug-ins by setting the Visualization Plug-In Directory and DSP/Effect Plug-In Directory options in the Plug-In Settings group box in the Winamp Preferences dialog box (Ctrl+P).

Selecting, Configuring, and Running a Plug-In

The following list shows the general steps for selecting, configuring, and running a plug-in. In the next three sections, we'll look at the specifics of three of the best plug-ins.

1. Press Ctrl+K, or choose Visualization ➤ Select Plug-In from the main menu, to display the Winamp Preferences dialog box with the Visualization page under Plug-Ins selected.

To choose a different sort of plug-in than visualization, choose Input, Output, DSP/Effect, or General Purpose in the Plug-Ins area.

2. In the list box, select the plug-in you want to run.

3. If this is the first time you've run the plug-in, click the Configure button to display a dialog box containing any configuration options that the plug-in supports. (Some plug-ins do not support any configuration options.) Choose options as appropriate and close the dialog box.

4. Click the Start button to start the plug-in.

5. Click the Close button to close the Winamp Preferences dialog box. The plug-in should now be running.

Adding RealAudio Functionality to Winamp

The RealAudio plug-in from innover lets you play RealAudio files and streams—both audio and video—from within Winamp. By using this plug-in, you can avoid using RealPlayer almost entirely.

Here's how to get, install, and configure the RealAudio plug-in:

1. Download the RealAudio plug-in from the main Winamp site or from another site of your choosing, and save it to your hard disk.

2. Run the EXE file to install the plug-in. The plug-in will detect your Winamp directory and will offer to install itself there, as shown below.

3. Usually, you'll do best to install the plug-in in the suggested directory, but if you want, you can click the Browse button and use the resulting Select Your Winamp Directory dialog box to select a different directory.

4. Click the Next button when you're ready to proceed. You'll see an installation dialog box flash by, and then a message box telling you that the installation was successful. The plug-in will also display an information page in your default Web browser.

This plug-in needs no configuration, so you're all done. (If you're in any doubt that it's installed correctly, fire up Winamp and press Ctrl+K to display the Winamp Preferences dialog box with the Plug-Ins page displayed. Check the Input page for an entry called innover's RealAudio Plugin for Winamp.)

You can now use Winamp to play RealAudio audio and video files and streams. If you already have RealPlayer installed on your computer, you may need to reassign the RealAudio file associations from RealPlayer to Winamp.

Ensuring a Supply of Eye Candy

Many of the plug-ins available for Winamp provide visual effects to accompany the music you're listening to. One of our current favorites is Climax by Sergej Müller, which provides amazing graphics.

Here's how to get, install, and configure Climax:

1. Download the latest version of Climax from `http://www.winamp.com`.

2. Run the EXE file to start the installation routine. You'll see the Climax for Winamp dialog box shown below.

3. Either accept the auto-detected Winamp directory or use the Browse button and the Select Your Winamp Directory dialog box to designate a different directory.

4. Click the Next button to install Climax. Once the installation has finished, Climax will display its readme file of information.

5. Press Ctrl+K to display the Winamp Preferences dialog box with the Visualization page displayed.

6. In the Visualization Plug-Ins list box, select the entry for Climax for Winamp.

7. Click the Start button. Climax will display the Climax window with visualizations running in time to the music. The next illustration shows Climax running in a window.

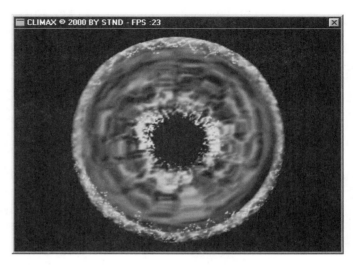

You can toggle Climax between a window and full screen by pressing the F4 key. Alternatively, right-click anywhere in the Climax window or the full Climax screen and choose Full Screen from the context menu. The illustration below shows Climax running full screen.

To configure Climax, press the F2 key. You'll see the Climax dialog box shown below, which offers a variety of information and configuration options that you can fiddle with by clicking the category on the left-hand side of the dialog box:

Display page On this page, you can set the resolution to use for running Climax full screen. This resolution doesn't have to be the same resolution at which you're running Windows—for example, you could be running Windows at 800 × 600 resolution and run Climax at 1024 × 768 if you wanted. But be sure that you don't choose a resolution higher than your monitor and graphics card support. The higher the resolution the more processing power is needed; unless you have a fierce graphics card, Climax may run slowly and jerkily at the higher resolutions. On the Display page, you can also choose a frame rate (in frames per second—FPS), whether you want to always start Climax in full-screen mode, and whether you want to minimize Winamp when Climax is in full-screen mode.

Keys page The illustration shows the Keys page of the dialog box, which gives the keystrokes that you can use for configuring and running Climax. For example, you can press the B key to move to the next song in Winamp or the Z key to move to the previous song—so you can control Winamp easily even when you're running Climax full screen.

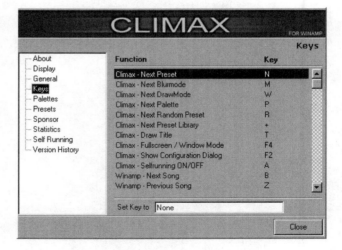

When you've set the options to your satisfaction, click the Close button to close the Climax dialog box.

To stop Climax running, press the Esc key with the Climax window or full-screen view active.

Adding Reverberation and Effects with DeFX

DeFX is a plug-in that lets you add effects such as reverberation, voice removal, and pitch modulation to MP3 playback.

Here's how to get, install, and configure DeFX:

1. Download the latest version of DeFX from http://www.winamp.com or another Winamp plug-in site.

2. Run the DeFX file to start the installation procedure. You'll see the DeFX DSP/Effects Plug-In for Winamp dialog box, shown next. Change the directory if necessary; if not, click the Next button. When the installation ends, you'll see an Installation Successful message box; dismiss it.

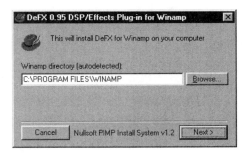

3. Press Ctrl+K to display the Winamp Preferences dialog box.

4. Click the DSP/Effect item in the left-hand list box to display the DSP/Effect Plug-In page.

5. Select the entry for DeFX in the right-hand list box. DeFX will automatically display its Console dialog box, as shown next.

6. In the Pitch Modulation, Voice Removal, and Reverberation group boxes, select the effects you want. Select the unnamed toggle button in the relevant group box to turn the effect on (when the button appears raised, it's deselected; when pushed in, it's selected). Voice Removal is good for karaoke (or Bob Dylan CDs), and Reverberation's great if you like to listen to music that seems like it's coming from a really big sewer pipe (without the smells).

WARNING The DeFX effects take a significant amount of processing power. In particular, heavy reverberation can swamp a less than macho computer and interrupt audio playback.

7. Click the Close button (the × button) to close the DeFX Plug-In Control Panel. (Alternatively, you can keep it open as you play music so that you can continue to make adjustments.)

8. Click the Close button to close the Winamp Preferences dialog box.

23 Play CDs with Winamp

As we mentioned earlier, Winamp can play CDs for you. If you chose the Autoplay Audio CDs option during setup, Winamp should already be set up for you to play CDs; if not, you need to set it up yourself.

To set up your copy of Winamp to play CDs for you, follow these steps:

1. Press Ctrl+P, or choose Options ➢ Preferences from the main menu, to display the Winamp Preferences dialog box shown below.

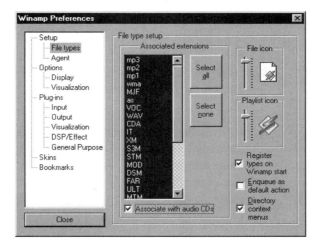

2. Select the Associate with Audio CDs check box.

3. Click the Close button.

When you insert an audio CD into your CD drive and close the drive, Winamp will automatically load the CD. If you're using Winamp's Internet features and are connected to the Internet, Winamp will contact CDDB and download the track titles.

You can then play the CD by using the Winamp controls. Better yet, you can use standard Winamp commands to manipulate the CD's playlist, removing and rearranging tracks as the fancy takes you.

24 Get and Install Sonique

Sonique is one of the leading MP3 players. It owes its popularity both to being free and to being a cool-looking and highly functional MP3 player that you can customize freely with skins.

You'll find a copy of Sonique 1.30 on the CD in the \Sonique\ folder. To check for the latest version of Sonique, point your favorite browser at http://www.sonique.com.

To install Sonique, double-click the distribution EXE file on the CD or wherever you downloaded it. The installation program will walk you through a standard InstallShield installation routine that includes accepting a license agreement and specifying an installation directory and program folder.

The first dialog box worth noting is the Supported File Types dialog box, shown next, in which you specify the file types for which you want Sonique to start automatically.

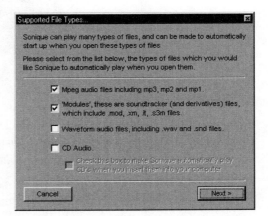

Unless you're using another MP3 player as your primary player, select the MPEG Audio Files Including MP3, MP2, and MP1 check box. Select the other check boxes, or leave them cleared, as seems appropriate to your needs. For example, if you want to use Sonique as your default CD player, select the CD Audio check box. When you select this check box, you can also select the check box below it (which is grayed out in the illustration) to make Sonique automatically play audio CDs when you insert them in your CD-ROM drive.

Click the Next button when you've made your choices. The installation routine will display the Internet Connection Configuration dialog box shown below.

In the Internet Connection Type group box, select the option button corresponding to the type of Internet connection your computer uses—a modem, a LAN, or none. If you don't want to use Sonique's Internet features, select the I Do Not Have an Internet Connection option button. These Internet features include online updates to Sonique, including some great visualizations. If you're online, you'll probably want to use these features.

If your computer connects to the Internet via a proxy server, select the I Connect via a Proxy check box. Then enter the address of the proxy server in the Address text box and the port number in the Port text box. The proxy server's address will probably be an IP address, something like 192.168.1.2. The port will be a number, such as 80. (Get these numbers from your network administrator if you don't know them—you won't be able to guess them unless you're psychic, and these examples are unlikely to be right for you.) If you need to log in to your proxy server, select the My Proxy Require a Name and/or Password check box, and enter the name in the Name text box and the password in the Password text box.

Again, click the Next button to proceed. The installation routine will install Sonique and create the program group and icons. It will then display the Setup Complete dialog box, from which you can view the readme file for the latest information on Sonique or launch the program file.

25 Understand Sonique's Interface

You can launch Sonique either from the Start menu item or Desktop icon it creates or from the Sonique QuickStart item it adds to your system tray. Click the Sonique QuickStart item and choose Open Sonique from the context menu. The first time you run Sonique, it will display the Register Sonique dialog box, shown next. Fill in the information as you see fit, select or clear the Send Me Sonique News check box and the Send Me Free Music News check box as appropriate, and click the Register Now button. Sonique will register you and will direct your browser to the Sonique Web site, where it will thank you for registering by offering you some free music to download.

Probably right around the time you're browsing the free music, Sonique will display the Sonique Online Updates dialog box, shown next, offering you Sonique updates and visualizations that you may want to download. Choose the items you want to download and click the Install Items button.

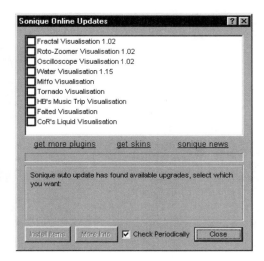

Sonique will download and install the items and will display a text-editor window (typically Notepad) containing their readme files. When it's finished, it will display an Upgrade Complete message box and will—finally—show you Sonique itself.

As you'll see, Sonique has a unique interface that can take a bit of getting used to. There are three modes and the main mode has multiple screens. We'll start with Navigation Console mode (*Nav mode* for short), the default mode Sonique initially runs in, with the Navigation screen displayed, as shown on the next page.

NOTE At first, Sonique may seem unnecessarily complicated. But once you've played with it for a few minutes, you'll identify the features most useful to you and concentrate on them.

The Navigation Console offers seven main screens, which we'll visit in the following sections:

Navigation screen   This screen (shown on the next page) gets you around Sonique.

Playlist Editor screen   This screen is used to create, save, and load playlists.

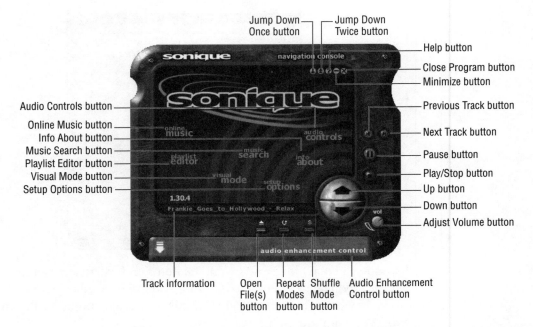

Visual Mode screen   This screen provides visual accompaniment to the music that's playing.

Setup Options screen   This screen lets you configure Sonique's system, audio, and visual options.

Info About screen   This screen displays Sonique's credits, the readme and what's new items, and the license information. We doubt you'll visit this screen frequently.

Audio Enhancements screen   This screen lets you set equalizations.

Music Search screen   This screen lets you search for music using Lycos Music Search or HotBot.

You can open and play tracks from any of the screens on the Navigation Console.

Sonique has two more compact modes designed for play: Mid-State mode displays Sonique as a shell-shaped player, as shown next.

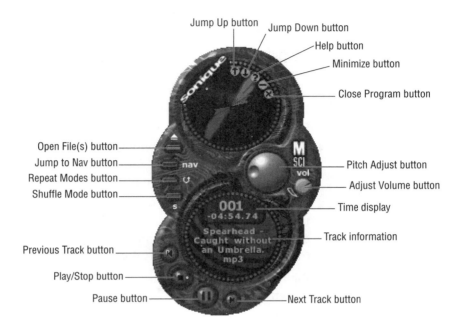

Jump Up button
Jump Down button
Help button
Minimize button
Close Program button
Open File(s) button
Jump to Nav button
Repeat Modes button
Shuffle Mode button
Pitch Adjust button
Adjust Volume button
Time display
Track information
Previous Track button
Play/Stop button
Pause button
Next Track button

Small-State mode, shown in the next two illustrations, takes up very little screen real estate. Small-State mode displays Sonique as a bar showing the track number and playing time, as you see in the upper illustration. When you move the mouse pointer over the Small-State Mode bar, it displays the drop-down panel of controls that you see in the lower illustration.

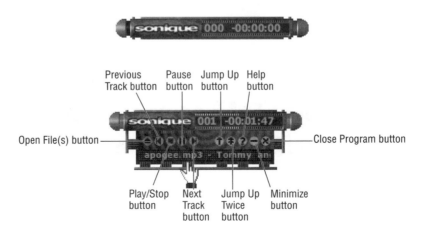

Previous Track button
Pause button
Jump Up button
Help button
Open File(s) button
Close Program button
Play/Stop button
Next Track button
Jump Up Twice button
Minimize button

You can navigate Sonique's modes with the keyboard or the mouse as follows:

◆ Use the navigation buttons (such as the Jump Up button) in the Sonique windows.

◆ Double-click any part of Sonique's chassis (the gray frame), or press Ctrl+Tab, to move between modes in the following sequence: Small-State mode, Mid-State mode, and Navigation Console. Double-click with the right mouse button to move through the modes in the reverse order.

◆ To quickly change modes with the keyboard, press Ctrl+N for the Navigation Console, Ctrl+E for Visual mode, Ctrl+M for Mid-State mode, or Ctrl+, (Ctrl+comma) for Small-State mode.

◆ To display different screens on the Navigation Console, press Ctrl+O to display the Online Tools, Ctrl+P to display the Playlist Editor, Ctrl+R to display the Audio Enhancement screen and Audio Enhancement Control, or Ctrl+S to display the Setup Options screen.

◆ Right-click to move from any screen back to main Navigation Console screen.

To move Sonique, click any part of the chassis and drag it to where you want it to appear. To minimize Sonique, click the Minimize button in any mode. To close Sonique, click the Close Program button in any mode.

To keep Sonique in front of other programs you're running so that you can always access it immediately, press Ctrl+T, or display the Setup Options screen by clicking the Setup Options button in the Navigation Console and select the Always on Top check box in the System Options area.

26 Play MP3 Files and SHOUTcast Streams with Sonique

Once you've gotten Sonique into the mode you like, play music with it by using the button controls as usual or the keyboard as follows:

◆ Press L to display the Add & Play Sonique Media dialog box (shown next). Select the tracks you want, or enter a SHOUTcast URL in the Enter URL text box, and click the Open button.

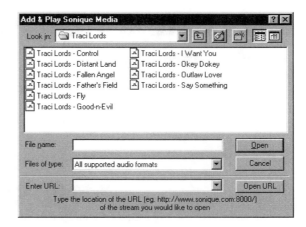

◆ Press X to start or stop the track playing.

◆ Press C to pause the track.

◆ Press D to clear the playlist.

◆ Press B or → to move to the next track. Press Z or ← to move to the previous track.

You can control the volume by using either the mouse or the keyboard as follows:

◆ To change the volume, click the Volume button and drag up or right (to increase the volume) or down or to the left (to decrease it).

◆ Press the ↑ key to increase the volume and the ↓ key to decrease it. (In the Playlist Editor, these keys move the selection up and down the playlist rather than changing the volume.)

◆ Press the ` key (not the apostrophe but the accent key that's usually on a key with the ~ on the upper-left corner of a regular keyboard) to reduce the volume to 0%.

◆ Press 1 for 10% volume, 2 for 20% volume, and so on up to 0 for 100% volume.

27 Create a Playlist with Sonique

To create a playlist, start the Playlist Editor (shown here with a number of songs added) by pressing P or by clicking the Playlist Editor button in the Navigation Console.

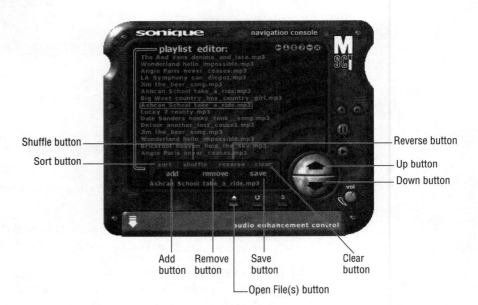

The Playlist Editor is straightforward to use. Here's the condensed version:

◆ Click the Add button to display the Add & Play Sonique Media dialog box. Select the tracks, playlists, or SHOUTcast streams you want to add, and then click the Open button.

◆ To remove a track or stream from the playlist, select it and click the Remove button. Shift+click or Ctrl+click to select multiple tracks.

◆ To sort the tracks in the playlist into alphabetical order, click the Sort button.

◆ To shuffle the tracks in the playlist, click the Shuffle button until Sonique produces an order that amuses you.

◆ To reverse the order of the current playlist, click the Reverse button.

◆ To move to a different track in the playlist, use the Up and Down buttons.

◆ To save the current playlist, click the Save button. Sonique will display the Save Sonique Media Playlist dialog box. Enter the name for the playlist (Sonique uses a PLS extension for playlist files), choose a suitable location for it (perhaps with your other playlists), and click the Save button.

◆ To open a playlist, click the Open File(s) button. In the Open & Play Sonique Media dialog box, select the playlist, and then click the Open button.

◆ To clear the current playlist, click the Clear button.

NOTE To display the ID3 tag attached to an MP3 file, click the File Info button on the Navigation Console in Visual mode. Sonique will display the tag information in your current browser. At this writing, Sonique does not support ID3 tag editing.

28 Tweak Sonique's Sound with the Audio Enhancement Control

If you like to tweak the way your music sounds, you'll be glad to learn that Sonique's Audio Enhancement Control is a full-featured graphical equalizer.

It lacks some of the features that Winamp's graphical equalizer provides, but it gives you even fuller control over the sound of your music.

Click the Audio Controls button on the main screen of the Navigation Console to display the Audio Enhancement screen and pop out the Audio Enhancement Control (shown below). You can also click the Audio Enhancement Control button on the Navigation Console to display the Audio Enhancement Control at any time. From the keyboard, press Ctrl+R to display the Audio Enhancement screen and the Audio Enhancement Control.

To turn on the equalizer, select the Equalizer Enabled check box on the Audio Enhancement screen. To hide the Audio Enhancement Control again, click the Audio Enhancement Control button.

To create an equalization, drag the sliders for the different frequencies up and down until you achieve the sound balance you want.

The Spline Tension check box on the Audio Enhancement screen controls whether the pitch sliders move independently or affect nearby sliders. When this check box is selected, moving a slider moves the adjacent sliders in the same direction to a lesser degree, producing a gradual change in the wave form, as shown next.

To change the preamplification, click the Amp button and drag up (or left) or down (or right). Similarly, use the Balance button to adjust the left-right balance and the control to change the pitch (the speed) at which the track is playing. Crank the pitch to make speech sound like chipmunks, or wind it down to make grinding noises grind to a halt. Use the readout in the song-title area to check the precise setting you're at.

To save an equalization:

1. Click the Save button. Sonique will display the Select a Preset Save Location panel on the Audio Enhancement screen shown next.

2. Click the preset save location to which you want to assign the equalization.

To load an equalization, click the Load button and choose the equalization from the Select a Preset Load Location panel that appears.

To reset the equalizer, click the Reset button on the Audio Enhancement screen.

29 Space Your Brain with Sonique Visualizations

Sonique comes complete with built-in visualizations that provide a psychedelic lightshow accompaniment to what you're playing.

Mid-State mode displays a small-scale visualization whenever you're playing music. You can change from one visualization to the next by moving the mouse pointer over the Vis Display window so that the Vis buttons pop up (as shown next), then clicking one of the buttons.

Sonique's best effects are accessible only from Nav mode. From any mode, press Ctrl+E to display Visual mode. (Sonique will switch to Nav mode if it's in another mode.) If you're already in Nav mode, you can also click the Visual Mode button on the Navigation screen to enter Visual mode, as shown next.

Click the Up and Down buttons, or press the , (comma) and . (period) keys, to change from one visualization to the next.

Click the Full Window Vis Mode button at the upper-right corner of the Vis display to enlarge the visualization to fill the Sonique screen area. You then have another choice at the upper-left corner of the Vis area—the No Extras Full Window Mode button, which removes all the information overlaid on the screen area. Click the button again to restore Full Window Vis mode with the overlaid information.

Full Window Vis mode is great for keeping your mind engaged when you're setting up monster custom playlists with Sonique. But when you've gotten a playlist rolling and are ready to kick back and enjoy a playlist, switch to Sonique's full-bore visualizations:

1. Click the Full Screen Vis button to have the visualization take over your entire screen.

2. Press the comma and period keys to switch from one visualization to another.

3. When you've found one you like, switch off the lights or draw the curtains.

4. Press Esc to return to normality.

WARNING Full Screen Vis mode can choke a slower computer and spoil playback. If you're running a classic Pentium, chances are that's the processor choking, not your eardrums popping—but check both to make sure.

NOTE To get more impressive visualizations out of a song at the same volume, turn up the preamplification and turn down the volume to balance things out.

30 Change Sonique's Skin

One of Sonique's coolest and most popular features is its support for different skins. By applying a skin to Sonique, you can completely change its appearance. The next illustration shows the Bubble Blues skin applied to Sonique.

Getting Skins

You'll have no problems finding skins for Sonique. Sonique maintains a stock of skins at http://www.skins.sonique.com. You'll also find them at other Web sites and on newsgroups.

Installing a Skin

The easiest way to install a skin is to download it directly into the \Sonique\
skins\ folder. You can also copy or move a skin manually into this folder.

Alternatively, right-click the skin file (which will have a SGF extension) in Explorer and choose Install into Sonique from the context menu.

Applying a Skin

You can apply a skin to Sonique in a couple of different ways:

◆ From the Navigation Console, click the Setup Options button to display the Setup Options screen. Click the Skins button on the right-hand side to display the setup options for skins with a thumbnail of the current skin. Then use the Up and Down buttons to browse through the skins you have available in your \Sonique\skins\ folder. To apply the skin, click the back arrow button or right mouse button. Sonique will apply the skin and will return you to the Navigation Console.

◆ To apply a skin immediately, double-click it in Explorer.

31 Extend Sonique with Plug-Ins

Another cool feature of Sonique is its support for visualization and audio plug-ins that extend its functionality.

Getting Plug-Ins

As you saw earlier, Sonique automatically alerts you to new plug-ins if you let it. If you don't let it, or if you simply must have the latest plug-ins the second they're released, point your favorite Web browser at the Sonique Web site (http://www.sonique.com) and follow the Plug-Ins link to get to the Plug-Ins page. Browse the categories and download anything that strikes your fancy.

Configuring Plug-Ins

Here's how to configure Sonique plug-ins:

1. Press Ctrl+S, or click the Setup Options button on the Navigation screen in Nav mode, to display the Setup Options screen.

2. Click the Plug-Ins button (just above the title display) to display the Plug-Ins screen.

3. On the right-hand side of the screen, click the tab for the plug-in you want to configure. The next illustration shows the configuration screen for the StarDust decoder plug-in.

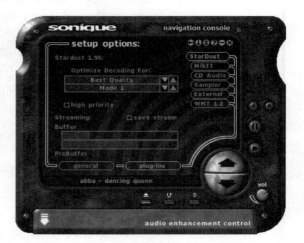

4. Select options for the plug-in. For example, the StarDust plug-in includes options for optimizing the decoding (for quality or performance) and streaming audio (saving the stream to the disk, and changing the size of the buffer and prebuffer to help avoid breakups).

5. Click the Navigation Menu button to return to the Navigation screen.

Windows MP3 Rippers and Jukeboxes

In this part of the book, we'll look at the two key MP3 player/ripper/jukeboxes for Windows. This is a field in which there's a huge amount of competition—as you'd guess, it's the most lucrative market for MP3 software—but we decided to stick with the products we've found the best: MusicMatch Jukebox and RealJukebox Plus.

MusicMatch Jukebox is one of the most popular ripper/player/jukeboxes currently available. MusicMatch Jukebox offers a Standard version that you can download for free but which is limited to recording at 96kbps—a sampling rate that most people find unacceptable for sustained music listening. (It's a bit like listening to AM radio when you're used to FM.) MusicMatch is betting that, after listening to low-quality audio for a short while, you'll be prepared to register and cough up $29.99 for the full version of MusicMatch Jukebox that can record at 128kbps (the standard for CD-quality MP3 files) and higher speeds to make music sound good again. We'd say this is a solid bet. MusicMatch Jukebox's killer feature is enabling you to create CDs directly from MusicMatch Jukebox.

RealJukebox Plus is a ripper/player/jukebox from RealNetworks. RealJukebox is available in a standard edition (called RealJukebox) that's free but is limited to recording at 96kbps (do you detect a little theme developing here?) and a Plus edition (called RealJukebox Plus) that costs $29.99 but lets you rip at decent quality. Because we figure you want decent quality, we concentrate on RealJukebox Plus, though we'll show you a screen or two from RealJukebox just so that you don't feel left out if you're stuck with the freebie.

Before we get started on these ripper-jukeboxes, we'll discuss quickly how to choose the right sampling rate for the MP3 files you'll create. Because you can vary the sampling rate for (almost) any ripper, this will be a general discussion.

NOTE Of the many other Windows rippers that we're not covering here, one that we've had great results with is AudioCatalyst from Xing Technologies (http://www.xingtech.com). AudioCatalyst is a ripper (not a player and not a jukebox) that comes in both Windows and Mac versions. We provide coverage of the Mac version of AudioCatalyst in the AudioCatalyst Web supplement to this book, which you'll find on the Sybex Web site (http://www.sybex.com). The Windows version of AudioCatalyst bears a strong family likeness to the Mac version, though (needless to say) there are the inevitable interface differences.

32 Choose the Right Sampling Rate

Minor alert: This section gets mildly technical. But as with the legal stuff earlier in this book, this is information you need to know—and we'll keep it short.

As we discussed in *1. Understand What MP3 Is and What It Does*, MP3 rocks because it compresses audio into a small file *and* it retains near-CD quality. To compress the audio, it uses sampling.

Before you start recording MP3 files, you need to set the sampling rate you'll use. To put it simply, the higher the sampling rate (within reason), the better the music will sound, and the larger the file size will be.

For example, a ripper such as MusicMatch Jukebox offers preset sampling rates of 64kbps (kilobits per second), 96kbps, 128kbps, and 160kbps, together with custom sampling rates that you can choose for yourself. (These rates are in the paid-and-registered version of the product; the free version tops out at 96kbps in the hope of your ears' forcing you to break open your wallet.) 64kbps is somewhat euphemistically termed "FM Radio Quality" (we reckon it's much worse), 96kbps is described as "near CD quality" (we'd say it's not within easy commuting distance of CD quality), and 128kbps and 160kbps are described as "CD quality" (which is almost true). Most people find music sampled at a rate below 128kbps to be unacceptable to listen to, but for spoken audio, higher-capacity options such as 64kbps or lower can be a good choice.

When recording music, you'll usually do best to use a sampling rate of 128kbps. Using a higher sampling rate generally produces little improvement in sound quality, and the file sizes will of course be larger. Some people swear by 160kbps, and others by 192, so try them yourself and see which suits you the best. Go all the way to 320kbps if your ears demand it and if you have the storage space to burn.

If you want to cram as much music as possible onto a device and are prepared to settle for poorer sound quality, experiment with lower bitrates and establish what you find tolerable for listening. But if you're looking to digitize any serious chunk of your music collection, be sure to do it at a sampling rate high enough that you'll enjoy the music for years rather than weeks.

Keep in mind that you won't be able to increase the sampling rate of any tracks you've already recorded—though with certain specialized programs, you can decrease the sampling rate if you really want to do so.

NOTE It doesn't take any more time to rip tracks at a higher sampling rate than at a lower sampling rate. (In fact, with most ripping programs, ripping at a higher sampling rate takes less time because it requires less compression and less processing power.)

33 Get, Install, and Configure MusicMatch Jukebox

We've included version 5 of MusicMatch Jukebox on the CD at the back of the book. To check for a newer version, browse http://www.musicmatch .com. At this writing, MusicMatch Jukebox is a little under 7MB—a hefty download. The application requires a minimum processor speed of 166MHz, preferably MMX, though needless to say you'll probably be much happier with performance if your processor is much faster than this.

To install MusicMatch Jukebox, double-click the distribution file. Install-Shield will walk you through a standard installation routine in which you accept a license agreement, are encouraged to register the software, and specify an installation folder, music folder, and Start menu group. We'll mention just the highlights here and leave you to handle the routine decisions.

The first thing to note is the User Registration Info dialog box, shown in the following illustration. You'll have to enter at least one character in the Name text box, the Email text box, and the Postal/Zip Code text box; select a year of birth; and specify a gender in order to enable the Next button, which is disabled by default. We feel that you shouldn't have to give this information, but you can't install MusicMatch Jukebox without appearing to give it. (If you have qualms about supplying this information, you might want to be less than honest here.) Either way, think twice before you leave the Notify Me When Software Upgrades Are Available check box and the Send Me Music-Related News and Special Offers check box selected, as they are by default.

Next, you get the Personalize Net Music dialog box, shown next, which invites you to let MusicMatch Jukebox upload to a MusicMatch server information on the music you listen to, save, and download. MusicMatch uses this information to deliver personalized recommendations to you, and assures you that "your personal music preferences…will never be sold or shared"—but the idea of MusicMatch Jukebox automatically uploading information about our listening habits creeps us out too much for us to recommend using this feature. However, your mileage will vary, so select the Yes (Recommended) option button rather than the No option button if you like. The option buttons are implemented a little strangely, and to access the No button via the keyboard, you'll need to press one of the arrow keys (for example, →) rather than the Tab key.

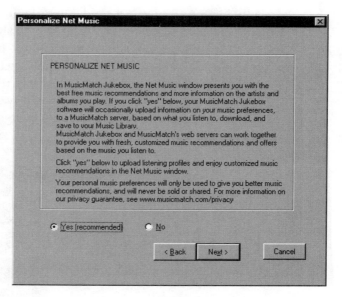

After you choose the destination location, your music folder, the program folder, and whether you want MusicMatch Jukebox icons on your Desktop, on your Quick Launch toolbar, and in your system tray, you get to a more serious decision in the Filetype Registration dialog box (shown below). For which file types do you want to use MusicMatch Jukebox?

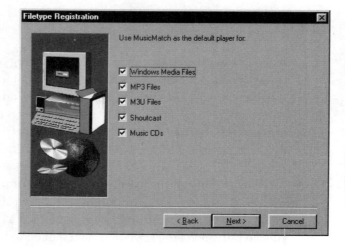

If you're using another MP3 player (such as Winamp, Sonique, or XingMP3 Player), you'll probably want to clear some or all of these check boxes. If you'll be using MusicMatch Jukebox primarily or exclusively, leave them selected.

If you do choose to make MusicMatch Jukebox your default MP3 player, it will monitor your file associations aggressively, even when you're not running it, to see if any have been stolen by another application. (Typically, this will happen when you install another MP3 player or jukebox after installing MusicMatch Jukebox; it may also happen when you run another player or jukebox that reclaims file associations it finds Music-Match Jukebox has stolen from it.) If MusicMatch Jukebox detects that it no longer has its associations, it will display the MusicMatch Jukebox File Associations dialog box, shown below.

To restore the associations, leave the Reclaim File Associations option button selected (it's selected by default) and click the OK button. To leave the file associations with whichever application has stolen them, select the Do Not Reclaim File Associations option button and click the OK button. You can prevent MusicMatch Jukebox from bugging you about this by selecting the Don't Ask Me Again check box before closing the MusicMatch Jukebox File Associations dialog box.

Once you're done with the file types, MusicMatch Jukebox will complete the installation and will display the Setup Complete dialog box. Leave the Run MusicMatch Jukebox Now check box selected and click the Finish button to close this dialog box. You're just about ready to rock.

The first time you run it, MusicMatch Jukebox will display the Search for Music dialog box, shown next. In the Look In drop-down list, select the drive or drives you want MusicMatch Jukebox to search. To limit the search to a particular folder, click the Browse button to display the Browse for Folder dialog box, navigate to and select the drive, and click the OK button.

MusicMatch Jukebox will automatically enter the appropriate drive in the Look In drop-down list. Make sure the Windows Media Files check box and the MP2/MP3 Files check box are selected or cleared as suits you, then click the OK button. MusicMatch Jukebox will search for music and will display the Adding *x* Songs to Music Library dialog box, shown below, until it has finished adding all the songs to its music database.

Next, you may see the Confirm Association dialog box, shown below, in which MusicMatch Jukebox is trying to grab some unspecified file associations from another application. You probably want to choose the Yes button in this dialog box, though it's tedious not to know which file associations MusicMatch Jukebox is after.

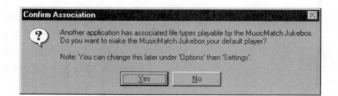

Finally, you'll be ready to start using MusicMatch Jukebox. The following illustration shows the Main window and the Music Library window. You'll probably be seeing them joined together, but we've pulled them apart so that we could label them better. You'll also be seeing the Recorder window, which we'll show you how to use in a few pages' time, and a Welcome Tips window, which we'll let you explore on your own.

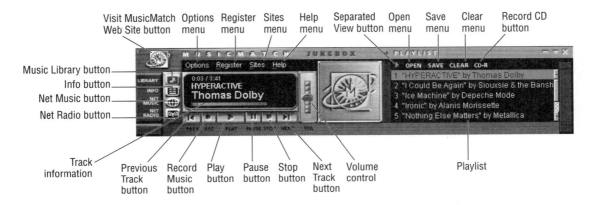

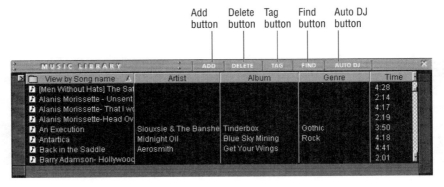

The MusicMatch Jukebox windows are easy to handle:

◆ You can drag the windows around as you want.

◆ You can click the Separated View button in the Main window to separate the Playlist window (on the right-hand side of the Main window in the illustration above) from the Main window. Click the resulting Integrated View button in the Playlist window to reunite the two.

◆ To make the Music Library window move with the Main window, drag the Music Library window so that one of its sides sticks to a side of the Main window.

◆ You can resize the Music Library window by clicking its border and dragging.

NOTE To register your copy of MusicMatch Jukebox, choose Register ➢ Enter Key to display the MusicMatch Enter Key dialog box. Enter the key in the Enter the Key (Include Hyphens) text box and click the OK button.

Configuring CDDB

If your computer has an Internet connection, make sure CDDB is configured correctly. You only need to configure CDDB once, and, as you'll see, it offers compelling benefits for most people.

CDDB is an online database of CD information from which PC CD-player applications (including MP3 players that play CDs) and rippers can download CD information—the artist's name, the CD title, track titles, and even lyrics for some tracks.

To configure CDDB, follow these steps:

1. Choose Options ➢ Settings to display the Settings dialog box, then click the CDDB Preferences tab to display the CDDB Preferences page, shown below.

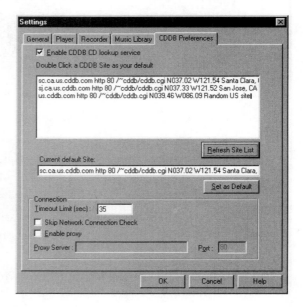

2. Make sure the Enable CDDB CD Lookup Service check box is selected. (If you don't want to use CDDB, clear this check box.)

3. Click the Refresh Site List button to get the latest CDDB sites available.

4. In the Double Click a CDDB Site As Your Default list box, double-click the CDDB site that you want to use. All other things being equal, you'll probably do best with one that's geographically close to you. But if your choice turns out to be slow or too busy, try another. Your selection will appear in the Current Default Site text box.

5. Click the Set As Default button to set the site as your default.

6. If you need to use a proxy server, select the Enable Proxy check box in the Connection group box and enter the server's details in the Proxy Server text box and the Port text box. (Consult your network administrator for this information if you don't know it.) You can also change the timeout limit from its default setting in the Timeout Limit (Sec) text box.

7. Click the OK button to close the Settings dialog box.

Choosing the Sampling Rate

Next, choose the sampling rate to use for your recordings. Like CDDB, this is something you'll typically want to set and forget, unless you suddenly need to make a low-quality recording for someone you dislike. Here's what to do:

1. Select Options ➢ Recorder ➢ Settings to display the Recorder page (shown below) of the Settings dialog box.

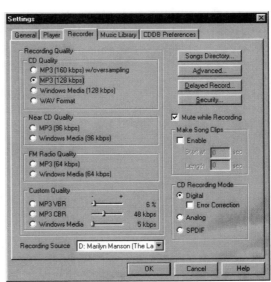

2. In the Recording Quality group box, select the sampling rate at which to record. For most music, you'll want to start with the MP3 (128kbps) setting, the default setting for the full version of MusicMatch Jukebox. (If you have the free version of MusicMatch Jukebox, you'll be able to record only at 96kbps or 64kbps.) If you find the quality not high enough, try the MP3 (160kbps) w/Oversampling setting. For spoken audio, experiment with the MP3 (96kbps) and MP3 (64kbps) settings found in the Near CD Quality and FM Radio Quality group boxes, respectively. For special purposes, you can use the MP3 VBR and MP3 CBR options found in the Custom Quality group box. Here's what you can do with them:

VBR   VBR stands for *variable bitrate* and lets you emphasize the quality of the audio—the amount of information recorded (the *bitrate*) varies according to the complexity of the music. Be warned that VBR can produce large files, and some MP3 players cannot play back VBR files successfully.

CBR   To squeeze even more audio into each megabyte of storage, select the MP3 CBR option button and drag its slider to the left to reduce the bitrate. CBR stands for *constant bitrate* and is best used for reducing the size of the MP3 files you're recording.

3. In the Recording Source drop-down list, select the CD or DVD drive from which you want to record. If you have an audio CD in the drive, the Recording Source drop-down list will show its title; if the drive is empty, the drop-down list will show a generic description, such as *Toshiba CD-ROM*.

4. Click the Songs Directory button to display the New Songs Directory Options dialog box, shown below.

5. In the Directory for New Songs text box, enter the name of the folder in which to store the folders and tracks you rip. Click the ... button to display the Browse for Folder dialog box, navigate to the folder you want to use, and click the OK button.

6. In the Make Sub-Path Using group box, select the Artist check box and Album check box as appropriate to include them in the name of the subfolders that'll be created. For example, if you're ripping the album *Exile on Coldharbour Lane* by A3, having the Artist and Album check boxes selected will produce the subfolder \A3\Exile on Cold-harbour Lane\. The Sample Path label at the bottom of the New Songs Directory Options dialog box will show a generic path reflecting your choices.

7. In the Name Song File Using group box, select the information to include in the track file by selecting the check boxes for Track Number, Track Name, Artist, and Album as appropriate. You can change the order of these items by selecting one of them and using the up and down arrow buttons to move it to where you want it. In the Separator text box, enter the separator character to use between these components. The default is an underscore, but you can use a different character (or several characters) if you prefer. For example, you might prefer to use two or three hyphens, or a space, a hyphen, and a space (for readability).

8. Click the OK button to close the New Songs Directory Options dialog box.

9. Select the Mute While Recording check box to make MusicMatch Jukebox rip the tracks without playing them back at the same time. Using this option lets MusicMatch Jukebox record much faster—at least, on a fast computer.

10. Make sure that the Enable check box in the Make Song Clips group box is cleared. (This feature lets you make a clip from a song: You select the check box and specify a start second and a length—for example, a 29-second clip starting at second 10. The main reason for creating clips is for providing a quick sample that will allow the recipient to identify or judge the song—for example, for sharing a small part of a copyrighted song without transgressing too horribly against the law.)

11. In the CD Recording Mode group box, make sure that the Digital option button is selected. If you want to use error correction in your recordings, select the Error Correction check box. (Error correction helps reduce clicks and pops that occur when a CD disagrees with your CD drive's read head during the recording. Using error correction slows down the recording, so you probably won't want to use it unless you're experiencing quality problems with your MP3 files.)

12. Click the OK button to close the Settings dialog box.

NOTE You can also quickly change the sampling rate by choosing Options ➢ Recorder ➢ Quality and choosing the appropriate setting on the Quality submenu.

34 Rip Tracks with MusicMatch Jukebox

Now that you've got CDDB and your recording options set up, you're ready to rip tracks with MusicMatch Jukebox. Here's how to proceed:

1. Slot a CD into your CD drive (or DVD drive) and close it. MusicMatch Jukebox will read the CD. If you're using CDDB, MusicMatch Jukebox will retrieve the information for the CD from CDDB and will display the album's name, the artist's name, and the track titles. If CDDB can't decide between a couple of possible listings for the CD, it will display a dialog box such as the one shown below to let you decide. Do so.

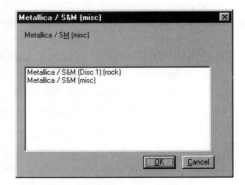

2. Click the Record Music CDs into Digital Tracks button to display the Recorder window, shown below, with a different CD recording.

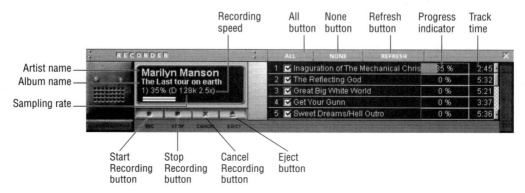

Recording speed / All button / None button / Refresh button / Progress indicator / Track time

Artist name — Marilyn Manson
Album name — The Last tour on earth
Sampling rate — 1) 35% (D 128k 2.5x)

1	☑ Inaguration of The Mechanical Chris	35 %	2:45
2	☑ The Reflecting God	0 %	5:32
3	☑ Great Big White World	0 %	5:21
4	☑ Get Your Gunn	0 %	3:37
5	☑ Sweet Dreams/Hell Outro	0 %	5:36

Start Recording button / Stop Recording button / Cancel Recording button / Eject button

3. Select one or more tracks to record by selecting the check boxes for the tracks or by clicking the All button.

◆ Click the None button to deselect all currently selected tracks.

◆ Click the Refresh button to make MusicMatch Jukebox reread the CD's contents. (This button is mainly useful if you have auto-insert notification disabled for your CD drive and manage to insert a fresh CD without MusicMatch Jukebox's noticing.)

4. Click the Start Recording button to start ripping.

The first time you go to rip tracks from a CD to MP3 files, MusicMatch Jukebox will configure your CD drive or drives. You'll see the CD-ROM Preparation dialog box, shown below. Make sure that each of your CD drives and DVD drives that you'll ever want to use for recording contains an audio CD, then click the OK button. MusicMatch Jukebox will configure the drive for you and will then start recording.

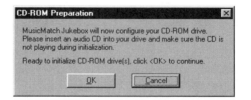

5. As MusicMatch Jukebox records the track, it displays a readout of its progress, as shown in the illustration in step 2.

6. When MusicMatch Jukebox has finished recording a track, it automatically adds the track to the music library.

Keeping Everything You Need to Know in a Track's Tag

MusicMatch Jukebox makes it easy to add tag information to all the tracks from the same album:

1. With a track selected in the Music Library window, choose Options ➤ Music Library ➤ Edit Track Tag, or right-click the track in the Music Library window and choose Edit Track Tag from the context menu, to display the Tag Song File dialog box, shown below.

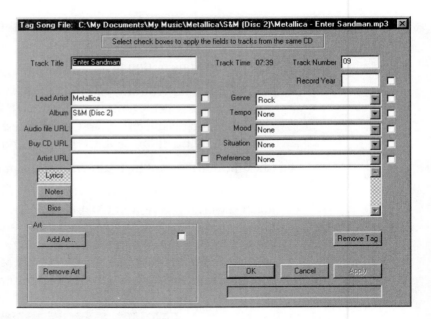

2. Enter information for the track by typing in the text boxes and by choosing items in the drop-down list boxes. If you want to apply the same information to all the tracks from the same CD, select the check box to the right of the text box or drop-down list box.

3. To add lyrics, notes, or bios to the track, click the Lyrics, Notes, or Bios button and enter the information in the text box.

4. To add a bitmap or JPEG picture to the track, click the Add Art button to display the Open dialog box. Navigate to and select the picture file, then click the Open button. The picture will appear to the right of the Remove Art button. Select the check box to the right of the picture if you want to apply the picture to all the tracks from the CD. So if you gotta have pix of Shania or Ricky on all your MP3 files, it won't cost you much effort. (To remove a picture from a track, click the Remove Art button. To remove a picture from all the CD's tracks, select the check box to the right of the picture before clicking the Remove Art button.)

5. Click the Apply button to apply your changes to the tag or tags. The readout at the bottom of the dialog box will show you which file's tag MusicMatch Jukebox is currently updating. If you're applying tag info to all the tracks from the CD, it'll take a little while, and MusicMatch Jukebox will display an MMJB message box telling you the results when it has finished.

6. To remove a tag from the track, click the Remove Tag button.

7. Click the OK button to close the Tag Song File dialog box.

35 Build Music Libraries with MusicMatch Jukebox

MusicMatch Jukebox's key feature is its ability to create music libraries that you can use to store, organize, and retrieve your music files. By using music libraries, you can manage your music much more easily than schlepping thousands of individual files in and out of your MP3 player.

You can create as many music libraries as you want. If you prefer to have all your music in one music library, that's fine, but be warned that it may become unmanageably large. We suggest segmenting your music into the different themes, moods, or occasions by which you'll want to play it. You can put any individual track into multiple music libraries, so creating music libraries isn't exactly difficult.

If you don't have the Music Library window displayed, click the Music Library button in the Main window to display it.

Planning Your Music Libraries

Before you create a music library, choose options for the music libraries you'll create. (You can choose options for a music library after creating it, but you'll save time by setting things up right before creating any music libraries.) Here's what to do:

1. Choose Options ➤ Music Library ➤ Music Library Settings to display the Music Library page of the Settings dialog box, shown below.

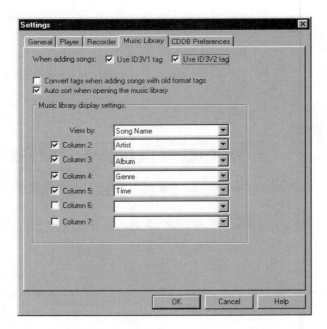

2. Make sure the Use ID3V1 Tag check box and the Use ID3V2 Tag check box are selected so that MusicMatch Jukebox adds all available tag information to the music library. (ID3V1 tags can contain title, artist, album, year, comment, and genre data; ID3V2 tags can add information, lyrics, and a picture.)

3. Select the Convert Tags When Adding Songs with Old Format Tags check box if you want to convert tags from older tag formats to new ones when you add them.

4. Select the Auto Sort When Opening the Music Library check box to have MusicMatch Jukebox automatically sort the tracks in the library each time you open it.

5. In the Music Library Display Settings group box, select the columns that you want to have appear in the Music Library window. For each column, select the appropriate contents in the list box.

6. Click the OK button to close the Settings dialog box.

Now drag the dividers on the column headings in the Music Library window left or right to resize the columns to display the information you want to see. For example, you might want to narrow the Time column so that it takes the minimum amount of space possible and leaves more room for the track title and album names.

Creating a New Music Library

To create a new music library, choose Options ➢ Music Library ➢ New Music Library. In the Please Specify the Name and Location of Your New Library dialog box (which is a Save As dialog box after a quick name-change operation), specify the filename and folder for the music library, then click the Save button. MusicMatch Jukebox will save the music library with a DDF extension.

Adding Tracks to a Music Library

MusicMatch Jukebox automatically adds to the current music library any new MP3 files you rip with it. But you'll need to add any existing MP3 files that you had to the database so that you can work with them through MusicMatch Jukebox. The same goes for any MP3 files that you download.

Here's how to add files to the current music library:

1. Click the Add button in the Music Library window to display the Add Songs to Music Library dialog box, shown next.

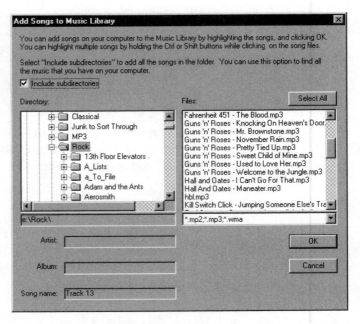

2. In the Directory list box, select the directory from which you want to add the MP3 files to the database.

3. If the directory contains subdirectories, select the Include Subdirectories check box.

4. In the Files list box, select the MP3 files you want to add to the database.

   ◆ To select all the files shown, click the Select All button.

   ◆ To view the information about a particular track (for example, to identify it more precisely), select it in the Files list box. The Artist, Album, and Song Name text boxes will display the information included for those categories in the file's tag.

5. Click the OK button to add the selected MP3 files to the database.

Deleting Tracks from a Music Library

To delete a track from a music library, select the track and click the Delete button (or press the Delete key). MusicMatch Jukebox will display the MusicMatch Jukebox dialog box, shown next.

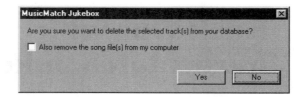

If you want to delete the file from your computer's hard disk, select the Also Remove the Song File(s) from My Computer check box. Then click the Yes button.

WARNING To nuke the contents of a music library, choose Options ➤ Music Library ➤ Clear Music Library. You won't usually want to do this, so MusicMatch Jukebox displays a confirmation dialog box to make sure you know what you're doing before it wipes your carefully built library. Of course, if a well-meaning relative ripped the *Titanic* soundtrack into your music library, go right ahead and tear it out root and branch.

Opening a Music Library

To open a music library, choose Options ➤ Music Library ➤ Open Music Library to display the Open dialog box. Navigate to and select the music library, then click the Open button. MusicMatch Jukebox will open the music library, closing any music library that is currently open.

Dropping a Music Library on a Friend

To inflict a music library on friends, export it to a text file by choosing Options ➤ Music Library ➤ Export Music Library, entering a filename in the Save As dialog box, and clicking the Save button. You can then e-mail the text file to your friends, and they can import it by choosing Options ➤ Music Library ➤ Import Music Library.

Sharing a music library like this gives your friends only the list of tracks in the library. They need to have the MP3 files that the music library references in order to play them back—but you knew that already.

36 Rock Out with MusicMatch Jukebox

Once you've got your music organized into music libraries, you can create playlists, save them, and play them back. You can also use the Auto DJ feature to create automatic playlists for you.

Creating, Saving, and Opening Playlists

The Playlist window initially appears docked to the Main window. When you're working with it, you'll usually want to display it separately so that you can expand it to see more of its contents.

Click the Separated View button to display the Playlist window as a separate window. Click the Integrated View button to attach the Playlist window to the Main window again.

Creating a Playlist

Here's how to create a playlist:

◆ If you have tracks in the Playlist window that you don't want to include in the new playlist, click the Clear button to remove them all.

◆ Add tracks to the Playlist window by dragging them from the Music Library window or by selecting them in the Music Library window, right-clicking, and choosing Add Track(s) to Playlist from the context menu.

◆ To preview a track, select it in the Music Library window and choose Options ➢ Music Library ➢ Preview Track. MusicMatch Jukebox will start playing the track without adding it to the playlist.

◆ To rearrange the tracks in the playlist, drag them to where you want them to appear. This is your opportunity to correct the crimes of the music publisher—now you can put all of the best tunes up front and kill the abysmal tracks they only included to pump up the CD's total running time.

◆ To delete a track from the playlist, select it and click the Delete button.

Saving a Playlist

When you've assembled your playlist, save it by clicking the Save button to display the Save Playlist dialog box, entering a name, and clicking the Save button.

MusicMatch Jukebox supports really long names for playlists, but anything over about 40 characters tends to be hard to work with. Best types of titles: Guitars That Killed Cleveland; Psychedelic Psongs; Lame Ballads Babes Love. Keep it short but descriptive so you don't confuse yourself.

Opening a Playlist

To open a playlist, display the Playlist window in Separated view. In the Saved Playlists list, click the playlist to display its contents in the panel to the right, or double-click the playlist to add its contents to the Current Tracks list.

Having MusicMatch Jukebox DJ for You

MusicMatch Jukebox's AutoDJ feature lets you specify vague guidelines by which MusicMatch Jukebox should put together automatic playlists for you. The AutoDJ feature isn't for everyone. If you've ever sat out a dozen songs in a row at a party waiting for the one track to which you *can* dance, you'd do better to give MusicMatch Jukebox more specific instructions on how to please you.

If you want to chance your luck at the AutoDJ feature, here's how to start:

1. Click the AutoDJ button in the Main window to display the AutoDJ dialog box, shown below.

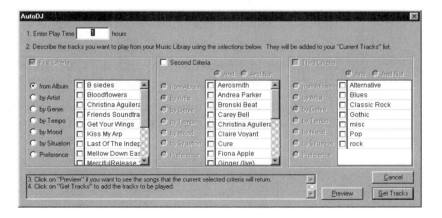

2. In the Enter Play Time text box, enter the number of hours that you want MusicMatch Jukebox to play for. Keep this number low until you see what kind of effect AutoDJ produces with your pet music collection.

3. In the First Criteria group box, select the first set of criteria by which MusicMatch Jukebox should select the music. Choose From Album, By Artist, By Genre, By Tempo, By Mood, By Situation, or Preference, as appropriate. The first list box will display check boxes for the category. Select the check boxes for the items you want to include. For example, you might select the By Genre option button and the Techno, Trance, and Trip-Hop check boxes.

4. Define a second set of criteria if you want to by selecting the Second Criteria check box, selecting the And option button or the And Not option button as applicable, and making a choice from the same list. Select check boxes as appropriate. For example, you might select the And option button, select the By Artist option button, and select the check boxes for artists such as Massive Attack, The Chemical Brothers, and The Orb.

5. Define a third set of criteria if you want to by selecting the Third Criteria check box, selecting the And option button or the And Not option button, making another choice, and selecting from the resulting check boxes. For example, you might select the And option button, select the By Tempo option button, and select the Pretty Slow check box to find mellow music to get wasted by.

6. Click the Preview button to display information about how many tracks MusicMatch Jukebox has found matching those criteria (up to the play time you specified in step 2).

7. Adapt your criteria as necessary to produce the play time you want.

8. Click the Get Tracks button to close the AutoDJ dialog box. Music-Match Jukebox will display a message box telling you how many tracks it has found and the total playing time.

9. Click the OK button. MusicMatch Jukebox will add the tracks to the current playlist, from which you can play them as usual.

37 Use MusicMatch Jukebox's Net Music Feature to Access Music on the Internet

To keep you up to date with what's happening in music on the Internet, and to deliver that customized music it promised you during the Setup routine, MusicMatch Jukebox provides its Net Music feature. To use Net Music, click the Net Music button in the Main window to display the Net Music window. As you can see in the illustration below, the Net Music window contains six pages: Home (shown below), Best Matches, Charts, New, Find Music, and More Music. You access each page by clicking its tab below the ever-changing and relentless ads that barrage you from the upper reaches of the window.

We'll leave you to explore the Net Music feature on your own, pausing only momentarily to show you the Find Music page of the window (see the following illustration), which provides not only a search text box but also lets you browse by different categories of music.

38 Play Net Radio with MusicMatch Jukebox

MusicMatch Jukebox provides a feature called Net Radio that lets you play Internet radio streams. Here's how to use the feature:

1. Click the Net Radio button in the Main window to display the Net Radio window, shown below with a station playing.

NOTE If you don't have the latest version of Microsoft Windows Media Player installed on your computer when you first click the Net Radio button, MusicMatch Jukebox will start your Web browser and encourage you to download that version. Comply and follow the installation procedure, then restart MusicMatch Jukebox and click the Net Radio button again.

2. Click the Station Selector button to display the Station Selector dialog box, shown below.

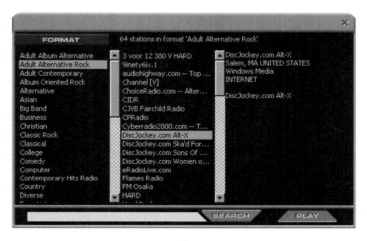

3. In the Format list box on the left-hand side of the Station Selector dialog box, select the type of music you want to listen to. The second column will display the available stations of that type.

Alternatively, enter a search term in the text box at the bottom of the Station Selector dialog box and click the Search button. Again, the second column will display the available stations that match the text you specified.

4. In the second column, select the station that interests you. The third column will display details of the station, as shown in the illustration.

5. Click the Play button to start playing the station. Depending on the speed of your Internet connection and the strength of the signal, MusicMatch Jukebox will need a few seconds to buffer the signal before it starts playing. You'll see a Buffering label and a growing percentage readout on the right-hand side of the Net Radio window while MusicMatch Jukebox is filling the buffer.

You can control the net radio station's play by using the controls in the Main window. For example, to quell the station when it starts playing something wretched, click the Stop button.

39 Equalize Out Mixing Errors with MusicMatch Jukebox

To keep up with the Joneses—or rather the Winamps and Soniques of the world—MusicMatch Jukebox provides a graphical equalizer that you can use to improve the sound of the music, or at least to make it sound marginally less horrible than its creators intended.

Strange to say, MusicMatch Jukebox seems to be ashamed of its MP3 Equalizer (as it terms it)—or perhaps to consider it a feature that most users shouldn't need too much of the time. Whatever the reason, MusicMatch Jukebox keeps the MP3 Equalizer tucked away and not directly accessible from the interface. But in our experience, the MP3 Equalizer works well enough, though it's definitely limited: It's implemented as a dialog box, so you can't keep it open and manipulate MusicMatch Jukebox at the same time, and it lacks the more stimulating features that some of its counterparts offer. (For example, the Winamp graphical equalizer offers an auto-load feature for preset equalizations.)

To display the Equalizer dialog box, choose Options ➤ Player ➤ MP3 Equalizer. The illustration below shows the Equalizer dialog box.

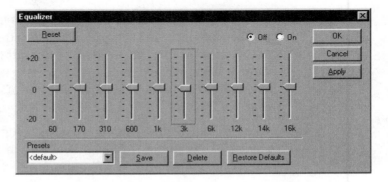

First, select the On option button to turn the Equalizer on. Then drag the ten sliders up and down to create the equalization you want. Alternatively, choose a preset equalization from the Presets drop-down list. Then click the Apply button to apply the equalization, and see how it sounds. Click the OK button to close the Equalizer dialog box.

You can't save new equalizations of your own, but you can change the preset equalizations that MusicMatch Jukebox provides: Choose the preset equalization from the Presets drop-down list, change the slider positions as necessary, and then click the Save button. (If you goof up, you can restore the default settings for all preset equalizations—not just the currently selected one—by clicking the Restore Defaults button.)

40 Burn CDs with MusicMatch Jukebox

One of MusicMatch Jukebox's newest (at this writing) and most compelling features is its ability to burn music CDs. Compared to a semi-professional CD-creation package such as Adaptec's Easy CD Creator, this feature is limited, but you'll probably find that it's good enough to get the job done.

Needless to say, in order to burn CDs, you need to have a CD-R or CD-RW drive, and it needs to be working. (If you don't have a CD recorder but want to get one, turn to *67. Choose a CD Recorder* to learn what your options are. And if you're looking for a CD recorder specifically for use with MusicMatch Jukebox, check the MusicMatch Web site for a list of supported CD recorders. At this writing, the URL is `http://www.musicmatch.com/jukebox/player/cdr.cgi`.)

Here's how to create a CD:

1. Assemble a playlist containing the tracks that you want to put on the CD, preferably in the order in which you want them to appear on the CD. If you're a careful person, you might even want to play through the playlist to make sure it sounds okay and that none of the juxtapositions of tracks are too grim.

2. Save the playlist in case things go disastrously wrong.

3. Click the Create CD button in the Main window (or in the Playlist window, if you're using Separated view), or right-click in the playlist and choose Create CD from Playlist from the context menu. Either way, MusicMatch Jukebox will display the Create CD from Playlist dialog box, shown below.

4. In the CD Format area at the top of the dialog box, make sure that the Audio (Default) option button is selected if you want to create an audio CD—one that you can play in a CD player. The Data (MP3, WMA, WAV) format lets you pack far more music onto a CD, but you'll need to play it in a computer (or in a special CD player that can handle the MP3 format, such as the D'music MP3 CD player from Pine Technology).

5. Scan through the tracks in the CD Song List and see how things look:

◆ Use the CD-ROM Disc Space readout to see if there's extra space on the CD.

◆ To add a track to the CD, click the Add Song button, use the resulting Open dialog box to specify the track, and click the Open button. MusicMatch Jukebox will add the track to the end of the CD, so you may well want to move it to a better position.

◆ To change the order of tracks, select a track and drag it up or down the list to where you want it to appear.

◆ To remove a track from the CD, clear its check box in the list.

6. To choose further options for creating the CD, click the Options button. The Create CD from Playlist dialog box will display a whole new right-hand part, as shown below, containing the following options:

Create CD in Drive drop-down list   This drop-down list lets you choose which CD recorder to use. If you're like most people, you'll have a maximum of one CD recorder, so you shouldn't need to change this option.

Setup group box   This group box lets you specify how MusicMatch Jukebox writes the CD. In the group of option buttons, use the Test Then Write CD option the first few times you burn a CD with Music-Match Jukebox and this CD recorder. After that, if all is well, you may want to use the Write CD Only option, which dispenses with the testing phase and so is quicker. In the Speed drop-down list, leave MAX selected unless you're having problems and need to try cranking the recording down to a lower speed. Leave the Beep When Done check box selected to have MusicMatch Jukebox beep when the recording is finished, and select the Eject When Done check box if you want MusicMatch Jukebox to open the drive as a visual cue that the recording is done.

Cache group box   This group box controls whether and how Music-Match Jukebox creates a cache space for buffering data that it's feeding to the CD recorder. Leave the Enable check box selected unless you have a very good reason for clearing it. Leave the Priority drop-down list set to Normal unless you're having problems burning CDs, in which case you may want to try setting it to High. And leave the Size slider at its default setting of 4MB unless you're having problems burning CDs; if so, try increasing it in gradual increments.

Audio CD-R Options group box   This group box offers three more options that you need to know about. First, select the 2 Second Track Gap check box if you want MusicMatch Jukebox to add a gap of two seconds between tracks on the CD. Second, choose one of the two option buttons to specify whether to decode the MP3 files directly to the CD or to use a cache on your hard drive. Writing directly is faster, but if you're not getting satisfactory results from it, try the cache, but be aware that you need 800MB of free space on the hard drive in question. Third, the Temporary Storage Directory button controls where Music-Match Jukebox places the disk cache. You need change this setting only if the default drive is short of that 800MB of space.

7. Make sure your CD recorder is loaded with a blank disk, then click the Create CD button to start creating the CD. MusicMatch Jukebox will display the CD Creation Progress dialog box, shown below, to show you how things are going.

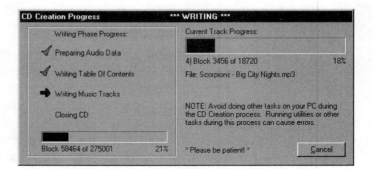

8. As you can see in the illustration, the CD Creation Progress dialog box enjoins you from doing other tasks on your PC while the CD is being created. If you have a reasonably powerful PC and you're using NT Workstation or Windows 2000 rather than Windows 95 or Windows 98, you may be able to get away with multitasking—but if your CD recorder is reasonably quick, you'd do better to take a break until the recording is finished.

9. When the recording is finished, MusicMatch Jukebox will display the MusicMatch Jukebox dialog box shown below, will beep (depending on the setting in the Create CD from Playlist dialog box), and eject the CD (likewise).

10. Click the OK button to close the MusicMatch Jukebox dialog box and return to the Create CD from Playlist dialog box.

11. If you want to create an insert card for the CD, click the Print CD Insert button, specify the details in the Print CD Insert dialog box, and click the OK button.

12. Click the Close button to close the Create CD from Playlist dialog box.

13. Remove the CD from the CD recorder, label it, and get ready to enjoy it.

41 Get, Install, and Configure RealJukebox Plus

One of the heavyweights in the all-round ripper/player/jukebox category is RealJukebox Plus from RealNetworks. RealJukebox Plus is a mean tool for settling your musical differences with the world; if you like it well enough, you may find it takes care of most of your MP3 needs.

RealJukebox Plus costs $29.95 but comes with a money-back guarantee—if you don't like it, scream loud enough and RealNetworks says they'll give you your money back.

In this section, we'll tell you what RealJukebox Plus's system requirements are, so that you can make sure it's a realistic choice for you. Then we'll give you a little history about RealNetworks and RealJukebox, because RealNetworks pulled a dirty enough trick on its users to make many people think twice about using any product from them. If you're still game after that, we'll show you how to get, install, and configure RealJukebox Plus.

> **NOTE** As you've probably inferred from the *Plus* in its name, RealJukebox Plus is the higher-end edition of RealJukebox. RealJukebox provides much of the functionality that RealJukebox Plus provides, except that it won't let you rip audio at a high enough quality for listening to music without suffering. (RealJukebox is limited to recording at a maximum of 96kbps; decent audio starts at 128kbps.) Because this severe (and deliberate) limitation wipes out a good half of RealJukebox's appeal, we decided to assume you would sooner or later choke up the 30 bucks for Real-Jukebox Plus—so that's the product we chose to cover in this book. To get you started, though, we've provided RealJukebox on the CD.

System Requirements

RealJukebox Plus's system requirements are Windows, a minimum of a modest-powered processor—a Pentium 200, a Cyrix 233, or an AMD K5 PR-200, 32MB RAM, 15MB of free space for software and 200MB for music, plus the obvious: a full-duplex sound card, speakers, and an Internet connection.

Brief History: A Gross Abuse of Privacy

Before we get into RealJukebox Plus, we should mention that RealJukebox and RealNetworks have some history that you need to be aware of because it may affect your decision to pay for and try RealJukebox Plus.

In 1999, RealNetworks made front-page headlines across the U.S. by perpetrating some truly disgusting marketing practices: Unknown to users, RealJukebox would send information on the user's listening and ripping habits to RealNetworks, together with a unique player ID number that identified the computer. The information included the number of songs the user had recorded onto their hard drive, the music CDs they were listening to, and even the type of portable MP3 player they had (if they were connecting it to the computer on which RealJukebox was installed).

As anyone who's taken Marketing 101 could tell you in a trice, this is the kind of information that marketing people lust for even more greedily than they lust for Rolexes and Z3s. If you had registered RealJukebox with your real e-mail address, RealNetworks was in a perfect position to market suitable music directly to you—or to sell your information to someone else for them to market to you.

As you can well imagine if you managed to miss the furor, the solids hit the air-conditioning most messily when this news came out. RealNetworks issued an apology for collecting this information and made available a patch that prevented RealJukebox from sending further information. However, by that time, more than 12 million people were using RealJukebox—and you can bet that a sizable percentage of them either never learned of the patch or were too lazy to apply it.

At this writing, RealNetworks has a Privacy Guarantee prominently displayed on their Web site that reads as follows:

> *We will not sell, rent, or give away your e-mail address or personal information. RealJukebox does not contain a unique identifier that could theoretically be used to track the actions or listening habits of individuals.*

If you choose to buy and try RealJukebox Plus, make sure you get the latest version of it and that you download and install any patches that are released. Even if you believe the Privacy Guarantee, you might also want to keep your eyes open for further news of RealNetworks savaging its customers' privacy—and if you hear any, bail from RealJukebox Plus and use another ripper/jukebox.

Getting, Installing, and Configuring RealJukebox Plus

In this section, we'll run you through getting, installing, and configuring RealJukebox Plus.

Direct your Web browser to `http://www.real.com`, and pay for and download the latest version of RealJukebox Plus. At this writing, you have the choice between just downloading RealJukebox Plus and downloading it and then getting the CD and manual a few weeks later. (That's a few weeks later unless you have a *really* slow Internet connection.) You get to pay a few bucks for shipping and handling on the CD and manual; it's very much your call whether they're worth having. The same goes for whether you choose to accept one or more of RealNetworks' aggressive upsells—first to sell you RealPlayer Plus at a discount along with RealJukebox, then to sell you a subscription to RealJukebox Plus and RealPlayer Plus (free updates), and finally to get the RealJukebox Plus Power Pack. The Power Pack includes a search tool called Copernic RealNetworks Edition for tracking down MP3, audio, and video files, and a tool called FreeMem Professional for freeing RAM. (We feel that you're better off investing in more physical RAM or simply practicing the self-restraint to run fewer applications at the same time rather than kludging about with software-based solutions, but feel free to disagree and prove us right.)

Once you've coughed up the plastic, RealNetworks presents you with a bewildering array of packages you can download, featuring RealJukebox Plus in different stages of completeness, with and without RealPlayer Plus (if you chose to get it); RealPlayer Plus on its own, in Complete, Standard, and Minimal incarnations; and so on. Usually you'll do best to get the most complete package available to you and then install only as much of it as you want.

WARNING If you're downloading RealJukebox (rather than RealJukebox Plus), be sure not to install it over an earlier version of RealJukebox Plus: Doing so will disable the RealJukebox Plus features, such as being able to record at an acceptable bitrate.

The following instructions lead you through installing RealJukebox Plus. If you chose to buy and download RealPlayer Plus as well, you'll have to go through some simple additional steps that we won't cover.

NOTE The setup procedure for RealJukebox (the free version) is similar to that for RealJukebox Plus, except that you don't have to enter a serial number, and you're limited to a maximum recording rate of 96kbps—much less than CD-quality audio.

Here's what to do:

1. Double-click the RealJukebox Plus file you downloaded to launch the Setup routine. You'll see the first Setup of RealJukebox Plus dialog box, shown next, which contains the end user license agreement.

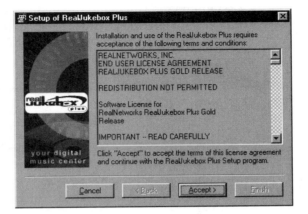

2. Read through the license agreement and click the Accept button if you can handle the terms and conditions. (If not, click the Cancel button to abort the installation, then demand a refund of your money.) Setup will display the second Setup of RealJukebox Plus dialog box, shown below:

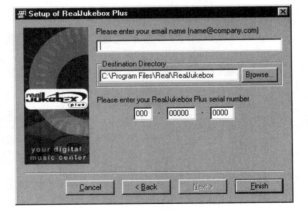

3. Enter your e-mail address in the Please Enter Your Email Name text box.

4. Check the directory shown in the Destination Directory text box. If necessary, change the path, either by typing directly into the text box or by clicking the Browse button to display the Choose Directory dialog box, selecting the directory you want to use, and clicking the OK button.

5. Enter your serial number in the sequence of three text boxes. You should have received this number in your browser when you placed your order, and RealNetworks should have sent you an e-mail containing it.

6. Click the Finish button to finish the installation. You'll see the installation routine running, then RealJukebox Plus will start and will display the Introduction dialog box, which sings the product's praises.

7. Click the Next button. RealJukebox Plus will display the Electronic Registration Card dialog box, in which you can enter your e-mail address, country, and zip code. If you don't want to have RealNetworks sending you RealJukebox Plus–related mail, clear the Inform Me of Updates and Events check box.

8. Click the Next button. RealJukebox Plus will display the first Portable Players/Storage dialog box, shown below, which asks you whether you have a portable music player or storage device—a portable player, a CD-R or CD-RW, or a portable drive such as a Zip, a Jaz, or an Orb. Select the Yes option button or the No option button as appropriate. If you select the No option button, skip ahead to step 11.

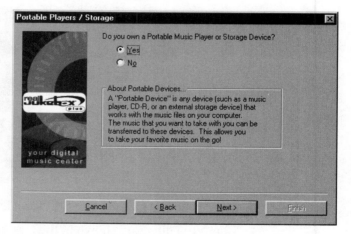

9. Click the Next button. RealJukebox Plus will display the second Portable Players/Storage dialog box, shown next. The list box may be blank, or may contain a list; in either case, click the Update List button to download the latest list of portable players and storage devices from RealNetworks. Then select the player or device you have.

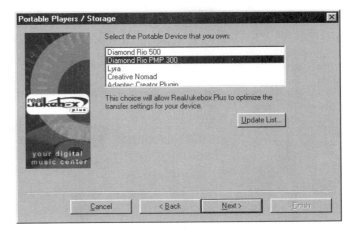

10. Click the Next button. Depending on which player or device you chose, you may see the Missing Plugin dialog box, shown below, which tells you that RealJukebox Plus needs to download a component to support the device. Click the OK button to let RealJukebox Plus download the component. It'll establish an Internet connection if you don't have a connection open, and you'll see message boxes about updating the component as it downloads it.

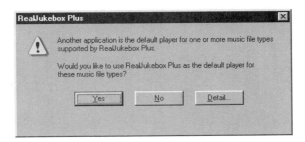

11. If any other application has had the temerity to assign to itself the file associations that RealJukebox Plus wants, you'll see the RealJukebox Plus dialog box shown below, asking for permission to grab the file associations so that it can be your default player.

12. If you want to see the gory details, click the Detail button to display the Reclaim – Advanced dialog box, shown below. In it, you can select and clear check boxes to specify which file associations RealJukebox Plus can have and which you want to leave with your current default player. Click the OK button when you're done, then click the Yes button in the RealJukebox Plus dialog box.

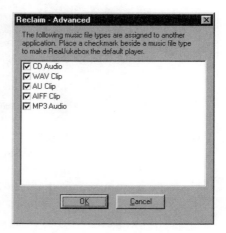

13. Next, RealJukebox Plus will display the Configuration Options dialog box, shown below, which lists the configuration options you've chosen so far.

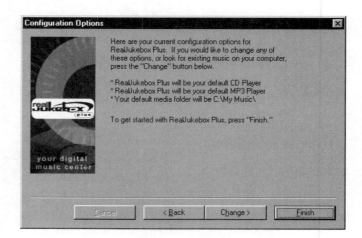

14. If all looks well—as it should—you can click the Finish button to finish configuring RealJukebox Plus. If you want to change one of the settings, or if you're just curious, click the Change button to display the first Configuration – Audio Playback dialog box, shown below.

15. In this dialog box, you'll probably want to make sure the Make Real-Jukebox Plus the Default Player for Playing These Music File Types check box is selected. Then click the Advanced button to display the second Configuration – Audio Playback dialog box shown below. Select or clear the check boxes for the different types of music files RealJukebox Plus wants to claim as its own, and click the OK button to apply your choices and return to the first Configuration – Audio Playback dialog box.

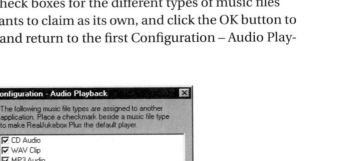

16. If you want to use another MP3 player or ripper as well as RealJukebox Plus, you may want to clear the Reclaim RealNetworks Music Types without Asking check box. If you leave this check box selected, as it is by default, RealJukebox Plus will grab the file associations for the music files at any chance it gets. This may prevent the other player or ripper from working as you'd like it to.

17. Click the Next button to proceed. RealJukebox Plus will display the Configuration – Find Music dialog box, shown below.

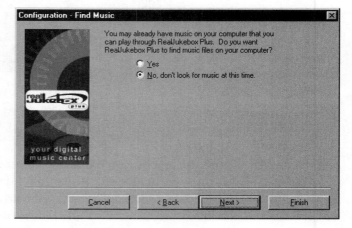

18. Select the Yes option button if you want to have RealJukebox Plus search your hard disk and other local drives for music files; otherwise, leave the No, Don't Look for Music at This Time option button selected, as it is by default. (You can make RealJukebox Plus search for music later if you want.)

19. If you chose the Yes option button in step 18, click the Find Music button, and RealJukebox Plus will display the Configuration – Find Music dialog box, shown next; if you chose No, click the Next button and skip ahead to step 22.

20. To search every drive, leave All Drives selected in the Look for Music In drop-down list. When All Drives is selected, you won't be able to change the setting in the Searching In text box: It will be set to All Folders, and the Browse button will be unavailable. If you want to restrict the search to a particular drive, select the drive in the Look for Music In drop-down list. You can then choose a particular folder in the Searching In text box by clicking the Browse button to display the Browse for Folder dialog box, navigating to and selecting the folder, and clicking the OK button. Then click the Start Search button. You'll see a readout of how the scan is going, as shown below.

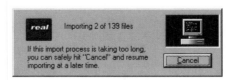

21. When RealJukebox Plus has finished searching your drives for tracks and playlists, it will display the Configuration – Find Music – Results dialog box, shown next, telling you what luck it had searching your drives or folders. If you want, you can click either Details button to display an Import Results dialog box listing the tracks or playlists found.

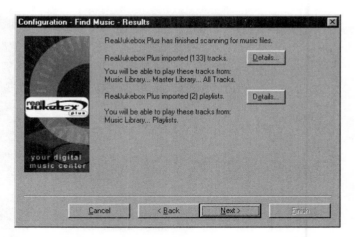

22. Click the Next button. RealJukebox Plus will display the Configuration – AutoStart dialog box, which contains just one check box, the Enable AutoStart for CD Recording check box. If this check box is selected, RealJukebox Plus will automatically start recording each new CD you put in your drive. We recommend clearing this check box because you won't want to record every CD, and you can start the recording process easily enough manually when you do want to record a CD.

23. Click the Next button. RealJukebox Plus will display the Configuration – CD Recording Options dialog box, shown below.

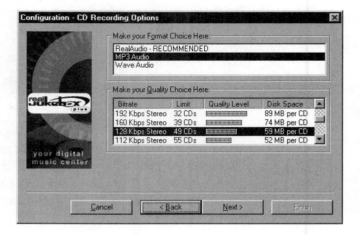

24. In the Make Your Format Choice Here list box, select the file format you want to use. We recommend the MP3 Audio format rather than the RealAudio format that RealJukebox Plus recommends: For most purposes, MP3 is a more flexible file format than RealAudio.

25. In the Make Your Quality Choice Here list box, select the recording quality you want. We recommend 128 Kbps Stereo—it provides high audio quality without taking up too much disk space—but this is a decision you'll need to make for yourself. (If you're slumming it with RealJukebox Standard Edition rather than RealJukebox Plus, you'll have a maximum rate of 96 Kbps Stereo.)

26. Click the Next button. RealJukebox Plus will display the Configuration – Music File Location dialog box, shown below.

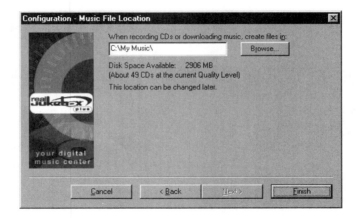

27. Check the location that RealJukebox Plus has entered in the When Recording CDs or Downloading Music, Create Files In text box. If necessary, change it, either by typing in the text box or by clicking the Browse button to display the Browse for Folder dialog box, selecting the folder, and clicking the OK button.

28. Click the Next button to proceed. RealJukebox Plus will display the Recording Options dialog box, which invites you to optimize your system for recording. To do so, leave the Yes option button selected, load an audio CD in the CD-ROM drive, and click the Start Test button; to skip this step (which we don't recommend skipping), select the No, Skip the Test option button and click the Skip Test button.

29. If you choose to test your CD-ROM, you may see the Use of Generic CD-ROM Driver dialog box, shown below, warning you that you may need to upgrade the generic driver you're using in order to record successfully. If your CD-ROM has been behaving to date, we suggest you stick with it and choose the Yes button in this dialog box to see if it will work for you—but leave the Don't Ask Me Again check box cleared until you've found out whether the driver is up to snuff. Then select the Don't Ask Me Again check box the next time RealJukebox Plus displays it.

30. Next, you'll see the System Test in Progress dialog box. It's best not to do anything else on your computer while the test is in progress, because you may confuse the test.

31. If worst comes to worst, you'll see the RealJukebox dialog box shown below telling you that your CD-ROM is not capable of digital extraction (ripping audio digitally).

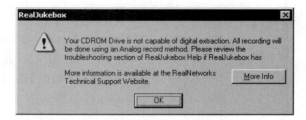

32. Once RealJukebox Plus has finished with the test, you may see the Recording Options dialog box telling you that the test is complete.

The illustration below shows the Recording Options dialog box reporting a drive that will only work for analog recording.

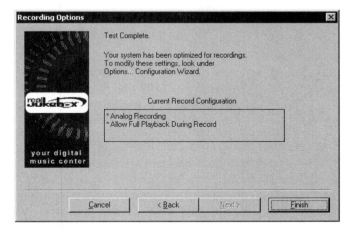

33. Click the Finish button to finish configuring RealJukebox Plus. Finally, RealJukebox Plus is ready for you to use.

NOTE If necessary, you can rerun the Configuration Wizard by choosing Options ➢ Configuration Wizard.

42 Navigate the RealJukebox Plus Interface

In this short section, we'll point out the main features of the RealJukebox Plus interface. Then, in the next section, we'll get you up and ripping with it.

Start RealJukebox Plus by clicking the RealJukebox Plus icon on your Quick Launch toolbar, by double-clicking the RealJukebox Plus icon in the system tray, by double-clicking the RealJukebox Plus icon on your Desktop, or by choosing Start ➢ Programs ➢ Real ➢ RealJukebox Plus.

NOTE If when you start RealJukebox Plus, it finds that another application has grabbed some of the file associations it considers to belong to it, it will display the RealJukebox Plus dialog box shown in step 11 of the previous section.

RealJukebox Plus has two very different visual modes: Full mode and Skin mode. Full mode is the one you're most likely to see at first—a conventional-looking application window, like the one shown below.

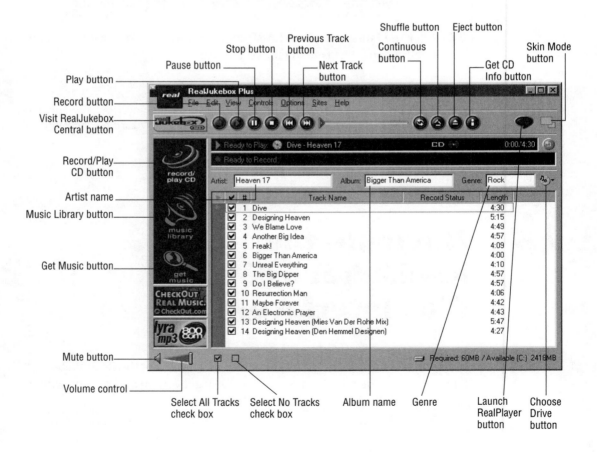

As you can see from the illustration, most of the buttons and other interface items are easy enough to understand, though a few perhaps could use a word of explanation:

◆ Clicking the Visit RealJukebox Central button launches (or activates) your default Web browser and takes you to the RealJukebox Central Web site.

◆ If you have multiple CD drives on your computer, you can switch from one to another by clicking the Choose Drive button and selecting the drive you want from the pop-up list that appears.

◆ Clicking the Skin Mode button displays RealJukebox Plus in Skin mode, a smaller and sleeker incarnation, as shown below.

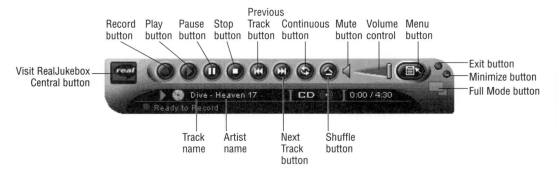

Again, these buttons and controls are easy enough to understand. As you'd suspect, clicking the Full Mode button returns RealJukebox Plus to Full mode.

You can change RealJukebox Plus's look further by applying other skins. We'll show you how to change the skin in *46. Change RealJukebox Plus's Skin*, a few sections later in the book.

43 Rip with RealJukebox Plus

In this section, we'll show you how to start ripping with RealJukebox Plus. (If you want to rock before you rip, turn ahead a few pages to the next section.) The process could hardly be simpler:

1. Slot a CD into your CD drive and close the tray. RealJukebox Plus will automatically contact the CDDB database and return the CD info—artist name, album name, and track names—if they're available, as in the illustration below.

If RealJukebox Plus isn't able to make a definitive match with an entry in CDDB, it may ask you to choose between two or more entries competing for your attention.

2. Select the check boxes for the tracks you want to record. By default, RealJukebox Plus selects all the tracks on the CD; to change this, you can either clear check boxes one by one or clear them all by clicking the Select No Tracks check box.

3. If necessary, check the options you've chosen for recording, encoding, and naming the tracks. Choose Options ➢ Preferences to display the Preferences dialog box.

General page   On this page, shown next, make sure the Start Playback with Record check box setting is suitable. When this check box is selected, you get to listen to the CD as RealJukebox Plus rips it, even if RealJukebox Plus is able to rip faster than real time.

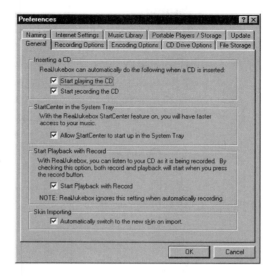

Recording Options page On this page, shown below, make sure the Digital option button is selected if your CD drive can handle digital extraction; otherwise, make sure the Analog option button is selected, and set an appropriate recording volume by using the Record Volume slider. If you're using digital recording, you may want to select the Use Error Correction check box to implement error correction on the recording. (Because using error correction slows down the recording, most people turn error correction on only if they're not getting good results from recording without it.)

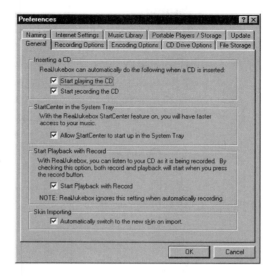

Encoding Options page On this page, shown below, select the format you want—probably MP3 Audio—in the Select a Format list box. Then, in the Select a Quality Level group box, select the Use Constant Bitrate option button and an appropriate speed (we suggest a minimum of 128 Kbps Stereo for music). In the Secure Files group box, you'll probably want to clear the Secure My Music Files When Encoding check box so as *not* to use RealJukebox Plus's security features. Why? Because if you do use them, you will be able to play the resulting file only in RealJukebox Plus, not with any other MP3 player, and only on the computer on which you recorded it (unless you install the same security key on another computer). We consider this security feature truly lame.

NOTE When you clear the Secure My Music Files When Encoding check box, RealJukebox Plus will display the Confirm Security Choice dialog box, warning you about copyright law and informing you that "by unchecking 'Security,' you are assuming the obligation to comply with all legal restrictions regarding extracted material." Read the information, select the I Accept the Above Terms option button, and click the OK button to close the dialog box.

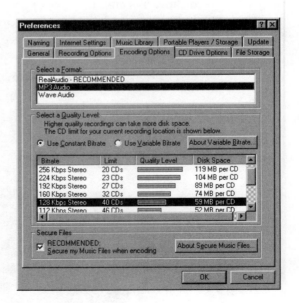

File Storage page   On this page, shown below, make sure you've set a suitable location in the Recorded Music Files Location text box.

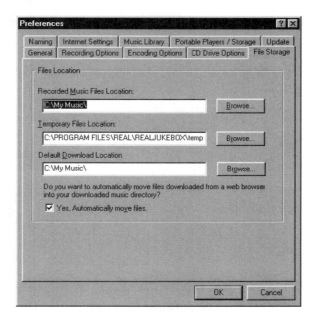

Naming page   On this page, (yes, the list goes on) of the Preferences dialog box, shown next, specify how RealJukebox Plus should name the files for the tracks you rip. In the CD Title group box, use the two drop-down lists to specify naming for a CD whose info CDDB fails to return. (This shouldn't happen often.) And in the Filenames Recorded on Your Drive from CD group box, use the four drop-down lists to specify how you want the artist, album, track number, and track name to appear. For example, you might choose Artist, Album, Track Name, and None (respectively) to produce naming such as **Beatles – White Album – Back in the U.S.S.R.**

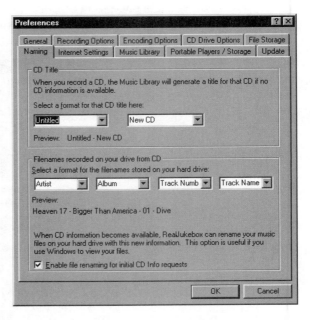

4. Click the OK button to close the Preferences dialog box.

5. Click the Record button to start recording the CD.

As RealJukebox Plus records the CD, it displays its progress, and changes the entry for the track in the Record Status column to *Recorded* when it has finished recording.

44 Rock Out with RealJukebox Plus

Once you've imported your existing MP3 files and learned how to rip files from your CDs, you're ready to get rocking. In this section, we'll show you how to play MP3 files, create playlists, and build libraries of your MP3 files.

To work with your music, click the Music Library button in the left-hand panel. RealJukebox Plus will display the Music Library window, as shown next. As you can see, RealJukebox Plus shows you an Explorer-style tree view whose three roots are the Master Library, your playlists, and any portable players or attached storage that you may have. You can expand any of these three items by clicking the + sign to its left, and collapse any item again by clicking the resulting – sign to its left. You can sort any of the items displayed in a category by a column by clicking its column heading: Click once for an alphabetical sort, and click again for a reverse-alphabetical sort.

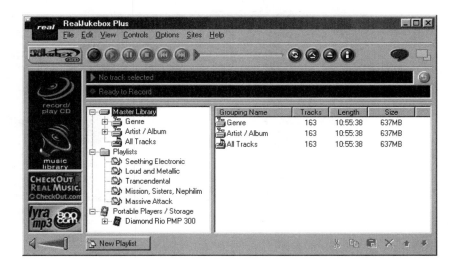

Building Your Master Library

RealJukebox Plus automatically adds to your Master Library any tracks that you rip from CD, import, or download using RealJukebox Plus.

You learned how to rip files from CD in the previous section. Importing files and playlists is even easier: Just choose File ➢ Import Files and Playlists to display the Import Files and Playlists dialog box, navigate to and select the files and/or playlists you want to import, and then click the Open button. RealJukebox Plus will import the tracks and then display the Import Tracks – Results dialog box, shown below.

To download music via RealJukebox Plus, click the Get Music button in the left-hand panel to display the Get Music pane, shown below.

Then follow the links to find music. When you hit upon something you want, click its link, and RealJukebox Plus will start to download it, as shown below. When the download finishes, RealJukebox Plus will automatically add the track to your music library.

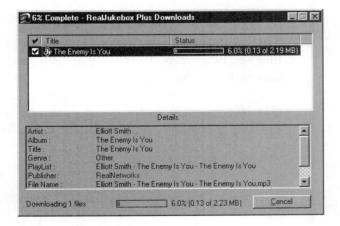

NOTE You can also download tracks by using your Web browser or an FTP client, then use the Import Files and Playlists feature to import them into your music library as described above.

Within the Master Library, RealJukebox Plus organizes your music by genre (<blank> for tracks not assigned a genre, Alternative, Blues, Hip-Hop, Pop, and so on) and by artist. You can expand the Genre tree or the Artist/Album tree to browse to the music you want. For example, in the illustration below, we're browsing by artist; we've reached Metallica, and we've descended into S&M.

Creating and Using Playlists

Here's how to create and populate a playlist:

1. From the Music Library window, click the New Playlist button at the bottom of the RealJukebox Plus window. RealJukebox Plus will display the New Playlist dialog box, shown next.

2. Enter the name for the playlist and click the OK button. RealJukebox Plus will create the playlist and will add it to the Playlists list.

3. Select the playlist's entry in the Playlists list.

4. Click the Add Tracks button. RealJukebox Plus will display the Add Tracks dialog box, shown below with selections made.

5. Drill down through the Master Library until you reach the tracks you want, select them, and then click the Add button. RealJukebox Plus will add them to the playlist, which you may be able to see behind the Add Tracks dialog box.

6. Repeat step 5 until you've added to the playlist all the tracks you want it to contain.

7. Click the Close button to close the Add Tracks dialog box.

8. Sort your playlist as necessary by either dragging the tracks up and down in the playlist or by selecting a track and using the Move Track Up button or Move Track Down button.

Once you've created a playlist, you can play it by selecting it in the Playlists list and clicking the Play button.

45 Use RealJukebox Plus with a Portable MP3 Player

You can use RealJukebox Plus to gas up a portable MP3 player with tracks—and in fact a number of portable MP3 players, including the Yepp (from Samsung), ship with RealJukebox Plus as their software.

To use a portable player with RealJukebox Plus (or vice versa, depending on how you view things), you typically need to do three things:

1. Install RealJukebox Plus as described a little earlier in this book.
2. Install the portable player. The installation routines for portable players vary wildly, so at this point we'll have to let you rely on your own initiative a bit.
3. Identify the portable player to RealJukebox Plus. Depending on whether your portable player's software is designed expressly to interoperate with RealJukebox Plus, you may or may not need to explicitly identify the portable player—but in case you do, we should tell you how to do so.

Identifying a Portable Player to RealJukebox Plus

To identify a portable player to RealJukebox Plus, follow these steps:

1. Connect the portable player to the cable that connects it to the PC.
2. Turn on the portable player.
3. Choose Options ➤ Preferences to display the Preferences dialog box.
4. Click the Portable Players/Storage tab to display the Portable Players/Storage page.
5. Click the Add button to display the Add Portable Players/Storage dialog box, shown next.

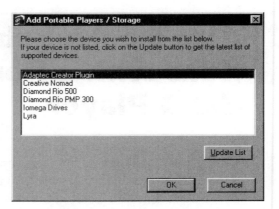

6. Click the Update List button to update the list of supported devices. Real-Jukebox Plus will connect to the Internet and download the latest list.

7. In the list box, select the entry for the portable player you have.

8. Click the OK button. Chances are good that RealJukebox Plus will display the Missing Plugin dialog box, shown below, telling you that it needs to download a component to add support for the device. Click the OK button and let it proceed.

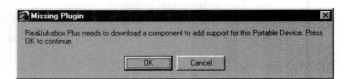

9. If you forgot to turn your portable player on, or if you turned it on but it got bored and went to sleep while RealJukebox Plus was entertaining itself fetching a plug-in, or if it's not connected, you'll see a dialog box such as the Driver Problem Detected dialog box shown below. Click the Done button.

10. You may have to restart your computer after completing the installation, as indicated by the RealJukebox Rio500 Installation dialog box shown below. Restart RealJukebox Plus, and you should be in business.

Configuring a Portable Player

RealJukebox Plus provides some options for configuring a portable player. The options available to you depend on which player you have. In this example, we'll use the Diamond Rio 500, because at this writing it seems to be the most widespread portable player.

Here's what to do:

1. Select the portable player in the Portable Players/Storage tree.

2. Click the Configure button that appears at the bottom of the RealJukebox window to display the Configure dialog box, shown below.

3. In the Track Conversion group box, specify conversion settings. Your best bet is usually to select the Convert Tracks Only If Necessary option button, so that RealJukebox Plus converts to MP3 only those tracks in other formats that the Rio can't handle. But if you want, you can select the Always Convert Tracks To option button and specify an appropriate rate in the Quality drop-down list. (We suggest 128kbps for the best balance of sound and track size.)

4. In the Initialize group box, you can click the Initialize Rio button to initialize the main memory on the Rio or the Initialize Flash Card button to initialize the flash memory card (if you have one). Clicking either button displays a confirmation dialog box, such as the Initialize External Flash Card dialog box shown below, to make sure you didn't mis-click. Choose the Yes button or the No button as appropriate; if you choose the Yes button, you'll see a message box telling you that the Rio was successfully initialized.

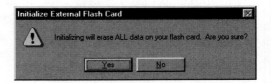

5. Click the OK button to close the Configure dialog box, then click the OK button to close the Preferences dialog box.

Removing a Portable Player

To remove a portable player from RealJukebox Plus's awareness:

1. Choose Options ➢ Preferences to display the Preferences dialog box.

2. Click the Portable Players/Storage tab to display the Portable Players/Storage page.

3. In the Installed Devices list box, select the entry for the portable player.

4. Click the Remove button. RealJukebox Plus will display the Remove Device dialog box, shown below.

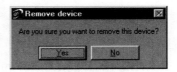

5. Click the Yes button. RealJukebox Plus will remove the portable player.

Loading Your Portable Player

To see what's on your portable player, select the entry for the portable player (or its external memory) in the Portable Players/Storage tree.

You can add tracks to your portable player in two ways: First, by working in the Music Library window; and second, by using the Add Tracks dialog box. Which method you prefer is entirely up to you.

Adding Tracks by Using the Music Library

Here's how to add tracks to your portable player from the Music Library:

1. Select the tracks in your music library.

2. Right-click the selection and choose Add to Device from the context menu to display the Add Tracks to Portable Device dialog box, shown below.

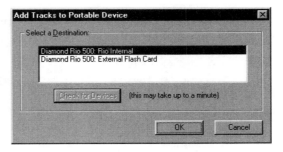

3. If the list box shows <*No devices detected*>, click the Check for Devices button to make RealJukebox Plus detect the portable player.

4. In the list box, select the player or the component of the player. For example, here we can choose between the Rio's internal memory and its external flash card.

5. Click the OK button. RealJukebox Plus will close the Add Tracks to Portable Device dialog next and will list the tracks in the tree for the device, as shown next. In our example, we've selected more tracks than will fit in the Rio's external flash card. RealJukebox Plus shows the tracks that will fit marked *Ready to Transfer* and those that won't fit marked *Will Not Fit*. At this point, you can adjust your selection as necessary.

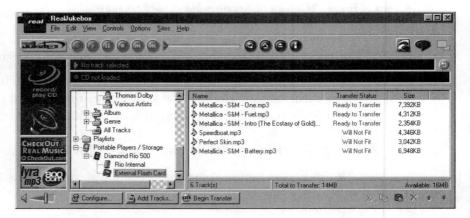

6. Click the Begin Transfer button to start transferring the tracks to the player. As RealJukebox transfers the files, it displays a readout of its progress, as shown below.

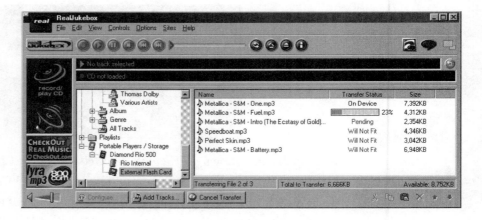

Adding Tracks by Using the Add Tracks Dialog Box

Here's how to add tracks by using the Add Tracks dialog box:

1. In the Portable Players/Storage tree, select your player. If the player has more than one memory storage unit, select the unit you want to use. (For example, some players have internal memory and external memory.)

2. Click the Add Tracks button at the bottom of the RealJukebox window to display the Add Tracks dialog box, shown below.

3. From the Master Library or the playlists, select the tracks you want to add, then click the Add button. Repeat till you've selected all the tracks you want to add.

4. Click the Close button to close the Add Tracks dialog box. RealJukebox Plus will list the tracks in the tree for the device, as described in the previous section.

5. Click the Begin Transfer button to start transferring the tracks to the player.

46 Change RealJukebox Plus's Skin

As you'd guess from its Skin mode, RealJukebox Plus is thoroughly skinnable—you can change its look by applying skins. It comes with several skins, which you can apply at will, and you can download a variety of other skins, both from RealNetworks and from other locations on the Internet.

NOTE You can create your own skins for RealJukebox Plus. We don't have space in this book to discuss this topic, but we cover it in *Mastering MP3 and Digital Audio,* also published by Sybex.

To change skin, choose View ➤ Skins to display the Skins submenu, then choose the skin you want to apply. The illustration below shows the Claymation skin.

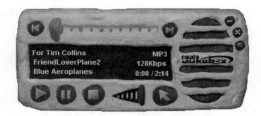

If you're looking for skins to download, you might want to start at the RealJukebox Central site. To get there, choose View ➤ Skins ➤ Get Skins. RealJukebox Plus will fire up your default Web browser and will connect to the site. Select a skin, and RealJukebox Plus will automatically download it.

By default, RealJukebox Plus switches view to a new skin as soon as you download it. To prevent RealJukebox Plus from doing so, choose Options ➤ Preferences to display the Preferences dialog box, click the General tab to display the General page if it's not already displayed, clear the Automatically Switch to the New Skin on Import check box in the Skin Importing group box, and then click the OK button.

Mac MP3 Players and Rippers

In this part of the book, we'll look at how to play and rip MP3 files on the Macintosh. There's both good news and bad news on this front.

The bad news is that, as with many other kinds of software, your choices for creating and playing MP3 files on the Mac are much more limited than they are for Windows. The Mac market is smaller than the Windows market, and fewer developers spend their precious time developing for it.

The good news is that some of the MP3 software written for the Mac is at least as good as its Windows equivalents, and you'll have no problem finding enough players and rippers to enjoy MP3 fully on the Mac. In this part of the book, we'll look at the following:

SoundApp   Created by Norman Franke, SoundApp is a freeware MP3 player that supports playlists and can perform batch conversions of files. SoundApp requires System 7 and Sound Manager 3.1 or greater; if you have System 7.5.3 or higher, you'll have Sound Manager already.

MACAST   From @soft, MACAST (formerly MacAMP) is a slick and friendly player whose features include support for SHOUTcast and icecast streaming audio, full graphical equalization, visualizations, skin support, and a sleep timer that can even shut down your computer (if you tell it to). MACAST is shareware that costs $24.95. It requires a PowerPC processor, System 7 or (preferably) System 8, and 4MB of available RAM. MACAST comes in a demo version that has only one limitation—but it's a killer: It can play only the first two minutes of each track. So, unless you live for the Ramones or the Buzzcocks, you'll need to pay for the registered version.

SoundJam MP   This is the first full-fledged ripper/player/jukebox for the Mac. Given this lack of competition, you won't be surprised to learn that SoundJam MP is currently enjoying significant popularity. Of course, SoundJam's popularity hasn't been hurt by its strong set of features. Aside from ripping like a pro and creating an effective jukebox database of your music, SoundJam also includes features such as a ten-band graphical equalizer, visualizations, skins, and a built-in Web connectivity that lets you download MP3 files directly from the Web. SoundJam costs $39.99.

N O T E   If you're looking for a Mac ripper, you may want to investigate AudioCatalyst from Xing Technologies (http://www.xingtech.com). Audio-Catalyst costs $29.99 and comes in Mac and PC versions; the Mac version requires a PowerPC processor, System 8 or better, and a compatible CD drive. You'll find coverage of AudioCatalyst for the Mac in the AudioCatalyst supplement to this book on the Sybex Web site (http://www.sybex.com).

If you want to play MP3 files on your Mac without installing any extra software, you may already have a program or two installed that will do the trick: QuickTime from Apple and RealPlayer G2 from Real Networks can both play MP3 files. Each was designed with a different purpose in mind, so neither rates high as an MP3 player, but they're more than good enough in a pinch, especially because you're likely to have at least one of the two already installed on your computer.

47 Get, Install, and Use SoundApp

We've included version 2.6.1 of SoundApp on the CD at the back of the book. At this writing, version 2.7 is expected to appear soon, so be sure to check for it—or for a newer version. Browse on over to `http://www-cs-students .stanford.edu/~franke/SoundApp/` and see what you find.

Once you unstuff SoundApp to a convenient location, you're ready to rumble. Double-click the SoundApp icon to launch SoundApp, or drag an MP3 file to the SoundApp icon and drop it there. SoundApp will take over the menu bar and will display the SoundApp Status window and Controls window, shown below. (If you don't see the Controls window, press Apple+H or choose Options ➤ Show Controls.) If you dragged and dropped an MP3 file, SoundApp will start playing it.

The SoundApp controls provide easy mouse control of playing and volume. You can also adjust the volume from the keyboard by pressing Apple+= to increase the volume and Apple+– to decrease it.

Once SoundApp is open and playing, you can drag further MP3 files to it to stack them up for play (in the order in which you drop them). You can also choose File ➤ Open and choose a file in the Open: SoundApp dialog box to add an MP3 file to the list of files to be played.

When you drag and drop MP3 files like this, SoundApp doesn't automatically create a playlist that you can save. To create a playlist:

1. Choose File ➤ New Play List or press Apple+N. SoundApp will open an untitled playlist window, as shown below.

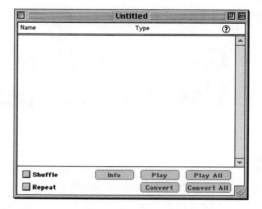

2. Add MP3 files to the playlist in either of these ways:

◆ By choosing File ➤ Add, or pressing Apple+D, to display the Add: SoundApp dialog box. Select the files to add and click the Add button to add them to the playlist.

◆ By dragging them to the playlist window and dropping them there.

3. To remove a track from the playlist, select it and press the Delete key.

4. To rearrange the playlist, drag the tracks up and down in the playlist window.

5. To save the playlist, choose File ➤ Save to display the Save: SoundApp dialog box. Choose a location for the file, enter the name for the playlist in the Name text box, and click the Save button to save it.

6. To play the playlist, click the Play All button in the playlist window. To shuffle or repeat tracks, select the Shuffle check box and Repeat check box first.

To close a playlist, choose File ➤ Close. To open a playlist, choose File ➤ Open, or press Apple+O, to display the Open: SoundApp dialog box. Select the playlist and click the Open button.

48 Get and Install MACAST

 We've included the current version (at this writing) of MACAST on the CD in the back of the book. To get the latest version of MACAST, visit http://www.macamp.net.

Double-click the distribution file to unstuff MACAST. MACAST automatically configures some Web browsers, such as Internet Explorer, to play MP3 files directly from your browser. If you're using Netscape, you're probably out of luck and will need to configure the MPEG Audio Stream item manually in the Preferences dialog box.

Once you've unstuffed MACAST, run its installer to install it. You'll get to wade through a General Information dialog box and a Licensing Information dialog box, after which you'll see the MACAST Installer dialog box shown below.

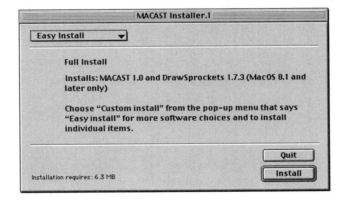

Choose the default Easy Install option to perform a full installation of MACAST. This takes around 6.3MB and is a good idea for most users. If you want to exercise some control over the parts of MACAST that are installed, select Custom Install from the drop-down list and choose the elements of MACAST to install from the MACAST Installer dialog box shown on the next page.

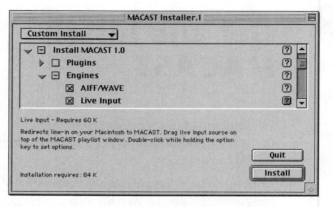

When you're satisfied with your Easy or Custom installation choices, click the Install button. MACAST will display the Select Disk to Install Onto dialog box shown below.

Select the appropriate disk and click the Install button. Try to divine a stereogram in your Mac's wallpaper as the installation routine unfolds, then click the Quit button in the message box that is displayed (see below) to inform you that installation was successful.

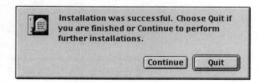

To launch MACAST, double-click the MACAST icon in the folder created by the installation routine.

The first time you run MACAST, it will display the Welcome dialog box, which sings the virtues of registration (it'll make MACAST work properly) and offers you information on how to get it. Click the OK button to proceed with your evaluation of MACAST.

N O T E MACAST Lite, MACAST's little brother, is made (you've guessed it) by @soft and can also be found at http://www.macamp.net. MACAST Lite provides fewer features than MACAST, but enough to be useful. It has a simple, unobtrusive interface and takes less memory than MACAST, but it supports playlists (through a somewhat clumsy pop-up menu) and skins.

49 Play MP3 Files with MACAST

In its default skin, MACAST offers a straightforward interface, as you can see in the illustration below.

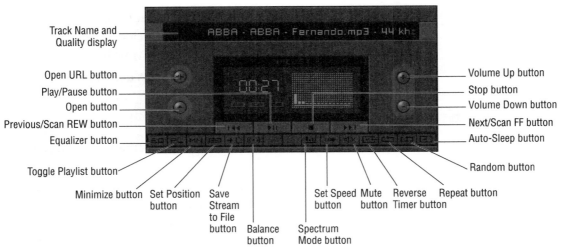

MACAST is easy to use with the mouse, but you can also use the keyboard, as follows:

- ◆ Press the spacebar to play the current track. Press it again to pause play.

- ◆ Press Tab to play the next track. Press Shift+Tab to play the previous track.

- ◆ Press ← to reduce the volume and press → to increase it.

MACAST is relatively modest in its demands on your screen real estate, but if you're pushed for pixels, minimize it by clicking the Minimize button, pressing the ` key (not the apostrophe—the key that also has the tilde [~] on it), and double-clicking its title bar or chassis. To restore MACAST to its regular size, press the ` key or double-click the title bar or chassis again. In its minimized state, MACAST looks like this:

To play music with MACAST, use any of the following methods:

- ◆ Choose File ➢ Open, select the file in the Open dialog box, and click the Open button.

- ◆ Choose File ➢ Open Location, specify the stream in the Open Location dialog box, and click the Open button. (Select the Add to Playlist check box if you want to add the stream to the playlist.)

- ◆ Drag files to the Playlist window. (More on this in a moment.)

Creating and Using Playlists

MACAST provides a standard but effective implementation of playlists. Here's what you need to know:

- ◆ Click the Toggle Playlist button to display the Playlist window, shown on the next page with a playlist created and playing. Tracks that haven't yet been played appear in white; tracks that have been played appear in dull green; and the active track is highlighted. The Elapsed Time readout at the bottom of the Playlist window shows how much of the playlist has been played so far, together with the total playlist time.

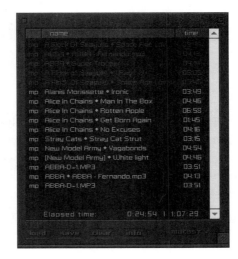

◆ To add tracks to the playlist, drag tracks to the Playlist window and drop them there. You can drag tracks from a CD to a playlist by opening a window for the CD.

◆ To arrange the playlist, drag tracks up and down.

◆ To save a playlist, click the Save button. In the Save dialog box, specify the name and location for the playlist, and then click the Save button to save it.

◆ To load a playlist, click the Load button. In the Open dialog box, select the playlist you want to load, and click the Open button to open it.

◆ To clear a playlist, click the Clear button.

◆ To make MACAST remember your current playlist between sessions, select the Remember Playlist check box on the Playlist page of the Preferences dialog box.

◆ To make MACAST pick up playing your playlist from where you ended your last session, select the Resume Playlist check box on the Playlist page of the Preferences dialog box.

50 Tweak MACAST's Sound with the Equalizer

Sometimes your bass nature gets the better of you, and you need your music to resonate more deeply in your guts. MACAST's graphical equalizer can help you out, providing preset equalizations including Live, Classical, Rock, Jazz, Dance, Uphill, Downhill, and PowerBook as well as letting you create your own equalizations.

Start by clicking the Equalizer button to display the Equalizer in the main MACAST window shown below.

Then proceed as follows:

◆ Click the up and down arrow buttons on the left of the display to move through the list of preset equalizations.

◆ To create a preset equalization of your own, click in the frequency bars to set equalization for the different frequencies. When everything sounds right, click the + button at the right-hand side of the Equalizer display to save the preset.

◆ To delete the current preset equalization, click the – button at the right-hand side of the Equalizer display.

MACAST automatically removes the Equalizer display when you leave it alone for a few seconds after messing with it.

51 Improve MACAST's Visuals

If you don't like MACAST's looks or you crave a little more visual excitement, no problem—MACAST's got you covered. You can change its skin, and you can run one or more visualizations at the same time.

Applying Skins to MACAST

Like many of the leading MP3 players, MACAST supports skins to change its look. MACAST comes with a couple of skins built in—TankAMP, subrad 4.2 (shown below), and QTAmp. You can find more skins on the Internet.

To apply a built-in skin, pull down the Skins menu and choose the skin from it. To apply a skin that's not built in, choose Skins ➢ Other and specify the skin in the resulting Open dialog box.

Watching MACAST's Visualizations

MACAST offers visualizations both within its main window (which are mildly entertaining but not worth caring about) and in separate windows.

To run through the main window visualizations, click in the track name display area in the main window.

To turn on the external visualizations, pull down the Plugins menu and select the G-Force, Reflections, RGB Spectrum, Star Lyrics, or WhiteCap item. Each opens in a separate window. You can run two or more at once if your processor can stand the strain. The illustration below shows WhiteCap keeping itself entertained.

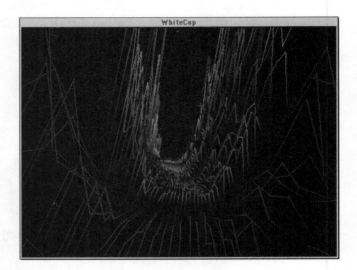

52 Go to Sleep with MACAST

One of MACAST's coolest features is AutoSleep, which enables you to use your Mac as a high-tech clock radio. AutoSleep can even turn your Mac off for you if you choose.

AutoSleep could hardly be easier to use:

1. Choose Edit ➢ Preferences to display the Preferences dialog box.

2. In the AutoSleep Action drop-down list on the Misc. page, select the action you want MACAST to take: Quit MACAST, Sleep, or Shutdown. (On some Macs, the Sleep option may not be available.)

3. Click the Save button to save your choice.

4. Click the AutoSleep button until the Sleep Timer message displays the appropriate length of time (shown below): 5, 10, 15, 30, 60, 90, or 180 minutes. (After 180, it loops back to Off.)

5. Load a soothing or seductive playlist and set it running.

6. Go to bed. To sleep, perchance to dream—whatever.

53 Play MP3 Files with QuickTime and RealPlayer Basic

In this section, we'll look quickly at how you can play MP3 files with two applications that you may already have on your Mac—QuickTime from Apple and RealPlayer Basic from RealNetworks. Neither is a dedicated MP3 player, but each can handle the file format—so if you need to listen to a track or three in a pinch, these applications can handle them for you. They don't have the sophisticated features of dedicated MP3 players, though, so we doubt you'll want to use them for playing MP3 files over the long term.

If you don't have RealPlayer Basic, you can download it from `http://www .real.com`. RealPlayer Basic is free, but if you want, you can drop $29.99 on RealPlayer Plus. If you don't have QuickTime, go to `http://www.apple.com` and see what you can scrounge up.

Playing MP3 Files with QuickTime

To play an MP3 file with QuickTime, choose File ➢ Open Movie (yes, we know *movie* doesn't seem right). Select the MP3 file in the resulting dialog box and click the Convert button. QuickTime will open the file, converting it along the way (don't worry—the MP3 file on the disk remains intact).

You can then play the file by using the QuickTime controls as usual. Quick-Time doesn't provide a full equalizer, but you can tweak the sound a little. From QuickTime's default compressed manifestation (shown on the left below), click the Expand button (the one with the four dots on it) to display the expanded window (shown on the right below) with the full set of controls. Now you have access to the balance, bass, and treble controls, which can help you remedy major equalization disasters, though they're insensitive enough to distress a gentle soul.

Playing MP3 Files with RealPlayer Basic

To play an MP3 file with RealPlayer Basic, drag the MP3 file and drop it on RealPlayer, which will start playing it. Alternatively, use the File ➢ Open File command to open a file or the File ➢ Open Location command to open a stream. You can then use the RealPlayer controls as usual. The illustration below shows RealPlayer Basic in Compact view (View ➢ Compact) playing an MP3 file.

54 Get, Install, and Configure SoundJam MP

In this section, we'll show you how to get, install, and configure SoundJam MP (which we'll call *SoundJam* from here on), the first full-fledged ripper/player/jukebox for the Mac. As you'll see, the process is easy, and you'll be ready to move on to ripping and rocking with SoundJam in just a few pages' time.

To get SoundJam via download, point your Web browser to `http://www.soundjam.com` and follow the links to buy it online. To get the physical package, either visit a good physical retail store or one of the online retailers, such as Mac Connection or Outpost.com.

NOTE If you're not sure you want to shell out forty bucks for SoundJam, download and try the seven-day demo first, then upgrade if you like it.

To install the downloaded version of SoundJam, unstuff the self-extracting archive and run the SoundJam MP Installer in the resulting SoundJam MP Demo folder.

To install SoundJam from the physical retail package, insert the CD-ROM into your CD drive. Your Mac will automatically open a window displaying the contents of the CD. Drag its folder from the distribution CD onto a convenient location on your Mac. For example, if you wanted to have the SoundJam MP folder on your desktop, you could drop it directly there. The Mac will copy the folder to where you drop it.

Double-click the folder to open it, then double-click the SoundJam MP folder to open that in turn. Then double-click the SoundJam MP icon.

The first time you run SoundJam, you'll see the SoundJam MP Software License Agreement dialog box shown next.

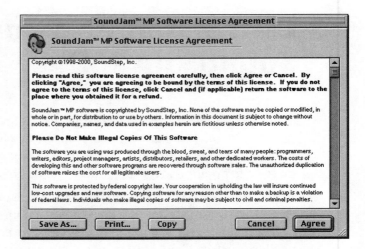

Read through the license agreement to you heart's content (print it, save it under a different filename, or copy it if you will), then click the Agree button if you want to proceed with the installation. SoundJam will display the Personalize SoundJam MP dialog box shown below.

Improve your name as necessary, add your company's name if appropriate, and type the serial number from the CD sleeve or the manual into the Serial Number text box. Then click the OK button.

If you're using virtual memory, SoundJam will display the dialog box shown next to alert you to that fact and to tell you that as a result of using virtual memory, you may experience slowdowns in playback. This won't necessarily happen; using virtual memory isn't a bad thing in itself—it just may indicate that your computer is light on physical memory (RAM), and this shortage of memory may cause problems with playback.

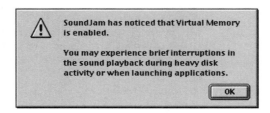

Next, SoundJam will ask if you want to set SoundJam as the handler for MP3 files and MP3 audio streams, as shown below.

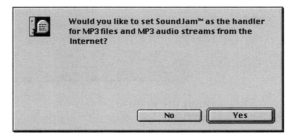

If you want to use a different MP3 player most of the time, click the No button. But for most installations, it makes sense to accept the default Yes button.

Once you've completed this little interrogation session, SoundJam will display itself. But we're not going to show you how to use SoundJam just yet—instead, we've decided to drag you through the seven pages of the Preferences dialog box first to make sure that you have SoundJam properly configured. Read on.

Setting Preferences in SoundJam

In this section, we'll walk you through the Preferences dialog box to make sure you've got the settings you need to run SoundJam effectively. If you feel you don't want all this information quite yet, but you want to learn how to get around SoundJam, move ahead to the next section, *55. Navigate the SoundJam Interface*, and come back here when you realize that it might be a good idea after all to make some configuration changes.

First, choose Edit ➤ Preferences to display the Preferences dialog box. As you can see in the next illustration, which shows the General page of the dialog box, the Preferences dialog box has seven pages, accessed through the items in the list box on the left-hand side of the dialog box.

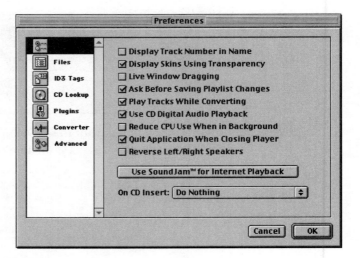

General Page

These are the options on the General page of the Preferences dialog box:

Display Track Number in Name check box This check box controls whether SoundJam includes the track numbers in the titles of tracks. Usually, the only reason to include track numbers is if you want to be able to play the tracks from a CD in order without needing to create a playlist.

Display Skins Using Transparency check box This check box controls whether SoundJam lets you see through lightly shaded parts of SoundJam skins to another application below.

Live Window Dragging check box This check box controls whether SoundJam displays the contents of a window when you drag it or just the outline.

Ask Before Saving Playlist Changes check box This check box controls whether SoundJam prompts you to save any unsaved changes to a playlist when you close the Playlist window. If you clear this check box, SoundJam saves the changes automatically without prompting you.

Play Tracks While Converting check box This check box controls whether SoundJam plays CD tracks as it converts them. Playing the tracks can be a good way to keep yourself entertained, and doing so doesn't slow down the recording speed: If you have a fast processor and CD drive, you can be ripping at 3× or 4× speed while listening at normal (1×) speed. If you have a slow processor and slow CD drive, you may need to turn this option off in order to rip effectively.

Use CD Digital Audio Playback check box This check box controls whether SoundJam routes CD audio through your Mac's sound circuitry or directly to the sound output. You'll almost always want to keep this check box selected because if you clear it, you won't be able to use SoundJam's visualizations or graphical equalizer.

Reduce CPU Use When in Background check box This check box controls whether SoundJam throttles back its demands on the processor (the CPU) when you have another application in the foreground. If you're experiencing a slow response in other applications when playing or ripping with SoundJam in the background, try selecting this check box to see if it improves matters.

Quit Application When Closing Player check box This check box controls whether closing the SoundJam Player window quits the application as well. This check box is selected by default.

Reverse Left/Right Speakers check box This check box controls whether SoundJam reverses left and right channels in output. You shouldn't need to use this option unless you've crossed your speaker wires and are too lazy to fix them.

On CD Insert drop-down list This drop-down list lets you specify what SoundJam should do when you insert a CD in your CD drive: Do Nothing, Begin Playing, Convert All Tracks, or Convert All Tracks & Eject. Pick the last option if you're trying to rip a stack of CDs quickly.

Files Page

On the Files page of the Preferences dialog box (shown on the next page), you get to set the following options:

Ask Before Removing Tracks check box This check box controls whether SoundJam prompts you for confirmation when you press the Delete key to remove a file from a playlist. If the confirmation dialog boxes bug you, clear this check box.

Change File Creator to SoundJam check box This check box controls whether SoundJam changes the creator code on MP3, MP2, AIFF, or WAV files to associate the file with SoundJam. (The creator code is a kind of tag on the file.) If you use SoundJam exclusively for your MP3 needs, make sure this check box is selected; if you use another player some or most of the time, clear this check box.

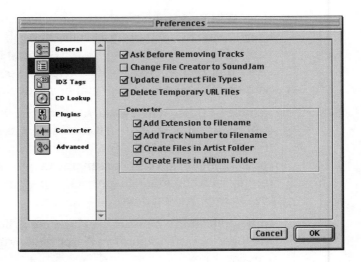

Update Incorrect File Types check box This check box controls whether SoundJam adds a creator code to a sound file that seems to be lacking one. Typically, the reason for a sound file lacking a creator code is that it comes from a non-Mac machine (for example, from a Windows machine). Leave this check box selected.

Delete Temporary URL Files check box This check box controls whether SoundJam automatically deletes temporary files created by playing streaming audio from the Web. Deleting these files automatically is usually clean, decent, honest, and helpful.

Converter group box The four check boxes in this group box control how SoundJam names MP3 files it creates, and where it stores them.

Add Extension to Filename check box Select this check box if you want the files to include a MP3 extension, which is useful if you plan to share them with people using computers other than Macs.

Add Track Number to Filename check box Select this check box if you want the filename to include the track number. (We don't find this option very useful.)

Create Files in Artist Folder check box Select this check box to have the MP3 files created in a folder named after the artist rather than directly in SoundJam's Music folder.

Create Files in Album Folder check box Select this check box to have SoundJam place the files in a folder named after the album. If you include the artist's name, the album folder is stored within the artist folder.

ID3 Tags Page

On the ID3 Tags page of the Preferences dialog box (shown below), you can select the following options:

When Editing Track Information options These two options—the Add Missing ID3 Tags check box and the Update Existing ID3 Tags check box— tell SoundJam to add missing tags and update tags using information you enter in the Track Information dialog box. Typically, you'll want to leave these two check boxes selected.

Create ID3 Tags As drop-down list Select the ID3 tag version you want to use. At this writing, v2.2 is selected by default, as it seems to be becoming the most widely used tag standard. If you're using SoundJam almost exclusively, you might want to choose v2.3, which can store more information.

Create ID3 Tags with Padding check box This check box controls whether SoundJam uses padding—extra space—in tags. If you're having problems using SoundJam-created files with padded tags in other MP3 players, try clearing this check box.

CD Lookup Page

On the CD Lookup page of the Preferences dialog box (shown below), you can select the CDDB server to use (in the CDDB Database Server text box) and the port (in the Port text box). At this writing, there's little reason to mess with the default settings, cddb.cddb.com and port 80. Make sure the Connect to CDDB Automatically check box is selected if you want SoundJam to use CDDB without prompting, and check that the e-mail address in the Your E-mail Address text box is the one you want SoundJam to give CDDB in exchange for the information that CDDB provides.

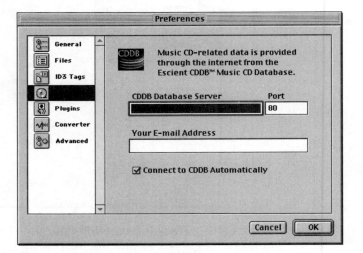

Plugins Page

The Plugins page of the Preferences dialog box offers options for the plug-ins that you're using with SoundJam. At this writing, SoundJam comes with the Eclipse, Melt-O-Rama, and Thumper plug-ins, but you can add other plug-ins to customize your copy of SoundJam as you feel necessary.

Some plug-ins provide configuration options. To access these options, select the plug-in in the list box and click the Configure button. Make the appropriate choices and click the OK button to close the configuration dialog box.

Converter Page

You'll find the following options on the Converter page of the Preferences dialog box (shown below):

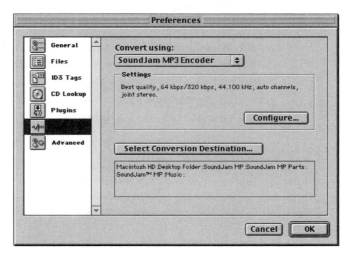

Convert Using drop-down list   Make sure SoundJam MP3 Encoder is selected—unless you really want to create MP2 or AIFF files.

Settings text box   This text box provides a cryptic summary of your current encoding settings—for example, *Best quality, 64 kbps/128 kbps, auto kHz, auto channels, joint stereo.* Click the Configure button to display the SoundJam MP3 Encoder dialog box shown below.

Bit Rate group box   Select suitable bitrates for the MP3 files you'll create in this group box. For example, select 128 kbps in the Stereo drop-down list.

Performance group box   Make sure the Best Quality option button is selected. (In our opinion, the Faster option button isn't worth using.)

Channels group box   Make sure the Auto option button is selected.

Stereo Mode group box   Make sure the Joint Stereo option button is selected.

Advanced button   To choose advanced encoding options, click this button and make choices in the second SoundJam MP3 Encoder dialog box, shown below. On the grounds that you won't need to mess with these options unless you already know what you're doing, we're not going to discuss them here.

Select Conversion Destination text box   Check the folder shown in this text box: This is where SoundJam will store the MP3 files you create. To change the folder, click the Select Conversion Destination button and use the resulting dialog box to specify the folder.

Advanced Page

Finally, these are the options you can set on the Advanced page of the Preferences dialog box (shown on the next page):

Add Encoded Files To drop-down list   In this drop-down list, select the playlist to which you want the ripped and encoded files to be added: Master Playlist, New Playlist, or None. The default setting is Master Playlist, which tends to be the most useful for conventional purposes.

Add Opened Files To drop-down list   In this drop-down list, choose the playlist in which you want files you open to be added. Again, your choices are Master Playlist, New Playlist, or None, and Master Playlist is the default and most widely useful setting.

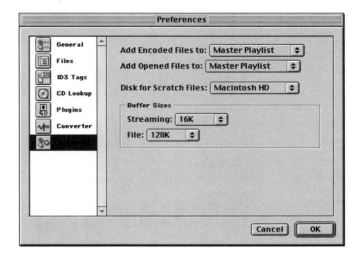

Disk for Scratch Files drop-down list   In this drop-down list, you can choose the location in which SoundJam should store temporary (scratch) files while processing audio. Unless you find yourself running out of disk space, you'll probably want to use your hard drive for temporary storage.

Buffer Sizes group box   In this group box, you can specify a buffer size for streaming and for writing to files. The Streaming buffer defaults to 16K, while the File buffer defaults to 128K. If playback seems choppy, try increasing the buffer sizes.

55 Navigate the SoundJam Interface

SoundJam's interface is friendly and easy to navigate, at least in its default skin. The illustration on the next page shows the Player window, all of whose controls are self-explanatory and straightforward to use.

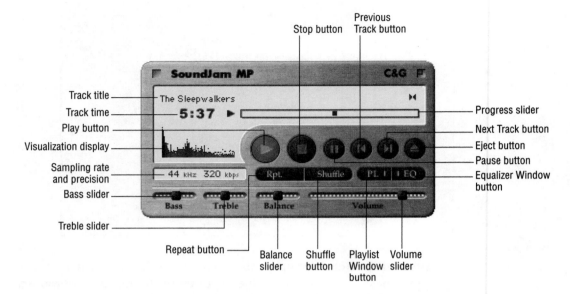

Stop button

Previous
Track button

SoundJam MP   C&G

Track title — The Sleepwalkers

Track time — **5:37** ▶   Progress slider

Play button   Next Track button

Visualization display   Eject button

Sampling rate   Pause button
and precision — 44 kHz 320 kbps   Rpt.   Shuffle   PL   EQ   Equalizer Window
                                                           button
Bass slider —

                  Bass   Treble   Balance   Volume

Treble slider —

Repeat button —   Balance   Shuffle   Playlist   Volume
                  slider   button   Window   slider
                                      button

In addition to the Player window, SoundJam uses an Equalizer window, a Master Playlist window, and a Converter window. You'll meet each of these in due course in the following sections.

56 Rip with SoundJam

Unless you've already got a massive collection of MP3 files stashed away on your computer, you're likely to want to use SoundJam's ripping capabilities straightaway. Like many of the other rippers, SoundJam uses the Fraunhofer MP3 compression technology, and in our experience it delivers consistently good results.

To get ripping, display the Converter window by choosing Window ➤ Converter or by pressing Apple+3. If you skipped our section on configuring SoundJam (*Setting Preferences in SoundJam*, a few pages earlier in this part of the book), check the Settings text box in the Converter window to make sure that all is in order. If anything looks wrong, click the Configure button to display the SoundJam MP3 Encoder dialog box, and check the settings there.

Now load a CD in your CD drive, then drag the CD's icon to the Converter window. (Alternatively, you can add tracks to the Converter window by selecting them in the Playlist window and clicking the Add to Converter button.) If you have SoundJam configured to access CDDB automatically, SoundJam will list the track names. The illustration below shows the CD *The Last Tour on Earth* by Marilyn Manson all ready for ripping.

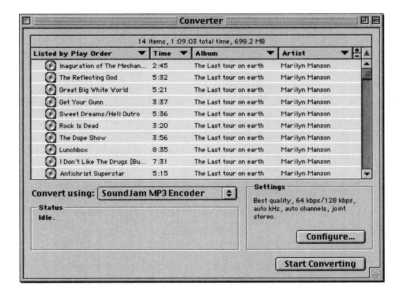

In the Convert Using drop-down list, make sure SoundJam MP3 Encoder is selected. (At this writing, the alternatives are SoundJam MP2 Encoder and SoundJam AIFF Encoder; we're betting you'll never need to use either of these.)

Once you're satisfied you've got the options right, click the Start Converting button to start ripping the CD tracks to MP3 files. SoundJam will spring into action, and as the ripping takes place, will keep you updated in the Status group box. The following graphic is an example from another CD.

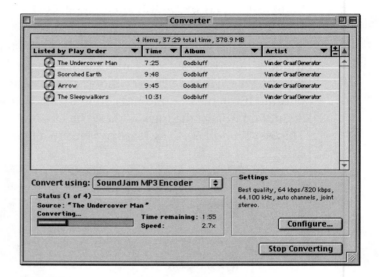

By default, SoundJam plays the tracks from the CD as it rips the files, which helps keep you entertained. You can prevent SoundJam from playing the files by clearing the Play Tracks While Converting check box on the General page.

If you need to interrupt the ripping, click the Stop Converting button, into which the Start Converting button will have changed itself.

NOTE You can convert files from other formats—such as AIFF, QuickTime, or WAV—into the MP3 format by dragging them to the Converter window and clicking the Start Converting button.

Adding and Updating Track Information

If you're building an MP3 collection for keeps—and you probably should be—from time to time you'll want to change the tag information for a track. The process could hardly be simpler: Choose File ➢ Get Info, or press Apple+I, to display the Track Information dialog box, shown on the next page. Change the information as appropriate, and then click the OK button to close the Track Information dialog box.

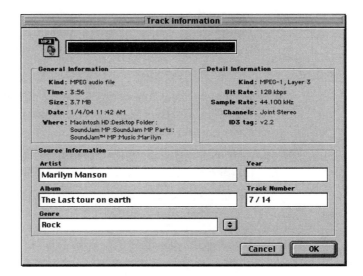

NOTE To make SoundJam update the tag information for the track, make sure the Update Existing ID3 Tags check box on the ID3 Tags page of the Preferences dialog box (Edit ➤ Preferences) is selected. Select the Add Missing ID3 Tags check box as well if you want SoundJam to add ID3 tags to tracks that are missing them.

57 Rock Out with SoundJam

To rock out with SoundJam, you'll typically want to create playlists. Take these steps:

1. Choose File ➤ New Playlist, or press Apple+N. SoundJam will open a new window named Untitled Playlist.

2. Populate the playlist by dragging tracks to its window. If you're keeping most of your tracks in the Master Playlist, you may want to simply drag tracks from there into the new playlist.

3. Drag the tracks in the playlist into the order in which you want them.

4. Save the playlist by choosing File ➤ Save or pressing Apple+S. SoundJam will display the Save: SoundJam MP dialog box. Specify a name and location for the playlist, then click the Save button to save it.

To start a track in a playlist playing, double-click it. Alternatively, select the track and then click the Play button in the playlist's window.

To open a saved playlist, choose File ➤ Open Playlist and select the playlist from the submenu that appears.

58 Use SoundJam's Graphical Equalizer

As we mentioned earlier, SoundJam includes a ten-band graphical equalizer, so you can tweak the music to sound more or less the way you want it to. SoundJam comes with a number of equalizations built in, including Arena, Classical, Hall, Jazz, Rock, and Vocal, to get you started, but you'll probably want to create your own equalizations to supplement them.

To display the equalizer, choose Window ➤ Equalizer, or press Apple+2. The illustration below shows the Equalizer window.

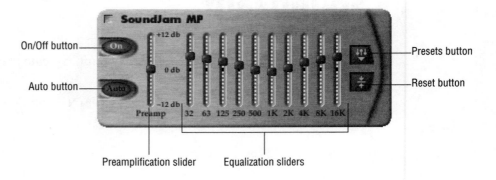

To use the Equalizer, make sure it's switched on. If the Off button is showing, click it to change it into the On button. Then either drag the Equalization sliders to adjust the current equalization, or choose an equalization by clicking the Presets button and making a choice from the pop-up menu.

Most of the time, you won't need to move the Preamplification slider from its default midline position. But if you do increase the preamplification, click the Auto button so that it's turned on. This feature monitors SoundJam's output and prevents you from slamming a higher level of sound through your Mac's audio circuitry than it can comfortably support. (If you manage to do this, you'll get a distorted sound that's called *clipping*.)

To save an equalization, move the sliders to create the sound you want, then click the Presets button and choose Save Settings from the pop-up menu to display the Save: SoundJam MP dialog box. Enter the name for the equalization and click the Save button to save it. You'll then be able to choose it from the pop-up menu like the built-in equalizations.

59 Enjoy SoundJam's Visualizations

As we mentioned earlier, SoundJam comes with a number of built-in visualizations, and you can add further visualizations as you find them on the Web.

To display a visualization, choose its entry from the Window menu. SoundJam will display the visualization in windowed mode, as in the illustration on the next page, which shows the Melt-O-Rama visualization interpreting Van der Graaf Generator's "Scorched Earth" visually.

To display the visualization full screen, choose Window ➤ Use Full Screen, or press Apple+F. To return from full-screen visualization to windowed visualization, click the mouse, press the Esc key, or press Apple+F again.

60 Change SoundJam's Skin

As you saw a few pages ago, SoundJam comes with a sleek, brushed-aluminum–style skin that's easy to understand and to use—but perhaps a little bland on the eyes for long-term use. You'll be glad to hear that SoundJam includes 17 other skins, any of which you can apply with just a couple of clicks of the mouse.

To apply a skin, pull down the Skin menu and choose the skin you want. The illustration on the left shows the WonderJelly skin, and the illustration on the right shows the Brass skin.

Linux MP3 Players and Rippers

In this part of the book, we'll show you one key MP3 player and one great ripper-encoder for Linux. Only one of each? Yes—because there are too many of both. Because of Linux's heritage as an OS developed by a multitude of loosely linked volunteer hackers, Linux players and rippers are plentiful, though many of them are less than finished and less than friendly to use. We're showing you ones that we've found effective, but of course your mileage may vary as usual.

The MP3 player we chose to discuss here is xmms, the player formerly known as x11amp and included (under that name) in Red Hat Linux 6 distributions. xmms is a terrific player, but we won't spend much time on it because it's essentially a Linux incarnation of Winamp, which we discussed earlier in the book. So we'll note only the key points about xmms, referring you back to the Winamp section for the features it shares with Winamp (almost everything).

....

NOTE Of the many other Linux players, you may want to try FreeAmp, which is available (free, as its name suggests) from `http://www.freeamp.org`. At this writing, FreeAmp offers fewer features than xmms, but has solid features for searching your computer for MP3 files.

After that, we'll move on to something more demanding: the freeware ripper Grip. Grip works effectively and the price is very right, but it takes a while to configure. You'll also need to have a good basic knowledge of Linux—but if you're using Linux exclusively, chances are that you have that anyway.

As you'll know from your experience using Linux, you can get many distributions of Linux, and you can install a distribution with different degrees of completeness. We can't see what you're looking at, so you'll need to be able to navigate the intricacies of Linux libraries, packages, tar, and make on your own.

The examples we present use Red Hat Linux 6, perhaps the most widespread distribution of Linux among Linux enthusiasts in North America at this writing. We're not putting down other distributions such as Caldera's OpenLinux, Mandrake Linux, Corel Linux, or S.U.S.E. Linux—they can rip and rock right along with Red Hat—we're just trying to pick the most common ground we can.

61 Get and Install xmms

As we mentioned, xmms—the X Multimedia System—used to be called x11amp. At this writing, x11amp is included with distributions of Red Hat Linux 6. So if you have Red Hat 6, you probably have it installed. If so, you'll probably want to upgrade to xmms, as it's fuller-featured and—in our experience—runs much faster.

To check for the latest version of xmms, point your Web browser toward `http://www.xmms.org`. Before you can install xmms, you need to have `gtk+/glib 1.2.2` or better. If you don't have these libraries, you can download them from various sources on the Web, including `http://www.xmms.org`.

To install xmms, right-click the distribution file and choose Upgrade (if you have x11amp already installed) or Install. Once the installation is finished, we suggest creating a launcher for it on your desktop so that you can launch it at a moment's provocation. Alternatively, crank up a terminal window or the Run Program dialog box and use it to start xmms.

62 Make Noise with xmms

Once you've got xmms started, you should be seeing something like the illustration below. (We've added in a number of MP3 tracks for visual excitement.)

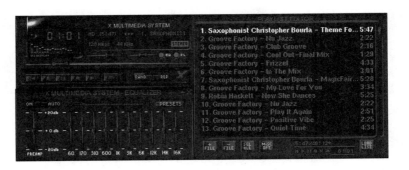

As you'll see, just about everything works the same as in Winamp—the Main window, the Playlist Editor, the Graphical Equalizer window, and so on. The most notable differences between xmms and Winamp are relatively minor:

Different default skin   xmms comes with its own slick-looking skin, rather than the Winamp-clone skin that x11amp sported. xmms can use Winamp's skins: Download a skin, install it in the `/skins/` directory, and then press Alt+S to display the Skin Selector dialog box to select and apply it.

No preset equalizations   At this writing, xmms doesn't have one of Winamp's strongest features—preset equalizations. You'll probably want to create equalizations of your own right away, perhaps taking a look at some of Winamp's preset equalizations for inspiration if you have Windows.

Different preference options   You'll find the Preferences dialog box is perhaps the area that is the most different than Winamp, though many of the preference options are the same. The illustration below shows the Options page of the Preferences dialog box.

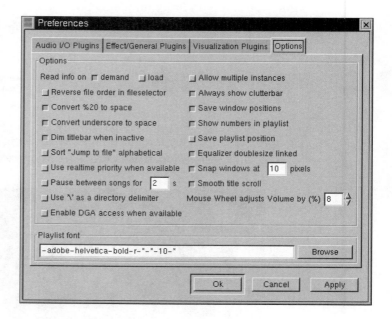

63 Get, Install, and Configure Grip

One of the better freeware Linux rippers that we've used is Grip by Mike Oliphant. You can find Grip at sites such as `http://www.freshmeat.net`. Download Grip and install it to an appropriate directory. (Consult the documentation for where to install Grip if you're root and if you're not root.)

Grip works with MP3 encoders such as bladeenc, lame, l3enc, mp3encode, and others. In our experience, bladeenc gives good performance, though you'll probably want to try Grip with the other encoders if you have them. If you don't, go ahead and download a distribution of bladeenc suitable for the Linux you're running.

Create a launcher for Grip, or simply launch it from a terminal window. The illustration below shows Grip with a fresh CD in the CD drive.

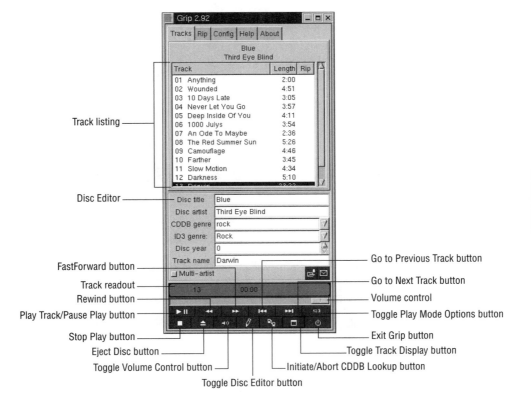

As you can see, the main Grip window has five pages: The Tracks page lists the tracks on the current CD; the Rip page contains options for ripping; the Config page contains configuration information; the Help page tells you to read the readme file and provides a button for submitting bug reports to the author; and the About page displays information about the version of Grip and the author.

Grip takes a while to configure, but after that, it's easy sailing. Take a deep breath; here we go:

1. Start by clicking the Config tab to display the Config page, which has six subpages. The four options on the CD page affect CD playback only, and we'll let you choose them on your own.

2. Click the Rip tab on the Config page to display the Rip subpage shown below.

3. Make sure the Ripper subpage of the Rip subpage is showing (yes, Virginia, this gets deep), and then choose ripper options as follows:

Ripper drop-down list Usually you'll want to choose grip (cdparanoia) in this drop-down list, but you can also use cdparanoia itself, cdda2wav, or another ripper if you have it installed.

Disable Paranoia, Disable Extra Paranoia, Detection, and Repair check boxes Leave these check boxes unselected. (The Disable Paranoia check box and the Disable Extra Paranoia check box are available only if you use the built-in cdparanoia ripper.)

Rip File Format text box   Enter **%n.mp3** to make Grip record the tracks as MP3 files that use the track's name. The switches for rip file format are as follows:

Switch	Designation
%n	Name of the track being ripped
%t	Number of the track being ripped
%a	Current track's artist
%A	Current disc's artist (they'll often be the same)
%d	Name of the CD
%b	Begin sector for ripping
%e	End sector for ripping
%c	CD drive involved
%i	CDDB ID of the CD in hex
%g	Number for the ID3 genre tag
%G	Word for the ID3 genre tag

4. Now click the Options tab to display the Options subpage of the Rip subpage, shown below, and choose options as follows:

Rip 'nice' Value text box   To change the priority given to Grip, enter a value in this text box.

Auto-Rip on Insert, Beep after Rip, and Auto-Eject after Rip check boxes   Select these check boxes as you see fit. If you select the Auto-Eject after Rip check box, you can specify a delay (in seconds) in the Auto-Eject Delay text box.

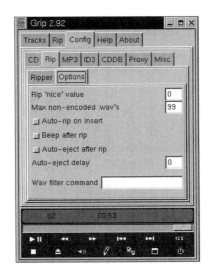

5. Click the MP3 tab to display the MP3 subpage (shown below). If the Encoder subpage isn't displayed, click the Encoder tab. Then choose options as follows:

Encoder drop-down list   Select the encoder you want to use: bladeenc, lame, l3enc, xingmp3enc, mp3encode, gogo, or Other.

Executable and MP3 Command-Line text boxes   Grip will enter the expected path to the encoder in the MP3 Executable text box and the command parameters in the MP3 Command-Line text box. Adjust these as necessary for your system: %b specifies the bitrate in kbps, %f the WAV filename, and %o the MP3 filename.

MP3 File Format text box   Change the default setting of ~mp3/%a/ %d/%n.mp3 if you want to name the MP3 file differently than by its name in a directory named after the CD in a directory named after the artist.

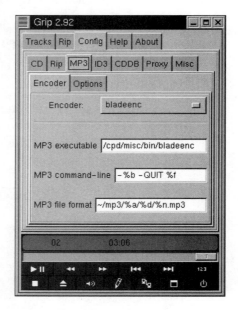

6. Click the Options tab to display the Options subpage (shown on the next page) and choose options as follows:

Delete .WAV after Encoding check box   Clear this check box if you want to keep the WAV file for whatever reason.

Insert Info into SQL Database check box   Select this check box if you're running a program such as DigitalDJ that logs audio tracks in a SQL database.

Encoding Bitrate text box   Make sure this text box shows a suitable bitrate, such as 128 or 160.

Number of CPUs to Use and MP3 'nice' Value text boxes   Change the numbers in these text boxes if appropriate for your system.

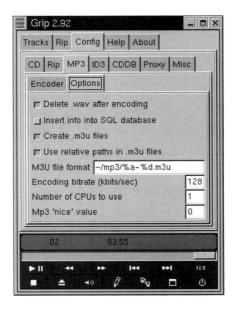

7. Click the ID3 tab to display the ID3 subpage, and make sure the Add ID3 Tags to MP3 Files check box is selected (unless for some reason you do not want to add tags to your tracks).

8. Click the CDDB tab to display the CDDB subpage (shown on the next page) and choose CDDB settings. On the Primary server subpage and Secondary Server subpage, enter settings for the CDDB servers you want to use. Unless you don't want to use CDDB, leave the Perform CDDB Lookup Automatically check box selected.

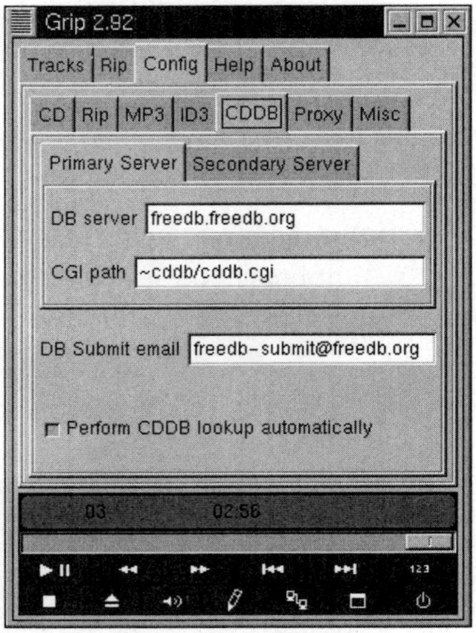

9. If you use a proxy server to connect to the Internet, click the Proxy tab and enter appropriate settings on the Proxy subpage.

10. Click the Misc tab to display the Misc subpage (shown on the next page) and choose options as follows:

Email Address text box Adjust the address in this text box as necessary.

Do Not Lowercase Filenames check box Select this check box if you don't want Grip to automatically lowercase filenames.

Do Not Change Spaces to Underscores check box Select this check box if you don't want Grip to automatically substitute an underscore for each space in a track name.

Characters to Not Strip in Filenames text box Enter any non-alphanumeric characters that you want to prevent Grip from stripping when it creates filenames.

Keep Application Minimum Size check box   Select this check box if you want Grip to minimize its demands on your screen estate.

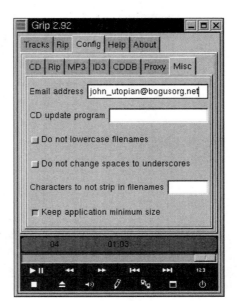

64 Rip with Grip

Finally, you're ready to rip. Insert a CD, and you're off:

1. On the Tracks page, right-click the tracks you want to rip. (Click the Rip column header to toggle selection of all tracks at once.)

2. On the Rip page, make sure that CDDB has entered an appropriate genre in the ID3 Genre drop-down list. Change the genre if necessary.

3. Click the Rip+Encode button to start the ripping and encoding of the tracks you selected. As Grip rips the tracks, the Rip meter and the MP3 meter will show its progress, as shown below.

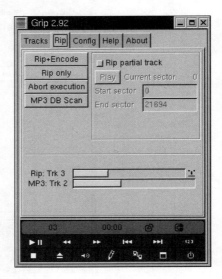

Ten Cool MP3 Maneuvers

In this part of the book, we'll look at some advanced and some semi-advanced MP3 maneuvers that you'll probably want to try once you've played a few dozen hours of MP3 music. We'll concentrate on Windows because it's the operating system that most of you are using most of the time.

In this section, you'll learn how to

◆ Designate a default MP3 player.

◆ Turn Windows' AutoPlay feature on and off.

◆ Choose a CD recorder (if you don't already have one).

◆ Create audio CDs that you can play in any CD player.

◆ Create data CDs of MP3 files that you can only play on a computer but which contain more hours of music than you have fingers. (If you're polydactylous, we don't want to know.)

◆ Convert MP3 files to WAV files (which you'll need to do when using some CD-burning software).

◆ Create executable files from MP3 files so that you can distribute them to people too lame to have MP3 players.

◆ Use Uncook 95 to clean up MP3 files that got trashed during download.

◆ Use MP3.com's Beam-it feature for storing MP3 files of tracks on your CDs online so that you can access them from whichever computer you're using, wherever you happen to be.

◆ Contribute a little to the online music community by plugging missing information into the CDDB database.

65 Choose a Default MP3 Player under Windows

As soon as you've loaded two or more MP3 players onto your computer, they'll start squabbling about which of them is the default player. As with young children, the newest MP3 player usually claims attention, but being the parent, you can overrule the newest player firmly if you so choose.

Winamp, Sonique, MusicMatch Jukebox, and RealJukebox each offers an easy way to do this:

Winamp   Choose Options ➤ Preferences from the main menu to display the Winamp Preferences dialog box. In the Associated Extensions list box, select the extensions that you want to associate with Winamp. If you want Winamp to grab these extensions back from any other application unwise enough to have stolen them each time you start Winamp, select the Register Types on Winamp Start check box; if not, clear this check box. Then click the Close button, and the deed is done.

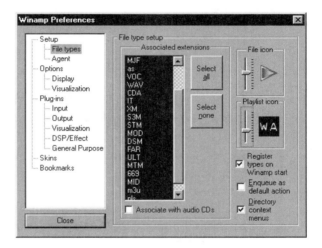

Sonique   Navigate to the Setup Options screen and click the File Types tab. Select the check boxes for the file types that you want to associate with Sonique—for example, MP3 and CDA. Navigate to a different screen, and Sonique will apply the choices for you.

MusicMatch Jukebox   Choose Options ➤ Settings to display the Options dialog box. On the General page, select the Use MusicMatch As Your Default .mp3 and .m3u Player check box and the Use MusicMatch As Your Default CD Player check box as appropriate. Click the OK button to apply your choice.

RealJukebox   Choose Options ➤ Preferences to display the Preferences dialog box, then click the Update page to display it. In the Music File Types group box, click the Settings button to display the Preferences – Advanced dialog box, shown below, and make sure that the appropriate check boxes are selected for the music file types that you want RealJukebox to reclaim.

Click the OK button to close the Preferences – Advanced dialog box, then click the Make RealJukebox Plus My Default Player button and choose the OK button in the Preferences – Confirmation dialog box that springs up to interrogate you. Click the OK button to close the Preferences dialog box.

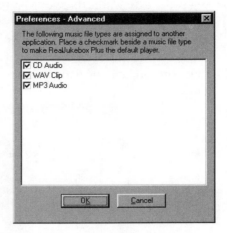

You can also open Explorer, choose View ➤ Options to display the Options dialog box, click the File Types tab to display the File Types page, select the file type you want to change in the Registered File Types list box, and click the Edit button to display the Edit File Type dialog box, in which you can associate a different application or action with the file type. Note that once you install Winamp, it craftily declares MP3 to be a *Winamp Media File* rather than any more conventional description that you'd imagine it to be filed under.

66 Turn AutoPlay Off or On on Your Computer

Depending on how you look at it, Windows' AutoPlay feature is either a blessing or a curse. AutoPlay is the feature that starts your default CD player running (and playing) when you insert an audio CD into the CD drive on your computer. If the CD you insert contains software, AutoPlay will start running or installing the software on the CD. Multiple unintended installations of operating systems and monster application suites tend to drive us up the wall.

To turn AutoPlay off or on in Windows 95 or 98:

1. Choose Start ➤ Settings ➤ Control Panel.

2. Double-click the System icon to open the System dialog box.

3. Click the Device Manager tab to display the Device Manager page.

4. If the entry for your CD drive is collapsed, click the + sign next to it to expand the entry.

5. Double-click the CD drive you want to affect. Alternatively, click the CD drive and click the Properties button. Windows will display the Properties dialog box for the CD drive.

6. Click the Settings tab to display the Settings page of the dialog box. The illustration below shows the Settings page of the Properties dialog box for a Mitsumi CD-ROM drive.

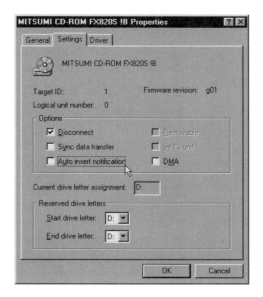

7. Clear the Auto Insert Notification check box.

8. Click the OK button to close the Properties dialog box, and then click the OK button to close the System Properties dialog box.

NOTE   To override AutoPlay temporarily when it's on, hold down the Shift key as you close the CD-ROM drive. This isn't infallible, but it almost always works.

67 Choose a CD Recorder

If you don't have a CD recorder but want to get one, here's what you need to know.

Get a Fast Recorder

First off, you'll probably want to get one of the fastest CD recorders you can afford. This doesn't necessarily mean the fastest CD recorder available to you—there are a couple of considerations that you need to keep in mind when choosing your CD recorder.

CD recorder speed is measured by the same rating system as CD drives: 1×, 2×, 4×, and so on. Each × represents 150kbps, so a 4× drive chugs through 600kbps, an 8× drive handles 1200kbps (1.2Mbps), and a 12× drive manages 1800kbps (1.8Mbps).

At this writing, CD recorders that write at 12× are becoming widely available; writing full bore, they can fill a whole CD in 6 minutes or so. (The speed will vary a bit depending on your system—if your other components are lame, chances are the CD recorder will have to scale back its speed so as not to choke them.) As you'd imagine, 12× writers are on the north end of the price spectrum, with external models costing as much as $500 or $600.

6× and 8× CD recorders are much more affordable, with many available between $200 and $400. 4× CD recorders tend to be cheaper still, but with prices on the 6× and 8× recorders dropping, you may want to forego a 4× recorder unless your primary interest is an incredible bargain.

That said, you shouldn't need to put yourself into Chapter 11 and buy a 12× drive unless you're cutting CDs all the time or you have savagely impatient chromosomes. A 2× drive takes 36 minutes to write a CD, which is far too slow for most people. The 18 minutes that a 4× drive takes is too long for some people, as well; but the difference between the 12 minutes that a 6× drive takes and the 9 minutes that an 8× drive takes is almost negligible unless you'll be holding your breath watching the CD being burned. Still, we're not denying that it'll be great when some friendly hardware manufacturer comes out with a 96× drive that can burn a CD in 30 seconds flat.

CD recorders almost invariably read data at a faster rate than they write it: Some now read up to 32×, making them almost as fast as a dedicated CD drive. Even so, unless you're out of space, look to add a CD recorder to your computer rather than replace your existing CD drive with a CD recorder. That way, you'll be able to duplicate a CD (assuming you have the right to do so) or install Quake at the same time as enjoying the cannons in Tchaikovsky's *1812* Overture.

Check out the range of CD recorders at your local friendly computer superstore or online paradise and choose a recorder that satisfies both your budget and your temperament.

Internal or External?

Generally speaking, an internal drive will cost you less than an external drive, but you'll need to have a drive bay free in your computer. An external drive will usually cost more, will occupy real estate on your desk, and will need its own power supply; most external drives are much noisier as well because they contain their own fans. But if your main computer is a notebook, or if you want to be able to move the drive from computer to computer as the fancy strikes you, you'll need an external drive.

Most external drives include a cable (SCSI, parallel, USB, or FireWire) for connecting to your computer—but many don't include an audio cable for connecting their audio output jacks to your sound card's input jacks. Before you go shopping for an external drive, determine what type of connection you'll need at the PC end (typically a ⅛-inch miniplug, but sometimes two RCA jacks). Then check the connection on the CD drive, find out whether the package includes the cable, and buy a cable if necessary.

EIDE drives are all internal. SCSI drives can be internal or external. Because the parallel port, the USB ports, and any FireWire ports are external connections, those drives are external only.

EIDE, SCSI, Parallel Port, USB, or FireWire?

The next question is: How will you connect the drive to your computer? If you have a SCSI card in your computer, you'll probably want to get a SCSI CD recorder because it will typically perform better *and* put much less burden on the processor than an EIDE CD recorder will. One restriction you need to know here if you need to copy CDs: Most SCSI CD recorders will copy CDs directly only from other SCSI drives, not from EIDE drives. If you have a SCSI CD recorder and an EIDE CD drive, you'll need to copy the CD to the hard disk and then burn it from there.

SCSI drives cost a bit more than EIDE drives of the same speed, but if your computer's already got SCSI, the extra cost is probably worth it. If you don't have a SCSI card, remember to factor in the cost of the card in your cost analysis—some SCSI CD recorders come with a bundled SCSI card, but most don't, so in most cases you'll have to budget for the card as well. (Check the specifications or the box to make sure you know what you're getting.) If you don't have SCSI, but you want the best, bite the bullet and cough up the cash for a good SCSI card and SCSI CD recorder.

If you don't want to pay for SCSI but you want an internal drive, or if your CD player is EIDE and you want to do a lot of CD-to-CD duplicating, EIDE is the way to go. Before you buy, make sure that you have an EIDE connector available on your computer. If it's already chock-full of drives (most modern machines can take four EIDE devices), you won't be able to add another without sacrificing an existing one.

If you're looking at an external non-SCSI drive, your current choices are a parallel port drive, a USB drive, or a FireWire drive. Parallel port drives suffer speedwise from being limited to the bandwidth (the transfer speed) of the parallel port, which is far less than EIDE and SCSI can transfer. But they're compatible with most computers ever built, and they get the job done— eventually. USB is much more promising, provided your computer has USB ports and your operating system supports USB. (If your desktop computer doesn't have USB ports, you can add them via a PC card.) USB delivers better speed and (in theory) the convenience of being hot-pluggable.

NOTE Though slow, a parallel port CD drive can have an additional benefit: If you have a computer without a built-in CD drive, you can use a parallel port CD drive to install an operating system (or to reload it after a fatal crash). Usually, you'll need to install a driver to access the CD drive, but you can install the driver after booting from a Windows 95 or Windows 98 boot diskette.

Barreling down the shoulder of the hardware turnpike are FireWire CD recorders. (*FireWire*, as you'll remember, is the most widespread snappy name for the IEEE 1394 high-performance serial bus. Sony, determined to continue its assaults on the English language, calls it i.LINK instead.) Consider a FireWire CD recorder only if you have a FireWire-capable computer. At this writing, FireWire ports are more or less confined to Macs and Sony computers, meaning that FireWire drives have a select and largely enthusiastic clientele.

CD-R or CD-RW?

Next, decide whether you want just a CD-recordable drive (CD-R) or a read/write drive (CD-RW). Burning a CD-R disc is essentially a one-time process: Once the data is written to the CD, you can't remove it or change it, though you can read it as many times as you want. With a CD-RW disc, on the other hand, you can write to it multiple times, changing the data as you see fit.

You've guessed the easy corollary: A CD-RW drive is more expensive than a CD-R drive. And a CD-RW blank is far more expensive (at $3 or so) than a CD-R blank, which you can get for much less than a buck if you buy in bulk and send in coupons. The good news is that over the past year or so, CD-RW drives have been dropping like the Hindenburg, and they now cost only a little more than CD-R drives. For most people, this price difference is negligible, and the benefits of a CD-RW drive over a CD-ROM drive are huge. And CD-RW drives can write both CD-RW discs and CD-ROM discs, making them a good investment.

NOTE Some stores, such as CompUSA, offer CD-R and CD-RW discs without jewel cases. This makes for a good discount, as the jewel cases are relatively expensive to manufacture and bulky to package (and easy to break, as you no doubt know from personal experience). The discs are typically sold on a spindle, which makes for handy storage until you use them—after which you'll have to find safe storage for them on your own. (One possibility to consider is a CD wallet, which can be especially handy if you need to take your CDs with you when you travel.)

The next factor is not so easy to guess: Because CD-RW discs use a different technology than regular CD-ROMs, they're not as compatible with all CD-ROM drives. If you want to share a CD with someone else, a CD-R disc is a better bet than a CD-RW disc. Likewise, only the most recent audio players can play CD-RW discs—most can play only prerecorded CDs and CD-R discs.

NOTE Some manufacturers try to sell you special CDs that are supposed to deliver greater writing speed. We're split on the virtues of these überCDs: On the one hand, you want your viciously expensive CD recorder to record as fast as possible; but on the other, chances are that you're paying enough for regular media anyway. You may want to spend extra on CD-RW discs if you find those higher-quality discs appear to deliver on the performance claim, but you're unlikely to want to spend extra on CD-R discs unless your time is mighty precious.

Choosing CD-Recording Software

At this writing, there are many dozen CD-burning applications, each of which would love to be your friend for life. You probably got some kind of CD-burning application with your CD recorder drive. Depending on how much you paid for the drive, you may have gotten a lite version of something good (quite likely), or you may have gotten the real thing (less likely, but refreshingly possible). If you got stuck with a lite version, you'll probably need to get something better before too long.

If you haven't already checked out the capabilities of whatever was bundled with your drive, stop reading and go check it out to see if it'll get the job done. There's more than a fair chance that you have a lameware version that will copy data files to CDs slowly and clumsily enough to persuade you to shell out for better software. (You gotta love those marketing folks.)

One of the heaviest hitters in the CD-recording ring is Adaptec's Easy CD Creator Deluxe, which costs a little less than $100. Easy CD Creator Deluxe is a solid product for general-purpose use, such as creating data CDs for backup, and it will create audio CDs with no problem. We'll show you how to use Easy CD Creator Deluxe to burn an audio CD from MP3 files a little later.

Other CD-recording packages that you may want to check out include PTS AudioCD MP3 Studio, MP3 Wizard from Data Becker, and HyCD Play&Record, to name just a few.

NOTE If you already have MusicMatch Jukebox and are mainly interested in creating audio CDs or data CDs of music tracks, you may not need to fork out the cash for CD-burning software. As we discussed in *40. Burn CDs with MusicMatch Jukebox*, MusicMatch Jukebox provides these capabilites.

Making the Tough Choice

As we mentioned, there are a huge number and variety of CD-R and CD-RW drives available. We haven't done any formal testing of CD recorders, but we can share with you some drives that we've used and liked. Don't take these as recommendations necessarily to be followed—they're more in the spirit of information. (Mind you, we *have* met several drives that we've decided not to tell you about here.)

The list below starts with the slowest drive and progresses to the fastest:

Parallel port   The Hi-Val EPP CD Recordable drive is a solid if uninspiring performer. Its main virtue is that it will attach to any computer with a minimum of fuss—no USB needed, no SCSI required, no mucking about with master and slave jumpers—and get the job done. We've caught it writing at a miserable 0.7× speed when it's been upset with something, but it gets the CD written eventually without choking.

SCSI internal   The Yamaha CRW4416S is a 4× write, 4× rewrite, 16× play drive that delivers good performance. We've used it for CD-to-CD copying (from a Toshiba SCSI CD-ROM drive) and found it reliable. Since we bought this drive, Yamaha has released a 6×4×16× CD-RW drive and an 8×4×24× CD-RW drive, so you probably won't want to go looking for the CRW4416S any more.

SCSI external   Our current king of the hill is a Smart & Friendly CD Rocket Mach 12, an external SCSI CD-RW drive. The CD Rocket Mach 12 is extremely fast and good tempered and comes with not only its own SCSI PCI card, but also a terrific selection of software, including Adaptec Easy CD Creator 4 Deluxe, Adaptec Toast for Macintosh, Power-Quest Drive Image (for creating an image—a backup—of your hard drive), Sonic Foundry CD Architect and Sound Forge XP, Diamond Cut Audio Restoration Tools 32 (for fixing messed-up audio tracks), and more. Its one detriment is that, as an external drive with its own power supply and fan, it does sound something like a rocket—a distant rocket, to be sure, but louder than comfort dictates.

68   Create Audio CDs with Easy CD Creator

In this section, we'll show you how to create audio CDs with Easy CD Creator from Adaptec.

Getting and Installing Easy CD Creator

Because Easy CD Creator is such popular software, it comes in a variety of packages. In this section, we'll run you through getting and installing Easy CD Creator Deluxe. If your package of Easy CD Creator uses a different installation routine, don't worry—the chances are good that it'll work just fine. You shouldn't have any problem getting Easy CD Creator. You can buy it online directly from Adaptec's Online Store (http://www.adaptecstore.com), from just about any online retailer (such as PC Connection, Outpost.com, CDW, the PC Zone, and all their competitors), or from a bricks-and-mortar retailer (such as Best Buy or CompUSA).

You'll probably start off with an installation screen that looks something like the one shown below.

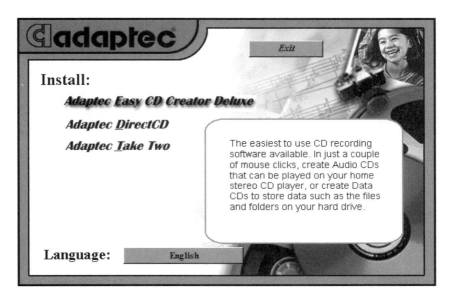

Click the Easy CD Creator Deluxe link, and follow the Setup program through a typical InstallShield routine. When (or if) the Setup Type dialog box (shown below) offers you the choice of a Typical, Compact, or Custom installation, choose the Custom option button.

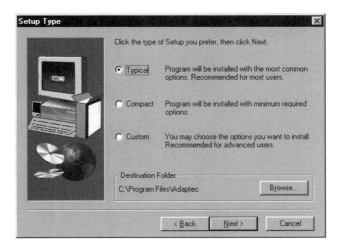

Setup will then present you with the Select Components dialog box, shown below, in which you can select the components you want. If you're short of space, you'll probably want to skip the 40MB PhotoRelay and the 50MB Video Postcard Templates. Click the Next button when you're ready to proceed.

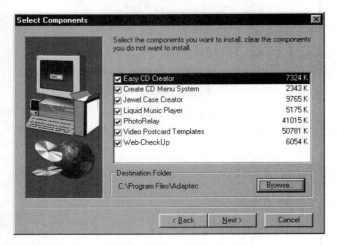

Your next treat will be the Personalization dialog box, in which you get to enter your name, your company's name, and your Tech Support ID (TSID—a.k.a. your serial number). After that, installation should be relatively swift and painless. Celebrate by installing Adaptec DirectCD as well, if your package includes it.

After that, six gets you one you'll need to reboot your computer before you can use the software. After you reboot it (and log in, if necessary), you'll probably see a splash screen like the one shown below.

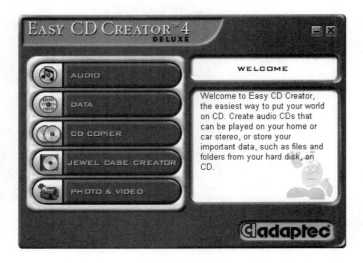

Creating an Audio CD

Follow these steps to create an audio CD with Easy CD Creator:

1. If you still have that splash screen facing you, click the Audio button. If not, choose Start ➤ Programs ➤ Adaptec Easy CD Creator ➤ Create CD, *then* click that Audio button. (Quick note: The menu choices may vary depending on the version of Easy CD Creator you have.) Easy CD Creator will display the Audio screen shown below.

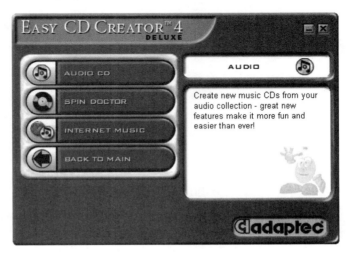

2. Click the Audio CD button to start Easy CD Creator. You'll see Easy CD Creator, probably as shown on the next page, with the CD Guide assistant demanding your attention.

3. Dismiss the CD Guide by right-clicking it and choosing Hide from the context menu.

4. Use the tree in the left-hand side of the upper part of the window to navigate to the folder that contains MP3 files you want to burn to CD.

5. Drag the tracks from the right-hand side of the upper part of the window to the CD.

6. Repeat steps 4 and 5 until you've added to the CD as many tracks as you want or as many tracks as it will hold. Use the graphical and text readouts at the bottom of the CD to see how much space you've used and how much you have left.

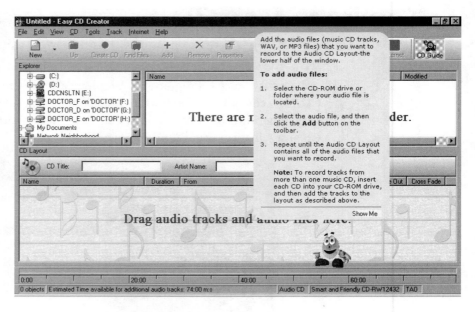

7. Drag the tracks up and down until they're in the order in which you want them to appear on the CD.

8. Enter the title for the CD in the CD Title text box and the artist's name in the Artist Name text box.

9. If you plan to use this CD layout frequently, save it by choosing File ➢ Save and specifying a name and location in the Save As dialog box.

10. Click the Create CD button on the toolbar, or choose File ➢ Create CD, to display the CD Creation Setup dialog box, shown below.

11. Make sure that Easy CD Creator has selected the right CD recorder in the Target Devices drop-down list, an appropriate write speed in the Write Speed drop-down list, and the number of copies you want in the Number of Copies text box.

12. Click the Advanced button to display the hidden section of the CD Creation Setup dialog box (shown below) that contains advanced options.

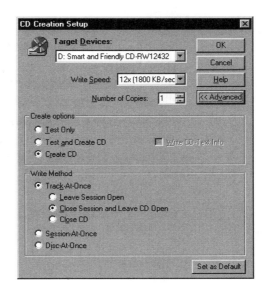

13. Choose advanced options as follows:

Create Options group box   In this group box, select the Test Only option button if you want to test the CD-creation process without writing any files to the CD. Select the Test and Create CD option button if you want to perform the test and then write to the CD. Otherwise, leave the Create CD option button selected to create the CD without testing. If your CD drive supports CD-Text information and you use the Disc-At-Once writing method (more on this in a moment), you can select the Write CD-Text Info check box to add the CD title and the artist and track names to the CD.

Write Method group box   In this group box, choose the writing method you want to use for creating the CD:

Track-At-Once option button   This button lets you record one track at a time. If you choose this option button, you can select the Leave Session Open option button if you want to add more tracks to the CD in the same session. Alternatively, you can select the Close Session and Leave CD Open option button to close the session (and make the first session's audio tracks playable on CD players) but leave the rest of the CD open for further sessions. (This is the default setting.) Your third choice is to select the Close CD option button, which closes the CD after writing the track. Writing Track-At-Once leaves a two-second gap between audio tracks.

Session-At-Once option button This button lets you record one session (typically of multiple tracks) at the same time, then record another session. Writing Session-At-Once also leaves a two-second gap between audio tracks.

Disc-At-Once option button This button writes and closes the CD in a single operation. This option is good for creating a full CD of music because it lets you eliminate the two-second gap between tracks.

Set As Default button When you've made your choices, click this button to set them as your defaults.

14. Click the OK button to close the CD Creation Setup dialog box. Easy CD Creator will start creating your CD, keeping you informed of its progress in the CD Creation Process dialog box, shown below.

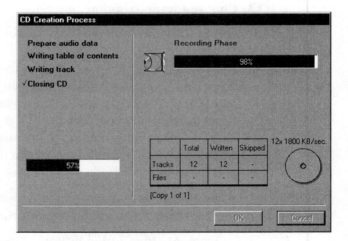

15. When Easy CD Creator tells you that the CD was created successfully, either pop it out and get ready to enjoy it, or click the Jewel Case button to use Easy CD Creator's Jewel Case Creator (if you installed it) to create a jewel-case insert for the CD.

69 Copy MP3 Files Directly onto CDs

If you have a CD recorder, you'll probably want to copy MP3 files directly onto CDs so that you can tote them around easily—directly, as in "without converting them to CD-DA format." By burning a CD full of MP3 files, you can put ten or so hours' worth of music on a single disc, but remember that you'll need a computer to read them—a regular CD player just won't cut it.

N O T E If you have Easy CD Creator, you can use it to create data CDs as well as audio CDs. Once Easy CD Creator is up and running, choose File ➤ New CD Layout ➤ Data CD, then drag tracks to the CD window provided.

Here's where that lameware program that came with your CD recorder comes into its own. The procedure you follow will vary depending on the program, but the sequence of steps is usually like this:

1. Unwrap a new blank CD-R and slip it into the drive.

2. Format the disc and assign a name to it (use descriptive names like **HEVYLECTRIC** and **GrrlGuitars** to help you keep your discs straight). Some CD-R programs will spring to life when you insert the disc; others you need to start manually.

3. Once the disc is under the program's control, you can add files to it by using standard Windows operations such as drag-and-drop or copy-and-paste. Again, the specifics will vary depending on the program, but many programs let you use Windows Explorer to copy or move files to the CD as you would to any other drive.

    Copying the files to the CD takes a while—up to an hour or more, depending on the speed of your CD recorder.

4. Issue the program's command for making the disc readable by CD drives; this command will probably say something about creating a "data" CD. Usually the program will then take a few minutes to convert the CD to the CD file system.

At this point, you may get to choose between an option for being able to write to the CD again and an option for fixing its contents permanently.

The program may require you to shorten very long path names and filenames so that the CD's file system can store them.

You then have a monster music CD that you should be able to read in any computer's CD drive.

70 Convert MP3 Files to WAV Files for Burning to CD

Depending on the CD-recording program you're using, you may need to convert MP3 files to WAV files before burning them onto the CD. You can get dedicated applications to perform this conversion, but you don't need to because Sonique and MusicMatch Jukebox can do the job for you.

Converting MP3 Files to WAV Files with Sonique

Sonique can turn an MP3 file into a WAV file that you can then burn to a CD. (When you write the WAV files to the CD, the writing program converts them to the CD-DA format that CDs use.) Before you start creating WAV files this way, be warned that doing so takes a fair amount of processing power—and remember that the WAV files will be about ten times the size of the MP3 files from which you create them.

To turn an MP3 file into a WAV file, follow these steps:

1. Load the file or group of files to convert. (For example, you can convert a whole playlist if you want.)

2. Display the Navigation Console if it's not already displayed.

3. Click the Setup Options button to display the Setup Options screen.

4. Click the Audio tab on the right-hand side to display the audio options.

5. Note the current setting in the Select Output list box (for example, Default Audio Device), then use the up or down arrow to choose WAV Disk Writer instead.

6. Click the WAV Disk Writer Path button to display the Browse for Folder dialog box.

7. Navigate to the folder in which you want to save the WAV files, and then click the OK button.

8. Click the Play button. Sonique will display the Sonique Diskwriter dialog box, shown below.

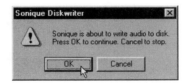

9. Click the OK button to write the audio to disk.

Other than listing the current track name and displaying the Stop button in place of the Play button till it's finished, Sonique doesn't give you any indication of how it's progressing, but you'll probably hear your hard drive writing busily. If you're in doubt, open an Explorer window to the folder you chose in step 6 and choose View ➢ Refresh periodically to watch the files being written to disk.

10. When you've finished writing WAV files, reset the Select Output list box to its previous setting.

Converting MP3 Files to WAV Files with MusicMatch Jukebox

To convert MP3 files to WAVs with MusicMatch Jukebox, follow these steps:

1. Choose Options ➢ File ➢ Convert to display the MusicMatch File Format Conversion dialog box, shown next with options selected.

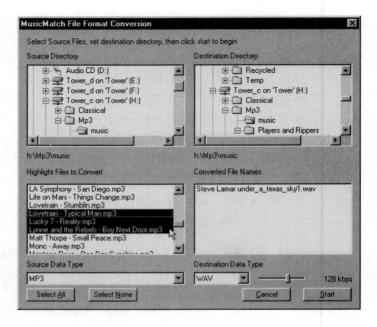

2. In the Source Data Type drop-down list at the lower-left corner of the dialog box, select MP3.

3. In the Source Directory list box, navigate to and open the directory that contains the files you want to convert. The files in that directory will appear in the Highlight Files to Convert text box.

4. In the Highlight Files to Convert text box, select the files you want to convert. Use the Select All button if appropriate.

5. In the Destination Directory list box, change the destination directory if necessary. By default, MusicMatch Jukebox makes the destination directory the same as the source directory.

6. Check that the slider next to the Destination Data Type drop-down list is showing a suitable bitrate for the conversion.

7. Click the Start button to begin the conversion. You'll see the Music-Match Jukebox File Conversion dialog box as MusicMatch Jukebox converts the files to WAVs. As it finishes each, the WAV shows up in the Converted File Names text box.

8. Click the Cancel button to close the MusicMatch File Format Conversion dialog box.

You can now burn the WAV files to a CD by using the CD-mastering software that came with your CD recorder.

71 Create Executable MP3 Files with MP3 to EXE

As you've seen so far in this book, you need a MP3 player to play MP3 files. Getting an MP3 player is no hardship—but what if someone doesn't want to (or cannot) install a player on their PC? For example, your company's MIS department may restrict employees from installing *any* program— even a screen saver—on company computers. If they catch you with an unauthorized MP3 player on your machine, you might as well just hang yourself from your cubicle's coat-hook (remember to keep your knees bent). Oliver Buschjost's MP3 to EXE converter provides the solution, allowing you to wrap an MP3 file into an executable file.

WARNING MP3 to EXE is a way cool utility, but it's problematic in this wicked world of ours. Because executable files can contain a multitude of sins that no virus checker yet invented can uncover, you may want to send executable MP3 files only to people who already trust you. Anyone else will nuke them on sight if they have any sense.

MP3 to EXE is a $15 shareware product that you can download from http://www.mp3toexe.com. Unlike some shareware, it's not a crippled version, so you can try it out thoroughly before doling out the *dinero*.

Once you've downloaded MP3 to EXE, unzip it and double-click the executable file to run the installation routine. As usual, you get to select a destination directory and Start menu group for it.

Launch MP3 to EXE and you'll see the MP3 to EXE Converter window, shown next with a track ready for conversion.

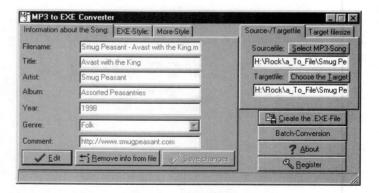

MP3 to EXE is easy to use:

1. Click the Select MP3-Song button to display the Open dialog box.

2. Select the track and click the Open button. MP3 to EXE will display its name in the Sourcefile text box and a suggested EXE name in the Targetfile text box, and will enter information from the track's filename and tag in the Information About the Song panel.

3. Change the Targetfile name if you want.

4. If you need to edit the track information, click the Edit button to enable the text boxes.

5. To choose options for the EXE file, click the EXE-Style tab to display the EXE-Style page, and make your choices. We recommend going with the standard settings, but if you must, you can do antisocial things like setting a default volume, locking the volume, and looping the track.

6. To choose yet more options, click the More-Style tab to display the More-Style page, shown below. Here you can enter a URL and caption to display, and you can choose to make the track expire at a given point in the future.

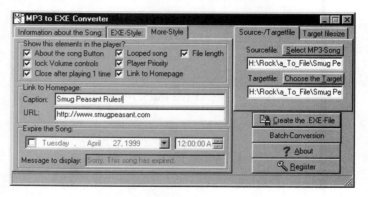

7. To split the executable file into several smaller files to make it easier to distribute, click the Target Filesize tab to display the Target Filesize page. Select the Split into Several Files check box, and then specify a maximum filesize in the Maximum Filesize group box.

8. Click the Create the .EXE-File button to create the executable. You'll see a progress bar in the lower-right corner of the window as MP3 to EXE builds the executable, then MP3 to EXE will display the Confirm dialog box offering to execute the file for you.

9. Click the Yes button or the No button as appropriate.

NOTE To convert multiple MP3 files to EXEs, click the Batch-Conversion button and work in the MP3 to EXE Converter – Batchmode dialog box.

The illustration below shows an executable MP3 file playing.

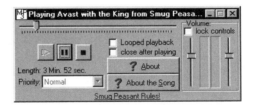

72 Uncook Cooked Files with Uncook 95

If an MP3 file you've downloaded from the Internet sounds not just bad but truly terrible—for example, it sounds as though it's nothing but squeaky noise—and you're sure that's not the way it's supposed to sound, it may have been *cooked*. *Cooking* is a type of mangling that occurs when a server sends a file as text rather than as a binary file; the text includes unnecessary carriage-return characters, which play havoc with the sound.

To undo the cooking, get and use the Uncook 95 utility as follows:

1. Download the current distribution of Uncook 95. You can find it at a number of locations, including `http://free-music.com/uncook95.htm`.

2. Expand the executable file or zip file you downloaded.

3. Run the resulting executable file. You'll see the Uncook 95 window, as shown below.

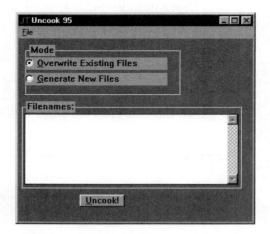

4. Choose File ➢ Open to display the Open dialog box, select the MP3 file or MP3 files you want to uncook, and click the Open button. Uncook will add the files to the Filenames text box, as shown below.

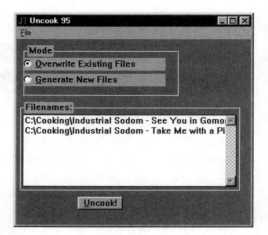

5. In the Mode group box, make sure the appropriate option button is selected:

Overwrite Existing Files option button   Select this button only if you're 200 percent sure that the files are cooked and that you want to overwrite the originals with the uncooked versions.

Generate New Files option button   Select this button if there's even the slightest doubt in your mind about the files being cooked. If you use this option, Uncook creates new files named "Copy of *the original filename.*"

6. Click the Uncook! button to uncook the files. Uncook will display the Files Are Uncooked! message box, shown below, telling you when the files are uncooked. Note that this message box lists only the first of the files that was uncooked.

7. Uncook more files as necessary, then choose File ➢ Quit to exit Uncook.

When you're done uncooking, test the uncooked files and make sure that they sound right.

....

NOTE Another program for removing extra carriage returns from an MP3 file is Detox.

73 Rename MP3 Files with MP3 Renamer

If you download enough MP3 files from the Internet, chances are you'll soon end up with tracks whose names include percent signs or underscores instead of spaces, making them impossible to decipher easily—for example:

```
sisters%20of%20mercy-under%20the%20gun.mp3
```

or

```
sisters_of_mercy-under_the_gun.mp3
```

Also, you'll probably find that some of the people creating the MP3 files you're downloading suffer from Morbid Phobia of Capital Letters, as in the above two examples. On special days, you may be lucky enough to run into files that exhibit all three of these characteristics.

You can of course rename these files manually in Explorer (or your other favorite file-management utility), but there's a better way—MP3-renaming tools. Several are available, among them MP3 Renamer from Digital Dreams Software, which we'll discuss here. We chose MP3 Renamer for several reasons, including that the price is right (it's freeware), it works well, and it's easy to use.

Here's how to get, install, and use MP3 Renamer:

1. To check for a more recent version of MP3 Renamer, aim your Web browser at the Digital Dreams Software Web site, `http://www.dgdr .com`. If there's a newer version of MP3 Renamer, download it.

2. Unzip MP3 Renamer to the folder from which you want to run it.

3. Run the executable file by double-clicking it in Explorer. (Create a shortcut on your Desktop or Quick Launch toolbar if you think you'll want to run MP3 Renamer frequently.) You'll see the MP3 Renamer window, as shown below.

4. In the Folder to Rename Files In drop-down list box, specify the folder that contains the MP3 files with offending names. Either type in the folder and path, or select a recently used folder from the drop-down list, or click the Browse button and use the resulting Browse for Folder dialog box to choose the folder.

5. If you want to apply a default artist to MP3 files that appear not to have one, enter the artist's name in the Default Artist text box. For example, if you've been downloading a couple of thousand Grateful Dead bootlegs into the folder in question, you could enter **Grateful Dead** in the Default Artist text box.

6. In the Filetype drop-down list, make sure *.mp3 is selected.

7. Click the More button to display the lower half of the MP3 Renamer window.

8. In the Presets drop-down list, you can choose one of the preset replacements it specifies. But usually you'll do better to leave the Auto Rename check box selected (as it is by default), in which case MP3 Renamer performs the following operations:

   ◆ Converts each underscore to a space.

   ◆ Corrects %20 to a space, %28 to an opening parenthesis, %29 to a closing parenthesis, and %7E to a tilde (~).

   ◆ Makes sure that there is a space on either side of each hyphen and ampersand.

   ◆ Makes sure that there is a space before an opening parenthesis and after a closing parenthesis.

   ◆ Replaces each double space with a single space.

9. Alternatively, choose Custom in the Presets drop-down list and use the Replace and With drop-down list boxes to specify the text to be replaced and the replacement text.

10. Leave the Capitalize Every Word check box selected if you want MP3 Renamer to capitalize every word in the track name. Clear this check box to leave the capitalization as is.

11. Click the Rename button to perform the renaming operation. MP3 Renamer will chug and whirr for a moment as it works and will then display the Results window (as shown below, with the window widened so that you can see all the results).

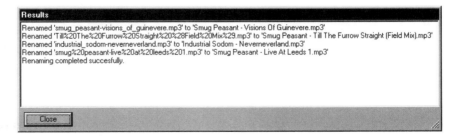

Results

Renamed 'smug_peasant-visions_of_guinevere.mp3' to 'Smug Peasant - Visions Of Guinevere.mp3'
Renamed 'Till%20The%20Furrow%20Straight%20%28Field%20Mix%29.mp3' to 'Smug Peasant - Till The Furrow Straight (Field Mix).mp3'
Renamed 'industrial_sodom-neverneverland.mp3' to 'Industrial Sodom - Neverneverland.mp3'
Renamed 'smug%20peasant-live%20at%20leeds%201.mp3' to 'Smug Peasant - Live At Leeds 1.mp3'
Renaming completed succesfully.

Close

12. Click the Close button to close the Results window. Then either rename more files or click the Exit button to close MP3 Renamer.

74 Store MP3 Files Online with MP3.com's Beam-it

If you live a mobile life and want to have your music available wherever you go, you may want to try the Beam-it service from MP3.com. Beam-it lets you quickly create virtual images of your CDs online at MP3.com. From there, you can listen to the tracks from the CDs whenever and wherever you're logged into the Internet by playing the tracks from MP3.com the way you would any other track that's available for download.

You'll notice we said *virtual images* in the previous paragraph. That's because MP3.com has set up Beam-it so that you don't actually have to upload the full contents of each CD to MP3.com—unless you have a honking connection, that would take an absurd amount of time. Instead, you slip the CD into your CD drive so that MP3.com can see that you own a copy, upon which MP3.com provides you with access to already ripped copies of the tracks on that CD.

The idea sounds great, but there are disadvantages. The first is that MP3.com doesn't have all the music in the world available—only the most popular CDs and only albums (no CD singles). But if the service expands, the available list of music may turn out to be reasonably comprehensive.

Notice that we said *if* the service expands rather than *when*. That's because, at this writing, the RIAA is suing MP3.com for copyright infringement for providing online copies of CDs. MP3.com is fighting back, saying that Beam-it is merely a (brilliant) example of *time-shifting*—the action of transferring content from one medium to another for convenience of listening. (Time-shifting was ruled legal back in the 20th century when the record and film industries were trying to prevent people from using cassette recorders and VCRs to make copies of audio recordings and videos.) MP3.com makes sure that the user owns the CD, then provides a time-shifted online copy for their listening enjoyment, wherever, whenever.

Both sides have published open letters more or less accusing the other of bad faith, and we confidently expect the lawsuit to be even more entertaining than the RIAA's lawsuit against Napster (also for copyright infringement).

The second obvious disadvantage of Beam-it is that unless you have a fast Internet connection, you'll need to spend a bunch of time downloading the files when you want to listen to them. If you have hard-disk space on your laptop, you'll do better to keep your favorite tracks with you and store less-used tracks on MP3.com, downloading them as necessary.

Not exactly a disadvantage, but definitely something you need to think about before using Beam-it, is your privacy. By using Beam-it, you're telling MP3.com which CDs you own (or have borrowed from your friends) and when you listen to them. MP3.com has a good privacy policy, and they seem to be on the up-and-up, but if you're concerned about people knowing more about you than they absolutely need to, you may choose not to use Beam-it.

Here's how Beam-it works. We'll assume that you've already set up a My.MP3.com account as described in the section *Creating a MyMP3.com Area* in *5. Find MP3 Sites on the Web*.

1. Steer your browser over to MP3.com and log in to your account.

2. Click the Add Your CDs link in the Add Music area.

3. Download the software for the operating system you're using. (At this writing, there's Beam-it software for Windows, the Mac, and Linux.) For the rest of this example, we'll use Windows.

4. Install the software following the procedure appropriate to your operating system. Be sure to read the license agreement, particularly the parts about registered content and verification. Restart your computer if you're running Windows.

5. Start the Beam-it software from the icon or shortcut that it installed. The following illustration shows the opening MP3.com Beam-it dialog box that you'll see if you're using Windows.

6. Click the Start Beam-it button to display the second MP3.com Beam-it dialog box, shown next.

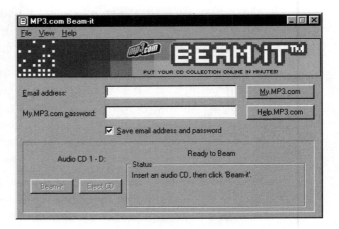

7. In the Email Address text box, enter the e-mail address you've used for your My.MP3.com account.

8. Enter your password in the My.MP3.com Password text box. Select the Save Email Address and Password check box if you want Beam-it to remember them. (Hint: Usual security warning here.)

9. Slot a CD into your CD drive and close it. The Beam-it button and the Eject CD button should become available.

NOTE If you have multiple CD drives and the CD title doesn't appear in the Audio CD area, choose Edit ➤ Preferences to display the Preferences dialog box, select the appropriate CD drive in the Default CD Drive drop-down list, and click the OK button.

10. Click the Beam-it button to start the beaming procedure. You'll see a progress update in the Status group box.

NOTE If you try to beam a CD that MP3.com does not have available, you'll see the message *Beaming unsuccessful: Insert another audio CD to Beam (message 17)*. Beam-it will activate or launch your Web browser and will direct it to the My.MP3.com CD Request page, where you can request that MP3.com add the CD. You'll need the artist's name, the CD's exact title, and the Universal Product Code (UPC). The UPC is the number printed under the barcode, usually on the CD's sleeve.

11. When beaming is complete, Beam-it will display a message telling you so.

12. Click the Eject CD button to eject the CD, slip in the next CD, and repeat the process.

13. Once you've finished beaming CDs, you can click the My.MP3.com button to access your music collection online, or choose File ➢ Exit to quit Beam-it.

To access your music collection by album, click the Albums link in your My.MP3.com area. You'll then see a list of the albums you've beamed, as shown below.

75 Enter Information in CDDB

As you've seen so far in this book, CDDB is a fantastic database of information about CDs, containing artist and track information about an amazing number of CDs. But if you have CDs that are old, new, borrowed, or blues, CDDB may well not have them.

When you run into a CD that CDDB can't identify, it's your chance to give a little back to the online music community by adding the CD's information to the CDDB. Most CDDB-compliant players and rippers provide a mechanism for adding this information.

Here's an example using MusicMatch Jukebox:

1. Slip the CD into the drive and close it.

2. Watch as MusicMatch Jukebox queries CDDB and comes up empty.

3. Open the Recorder window.

4. Enter the album name in the Album text box, the artist's name in the Artist text box, and the names of the tracks in the track list text boxes.

5. Choose Options ➤ Recorder ➤ Send Album Info to CDDB. MusicMatch Jukebox will grind for a moment and then display the Submit to CDDB dialog box, shown below. MusicMatch Jukebox will have filled in the artist's name, the album name, and the track names from the Recorder window, together with the CDDB DiscID (from the CD).

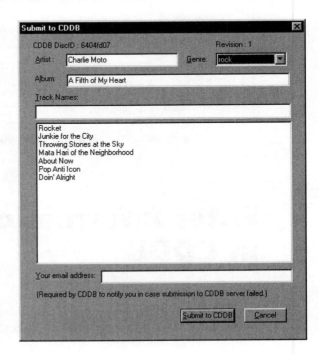

6. Check the artist, album, and track names. (Any typos or errors in capitalization may result in CDDB users cursing you for years to come.)

7. Select the appropriate genre in the Genre drop-down list.

8. Enter your e-mail address in the Your Email Address text box.

9. Check everything once again, then click the Submit to CDDB button. MusicMatch Jukebox will display the snappily named MMSITESERV message box shown below. Wait till the excitement subsides, then click the OK button to dismiss the message box.

If your submission is new, you won't hear anything from CDDB. Nothing. Nada. Zip. (To make sure that the information took, visit the CDDB site in a day or two and plug the artist's name and the CD into the search engine.) But if your submission is a duplicate, CDDB will probably send you an e-mail telling you politely to go climb a medium-sized tree. Do so with joy.

Find and Share Music with Napster

In this part of the book, we'll introduce you to Napster, the current state-of-the-art way of finding the MP3 files you want. Napster is a resource-pooling software that links all connected PCs into a group, enabling them to share MP3 files easily and swiftly.

Napster was originally developed for Windows, but it's rapidly proved such a hit that it's been implemented on most operating systems and graphical environments known to turn-of-the-millennium mankind. In this part of the book, we cover Napster (for Windows), Macster (for the Mac), and Gnapster (for Linux running Gnome).

If you're interested in Windows, start from the top and keep reading until you hit the Mac section. If you're interested in the Mac, read the section *76. Understand Napster* first, then jump ahead to *80. Use Macster—Napster for the Mac*. And if you're interested in Gnapster, read *76. Understand Napster* first, then put on your seven-league boots and skip ahead to *81. Use Napster on Linux*, in which we discuss the various Linux implementations before knuckling down and discussing Gnapster.

Before you start reading this part, we need to give you a quick heads-up: The RIAA has sued Napster for encouraging copyright violations. If the RIAA wins this lawsuit, it's possible that all Napster servers might be shut down—in which case, this section would be of use to you only as an historical document or as a replenishment for that tattered old almanac in the outhouse. So you might want to check the current status of Napster (for example, by visiting `http://www.napster.com`) before reading this part.

NOTE If Napster is gone or *resting* when you read this, look for similar programs named Wrapster and Gnutella. At this writing, these programs are under development, and they let you share various kinds of files in a way similar to how Napster lets you share MP3 files.

76 Understand Napster

In this section, we'll show you how to use Napster, the latest sensation in the MP3 world.

As you saw earlier in the book, there are a couple of problems with getting MP3 files online:

◆ First, it's hard to find the tracks you want. Despite the best efforts of sites such as Scour.net, there's no central repository of the tracks available and where to get them, so you'll usually have to traipse through a number of sites in order to get what you're after—and there's no guarantee that you'll find it.

◆ Second, there's no easy way for you to share any music you can legally distribute. Sure, you *could* set up an MP3 server—but you probably don't have the hardware or software to do so, or perhaps you don't have the always-on Internet connection that a server needs in order to be effective.

Napster solves both problems, the second problem rather more elegantly (or perhaps we should say *legally*) than the first.

Simply put, Napster creates a virtual community on the fly for sharing MP3 files. Each user can designate files to be shared and can download any files that other people currently logged in have shared. When you start Napster, it touches base with the central Napster server, which balances the Napster load and farms you out to one of the group of member servers.

Once you're logged in to the member server, Napster adds any MP3 files that you're sharing to its current list of what's available. Other people logged in can then download the files you're sharing, and you can download any of the files that everyone else is sharing. You can search through the list of files for ones that match specific criteria, and you can download multiple files at once if you feel so inclined. You can even chat with any of the other people who are logged on. And when someone logs off, Napster removes their files from the list, so that they no longer appear to be available.

NOTE At this writing, there are a number of different Napster servers that act more or less independently rather than being tied together into one humongous network. The result is that each time you log into Napster, you don't know which server you'll be using, and you'll see only the users and tracks available on that server. Even if you know that a particular person is online, you may not be able to locate them because they may be on a different server. Sooner or later all the Napster servers should be tied together, but it hasn't happened yet.

Napster Legal Issues

So far, so wonderful—Napster provides quick and easy MP3 file–sharing over the Internet (or over an internal TCP/IP network, such as a campus network, if you're connected to one), with powerful searching capabilities for finding the files you want. The only fly in the ointment is a juicy big legal bluebottle—what if the MP3 files that people are sharing are ones that they don't have the rights to share?

The brief answer to this question is: Yup, it's a problem. A big one. Many of the MP3 files that you'll find being shared via Napster are ripped from CD and distributed without permission. Obviously, we haven't been able to check out all the MP3 files on all the Napster servers around, but we'd guess that somewhere north of 95 percent of all files we've seen shared via Napster are illegal.

At this writing, Napster, Inc. has been hit with a lawsuit by the RIAA for a sum of money large enough to solve the debts of several emerging countries *and* buy another lifetime's worth of shoes for Imelda Marcos. This lawsuit is hardly surprising, for two reasons:

- ◆ First, the RIAA is big into suing people and companies who have anything to do with distributing digital audio online. At this writing, the RIAA is also suing MP3.com (for their Beam-it feature), and MP3.com is making things more interesting by counter-suing the RIAA (for defamation).

- ◆ Second, it would be hard to deny that Napster helps people illegally share music. When you fire up Napster and search for a thing or two, any remaining doubts you have on this subject are likely to be instantly dispelled.

That said, there's also no question that Napster helps people *legally* share music. So you could argue that the technology is neutral and the problem lies only in the way that people use it: If you have the legal right to distribute the MP3 files, it's good; and if you don't, it's bad. You can make the same argument about knives—they're good for chopping up meat and vegetables, but also good for chopping up humans—chainsaws, cars, and most legitimate tools. It's harder to make the argument for, say, assault rifles, which are good for, um, shooting people and shooting more people (or shooting those same people more quickly or more frequently).

At this writing, a number of universities have banned Napster, some for intellectual-property concerns, but more of them for the massive amount of bandwidth that it consumes. Napster is working on adding features that allow administrators to allocate bandwidth effectively to resolve such problems.

77 Get and Install Napster

In this section, we'll walk you through the process of getting and installing Napster (the Windows version). Follow these steps:

1. Download the freshest version of Napster from `http://www.napster.com`.

2. Double-click the Napster distribution file to start the Setup routine.

3. Click the Next button in the Welcome dialog box. Setup will display the Software License Agreement dialog box.

4. Agree to the license in the Software License Agreement. You should (of course) read all the licenses on all the software you install, but this license is more entertainment than most because it essentially tells you to behave yourself. Check this out—you'd almost think the RIAA was after them or something…

   Napster, Inc. makes no representations or warranties regarding MP3 files owned by Napster, Inc. users. Many MP3 files have been authorized for distribution by their respective copyright owners. You should be aware that MP3 files may have been created or distributed without copyright owner authorization and Napster, Inc. refers you to the terms and conditions above. Copying or distributing unauthorized MP3 files may violate U.S. and foreign law and compliance with such law is entirely your responsibility.

5. In the Choose Destination Location stage of the Setup program, choose the directory into which you want to install Napster.

6. Click the Next button. Napster will display the Select Program Folder stage of the Setup program.

7. Click the Next button. Napster will display the Ready to Install stage of the Setup program.

8. Click the Next button. Napster will install itself and will display the Finished stage of the Setup program when it has finished.

9. Make sure the Start Napster Now! check box is selected, then click the Close button to end the Setup program.

10. Napster will then start. You'll see the Napster, Inc. Software License Agreement and Disclaimer dialog box.

11. If you agreed to the license agreement in the distribution file, you'll agree to this one too, because it's the same. Click the Yes button to proceed. Next, Napster will display the Connection Information dialog box, shown below.

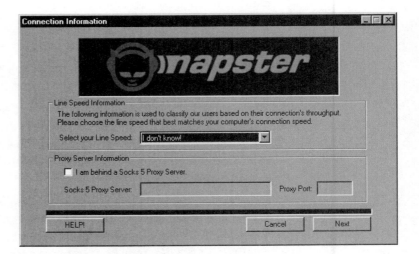

12. Specify the speed of your Internet or network connection in the Select Your Line Speed drop-down list. The choices go from 14.4K Modem to T3 or Greater. A T1 line is a fast business connection—1.5 million bits per second, or Mbps for short. A T3 line is a *very* fast business line. You're more likely to be choosing one of the faster modem choices (for example, 56K Modem) or Cable or DSL.

NOTE The speed you choose in the Select Your Line Speed drop-down list controls the line speed Napster displays in the information it lists about you, not the line speed that Napster uses for uploading and download files. (Napster uploads and downloads files as fast as it can.) As you'll see in a few minutes, the information Napster displays for you influences how other users interact with you—so you may choose to display disinformation rather than the truth. For example, if you have a 128K ISDN line, you'll get hit for downloads frequently because people will assume you'll deliver speedy downloads, whereas if you seem to have a slow modem connection, people may well shun you. But if you choose to declare a slower connection than you have, don't claim a 14.4K modem—hardly anyone uses them anymore, so people will assume that you're hiding a fast connection and will hit you to find out if they're right.

13. If your computer connects to the Internet through a Socks 5 Proxy Server, select the I Am Behind a Socks 5 Proxy Server check box, then specify the name of the server in the Socks 5 Proxy Server text box and the proxy port in the Proxy Port text box. (You're most likely to be behind a proxy server in a company or campus environment, in which case you will probably need to ask your network administrator for this information.)

14. Click the Next button to proceed. You'll see the Napster Configuration dialog box, shown below.

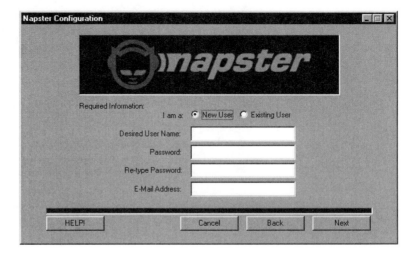

15. Enter your desired username, password (twice), and e-mail address in the text boxes. Make your password a good one—between 8 and 15 characters long, not a real word in any language, and using letters, numbers, and symbols—because you don't want anyone hacking you.

16. Click the Next button. If the username you chose is already in use, Napster will display the Napster Notification dialog box, shown below, to warn you of the problem. Click the OK button. Napster will then display another notification dialog box telling you that the password you entered for the name is incorrect. Click the OK button again, and Napster will return you to the Napster Configuration dialog box, where you can choose another username.

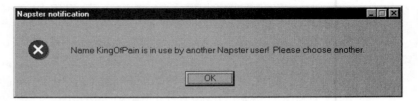

17. Once you've successfully chosen a username, Napster will register the name with the Napster servers and will display the Optional Information dialog box, shown below.

18. Fill in the optional information if you want. (We don't see any benefit in your giving Napster this information. At this writing the information goes to Napster only: It is not divulged to other Napster users.) Then click the Next button. Napster will display the Scan for MP3s? dialog box, shown below.

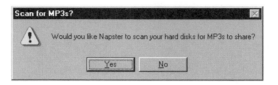

19. We recommend clicking the No button because for most people, it's much more sensible to share folders manually. If you click the Yes button, Napster will scan your local hard drives, removable drives, and CD (and DVD) drives for MP3 files, making a list of them. As it does so, you'll see the User Status dialog box. After that, Napster will display the Audio Information dialog box, shown below.

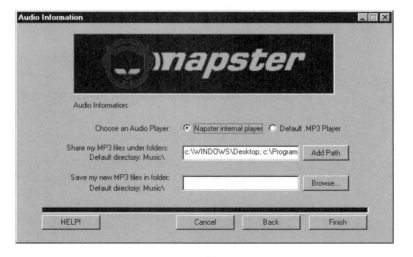

20. Select the audio player you want to use by clicking the Napster Internal Player option button or the Default .MP3 Player option button. This is the player that Napster will automatically use for playing MP3 files, but you can use another player manually if you so choose. The Napster internal player is fine for basic playing, but if you're used to the bells and whistles that a player such as Winamp or Sonique offers, you'll probably want to stick with that player.

21. In the Share My MP3 Files under Folders text box, enter the folder or folders that contain music that you want to share:

◆ Separate multiple folders with semicolons.

◆ If you let Napster scan your local drives for MP3 files, Napster will have entered in the text box the paths to any folders containing MP3 files. Edit these entries as necessary.

WARNING At this writing, there's a bug in Napster's implementation of this text box: After you use the Add Path button to add a path to the text box, Napster adds that path to the previous contents of the text box—*even if you have modified the contents of the text box*. For example, if you let Napster scan for MP3 files, it will enter paths in the Share My MP3 Files under Folders text box. Say you then delete one or more of these paths and use the Add Path button to designate a different path. When you click the OK button in the Browse for Folder dialog box, Napster will restore the list of paths to its unedited state and will add the new folder to it. Once you've finished adding paths, you'll need to edit out the ones you don't want to use.

◆ To add another path, click the Add Path button, use the resulting Browse for Folder dialog box to select the folder, and then click the OK button to enter the path in the text box.

WARNING Remember that in order for you to stay on the right side of the law, you need to have the right to distribute this music.

22. In the Save My New MP3 Files in Folder text box, enter the path to the folder in which you want to save the MP3 files you download. You can either type the path in or click the Browse button, use the resulting Browse for Folder dialog box to select the folder, and click the OK button.

23. Click the Finish button to finish installing Napster. You'll then see the Napster window, which we'll discuss in the next section.

24. If your computer is behind a firewall (a hardware device or software program that monitors incoming network traffic), you'll see the File Server Settings dialog box, shown next.

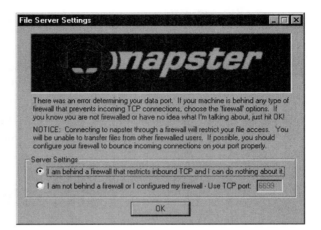

25. If you have no control over your firewall, select the I Am Behind a Firewall That Restricts Inbound TCP and I Can Do Nothing About It option button. Napster will then not be able to transfer files from other users whose computers are behind firewalls, but files from computers not behind firewalls will transfer fine. If you have control over your firewall or are able to specify a TCP port for data use, select the I Am Not Behind a Firewall or I Configured My Firewall – Use TCP Port option button and specify the TCP port in the text box. Then click the OK button. (TCP is the Transmission Control Protocol, part of the TCP/IP protocol suite.)

26. Napster will then display the Channel List dialog box, shown below, and will populate it with the current list of chat channels.

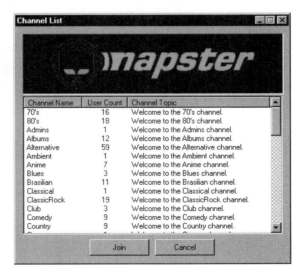

27. To join one or more channels, select it or them (Shift+click to select a contiguous range of channels; Ctrl+click to select multiple individual channels), and then click the Join button. Alternatively, click the Cancel button to avoid joining any channels. You can join chat channels at any point using Napster, so there's no need to join any now unless you want to. (We'll discuss how to use chat in *Chatting on Napster*, a little later in this section.)

28. Once you've dismissed the Channel List dialog box, you'll see the Napster window in all its glory, with the Chat page selected, as shown below. The Chat page displays the message of the day, which in this example tells you how wonderful Napster is and warns you about illegal MP3 files.

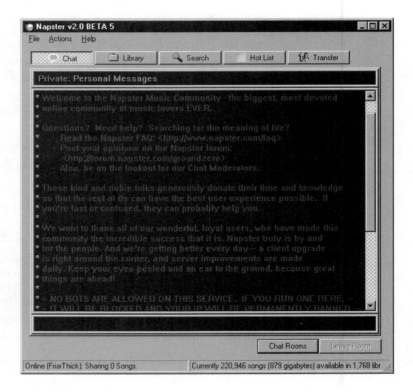

Choosing Further Preferences

Napster offers a half-dozen more configuration settings that do not appear in the current setup routine. To set these settings, or to change any of the

Napster settings you chose during setup, choose File ➤ Preferences to display the Preferences dialog box, shown below, which gathers together all the changeable information that you entered during setup. (You cannot change your username without reinstalling Napster.)

Now change your existing settings or set the extra settings:

Swear Filter drop-down list   Choose Off in this drop-down list if you want to turn the swear filter off for chat. The swear filter, which replaces common obscenities in chat with symbols, is switched on by default. For example, if someone types **f***** (yes, yes—without the asterisks, rhymes with *luck*), you'll see something like @$%& when you have the swear filter on.

Ping Search Results check box   Leave this check box selected if you want to see ping times for the search results. (We'll discuss ping times more in the next section.) If you have a slow connection, you might try turning ping times off in order to improve search times a tad.

Show Joins and Parts in Channel check box   Leave this check box selected if you want your chat rooms to notify you when people join and leave your chat channels. Clear this check box if you find constant notices are a distraction.

Auto Join Previous Channels on Connect check box   Select this check box if you want Napster to automatically join your previous chat channels each time you fire up Napster.

Auto Delete Transfer Entry upon Success check box   Select this check box if you want the Transfer page to automatically remove entries for files when they've been downloaded successfully.

Transfer Settings group box   In this group box, you can adjust the Max Simultaneous Uploads (Per User) setting and Max Simultaneous Downloads setting to match your line speed. If you use a modem connection, reduce the upload number to 1 in order to give visitors the maximum speed possible. (If multiple visitors connect at the same time, they'll still get slow speeds.) If you have a fire-hose connection such as a T1, choose a larger number. Likewise, adjust your download number. If you have a DSL or cable modem (or T1 or T3 line), you'll probably want to enter a number between 5 and 10 (or between 5 and 25) so that you can pull down a number of songs at the same time from lower-bandwidth sites. If you have a modem, you'll want to keep the number low—perhaps 2 or 3—so that each song you're downloading gets a significant chunk of your bandwidth and none takes too long to download.

Once you've made your choices, click the OK button to close the Preferences dialog box.

78 Find Music with Napster

Once you've configured Napster, you're ready to use it to find music—and to share music of your own. (We'll discuss sharing music of your own in the next section, *79. Share Music with Napster.*)

Navigating the Napster Interface

The Napster interface consists of five pages—Chat, Library, Search, Hot List, and Transfer—which you navigate between by clicking the five corresponding buttons at the top of the Napster window or by pressing Tab (to move from left to right). We'll introduce you to these pages in due course.

Finding a Track

With Napster, you can perform either a simple search, specifying only one or two criteria, or a complex search, using up to seven criteria. For example, you might want to search for any MP3 files from a certain artist, in which case you would need only to specify the artist's name. Or you might want to search for a specific track by a particular artist, looking for only copies at or above a certain bitrate (say, 128K) and available on ISDN or faster connections—in which case you would specify each criterion.

Here's how to use Napster to search for a track:

1. If you don't have the Search page displayed, click the Search button to display it. The illustration below shows the Search page with some search criteria specified.

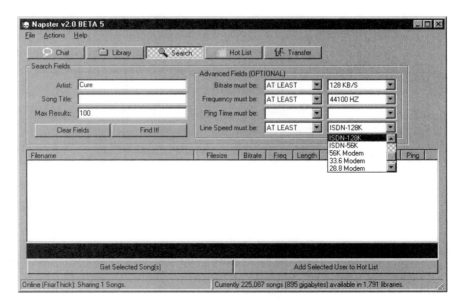

2. In the Search Fields group box, enter the basic criteria for the search:

◆ If you want to search for tracks by a particular artist, enter the artist's or band's name in the Artist text box.

◆ If you want to search for a particular track by the artist, or if you want to search for a particular track without specifying the artist, enter the song title in the Song Title text box. (In the previous illustration, we've left the Song Title text box empty in order to search for any tracks by The Cure.)

◆ At this writing, Napster only supports returning 100 results or fewer—you can enter another number in the Max Results text box, but doing so won't make any difference.

3. In the Advanced Fields group box, you can specify further criteria for the search if you want. Each of the drop-down lists in the left-hand column offers four settings: the default blank setting (meaning that the criterion is not used), AT LEAST, EQUAL TO, and AT BEST. Each of the drop-down lists in the right-hand column offers a range of settings appropriate to the subject:

Bitrate Must Be row In this row, you can specify the minimum, exact, or maximum bitrate you want. Usually you'll want to specify a minimum bitrate or an exact bitrate rather than a maximum bitrate. For example, you might choose AT LEAST in the left-hand column and 128 KB/S in the right-hand column to find only tracks with a bitrate of 128K or better.

Frequency Must Be row In this row, you can specify the minimum, exact, or maximum frequency you want. Again, you'll usually want to specify a minimum frequency or an exact frequency rather than a maximum. For example, you might choose EQUAL TO in the left-hand column and 44100 HZ to find only tracks sampled at CD frequency.

Ping Time Must Be row In this row, you can specify your desired ping time—the time it takes for a packet of information to get from your computer to the host computer and back. A longer ping time typically means there are more *hops* (stages) in the connection between your computer and the host, which translates to a greater burden on the Internet and a potentially longer download time. Usually you won't need to specify a ping time; instead, you can sort your search results by ping time and take the fastest relevant result. (If you do want to try setting a ping time, you might choose AT BEST 500 ms to avoid ultra-slow connections.)

Remember that 56K modems, DSLs, and cable connections have much slower upstream speeds—33.6K upstream for a 56K modem, and often 128K for a DSL or a cable connection (depending on the carrier and the service plan). In particular, don't scorn ISDN connections—they deliver the data rate advertised, and an ISDN-128K connection will often outperform a DSL or cable on the upload. And if you're prepared to use modem connections, set a minimum of 33.6K or even 28.8K rather than 56K—33.6K is the maximum speed you'll get when downloading from a 56K modem, so there's no sense in excluding 33.6K modems; and 28.8K is only about 15 percent slower than 33.6K, so it's still worth using. Also, remember that a number of Napster users will be deliberately hiding speedy connections in order to avoid downloads—so you may want to try barraging some ostensible 14.4K connections or Unknown speed connections to see what you can turn up.

Line Speed Must Be row   In this row, you can specify the speed you want for the host's connection. For example, you might choose AT LEAST in the left-hand column and ISDN-128K in the right-hand column to make sure that the hosts you find have a 128kbps ISDN connection or better. In most cases, it doesn't make sense to specify the exact line speed you want—unless you're overwhelmed by search results and need to winnow them down to, say, T3 connections only. And there's no sense in specifying a *maximum* line speed—unless you're very strange, you'll want the fastest connection you can find.

NOTE   Start by performing a gross-grained search and seeing how many results you get. If you get plenty, trim the search back by specifying quality criteria until you get down to a manageable number of results. Here's something else to try: Instead of searching for particular titles by the artist you're interested in, search for words like *rare, bootleg,* and *live.* Doing so may turn up some true treasures, along with more Grateful Dead tracks than the average human can handle.

4. Click the Find It! button to perform the search with the criteria you've specified. Napster will search through the songs available in the libraries and will return a list of what it has found. The next illustration shows Napster having found 32 Cure tracks from a variety of sources.

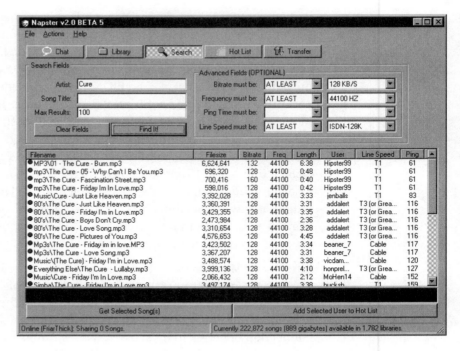

Most of the fields on the Search page are easy enough to understand: Filename, Filesize, Bitrate, Freq (frequency), Length (time in minutes and seconds), User (the host's name), Line Speed, and Ping (the ping time).

The colored circles next to the filenames provide a quick guide to the line speed:

◆ A red circle denotes a 33.6K or slower modem, or an unknown speed.

◆ A yellow circle denotes anything from a 56K modem to a 128K ISDN line.

◆ A green circle denotes anything faster than a 128K line—a cable modem, a DSL, a T1, or a T3.

For most of your downloads, you'll do best to avoid red circles because typically they'll give you the worst performance. But it's worth checking the Line Speed column to weed out the unknown line speeds from the slow modems. Some unknown line speeds are in fact cable modems and DSLs, others even T1s and T3s, and because many users automatically shun unknown line speeds, you may get blazing performance from them. Your mileage *will* vary here.

NOTE Because Napster is a dynamic community, with people logging on and off all the time, and is split across multiple servers, the pool of tracks available changes constantly. If you don't find what you're looking for, try either of these two tactics: Choose File ≻ Disconnect to disconnect from your current server, then choose File ≻ Connect to connect again until you get a different server (you're unlikely to get the same server twice in a row, but it could happen), or just search again in a few minutes or a few hours.

Downloading a Track

If you find one or more tracks you want, you'll probably want to download them.

To download one or more tracks, select it or them on the Search page, then click the Get Selected Song(s) button at the bottom of the page or right-click one of the tracks and choose Download from the context menu. Napster will display the Transfer page, as shown below with multiple Cure tracks being downloaded. Note that at this point we're almost certainly breaking the law—last we heard, The Cure hadn't granted all these people permission to shunt their copyrighted material around on the Internet. (Don't worry—we deleted the tracks straightaway after downloading them, yessir, Mr. Feebo, yes indeedy we did.)

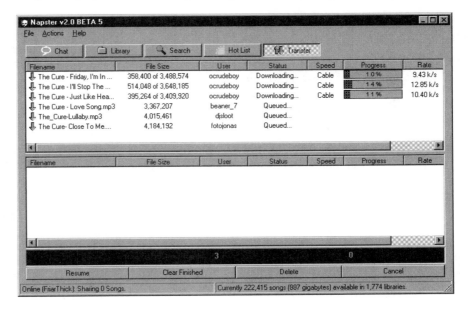

As each download runs, Napster will show you its status (Getting Info, Queued, Downloading, File Complete, Unavailable, or Transfer Error), the line speed, a progress bar for it, the download rate (as in the illustration), and the time left on the download.

NOTE Occasionally a download will fail, and Napster will mark the track Unavailable on your Transfer page. This happens especially if your computer and the host are both behind firewalls, preventing Napster from communicating effectively via TCP. It also may indicate that the host has decided, for whatever reason, to cancel your download request. If a host goes offline or exits Napster, you'll get a Transfer Error message instead.

When you're downloading multiple files, Napster starts downloading the number of files you have set in the Max Simultaneous Downloads text box in the Preferences dialog box (discussed in *Choosing Further Preferences*, a few pages earlier in this section). It queues the rest of the tracks, marking them *Queued*, and starts downloading them once it has finished with the first batch. You can download from any host up to the number of tracks the host has set in their Max Simultaneous Uploads (Per-User) text box (again, in the Preferences dialog box); any tracks beyond that will be queued at the host's end and will appear as *Remotely Queued*.

NOTE When downloading, try to spread the load as much as possible: Don't try to download multiple files from the same host at the same time unless both you and the host have fast connections. For example, if you try to download ten tracks at once from a host that has a 56K modem, you'll get a miserable transfer rate of a few hundred bytes a second and each track will take several hours to download (assuming the host allows each user to download that many tracks at once). Instead, hit multiple 56K hosts for a track apiece, and you'll get them much quicker (provided you have the bandwidth yourself). This strategy of not overburdening a host may be foiled by other people hitting the same host and downloading files, but at a minimum, you should make sure that you don't throttle any host by yourself.

When you try to download a file that has the same name as a file that's currently in your library, Napster displays the File Exists! dialog box, shown below. From the drop-down list, you can either choose the default setting, Overwrite Existing File, to overwrite the file currently on your hard drive with the file you're downloading, or choose Rename Remote File and adjust the filename in the text box. (Renaming the remote file works only if you can access the machine, so you'll probably want to avoid this choice.) Then click the OK button.

While downloading, you can use the four buttons at the bottom of the Transfer page to manipulate selected transfers:

Resume button   Click this button (or choose Actions ➤ Resume) to resume a download you haven't completed. Napster will display the Resume Files dialog box, shown below. Select the file or files whose transfer you want to resume, then click the Resume button in the dialog box. Napster will enter the file on the Transfer page and will search for a user online with the current server who has a copy of that file for download.

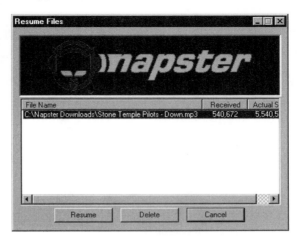

Clear Finished button Click this button to remove completed downloads from the Transfer page. (This action also removes from the Transfer page files that were unavailable.)

Delete button Click this button, or right-click the transfer and choose Abort/Delete Transfer from the context menu, to delete a transfer in progress.

Cancel button Click this button, or right-click the transfer and choose Cancel from the context menu, to cancel a transfer. Canceling a transfer leaves the entry in your Transfer list, so you can try it again later; aborting the entry removes the entry from your Transfer list.

NOTE If a file suddenly becomes unavailable, it usually means that the host has logged off from Napster (or that their computer has crashed). Perform your search again and find another host. Disconnect from Napster and reconnect if necessary.

Using the Library Features

Once you've downloaded a file via Napster, it appears in your library. You can then play it directly or add it to a playlist. You can also add files to your library by moving them to the library folder (the folder you designated during setup) using Windows Explorer or another file-management application.

To view the library, click the Library button (or press the Tab key until Napster displays the library). The illustration below shows a library with a modest selection of tracks.

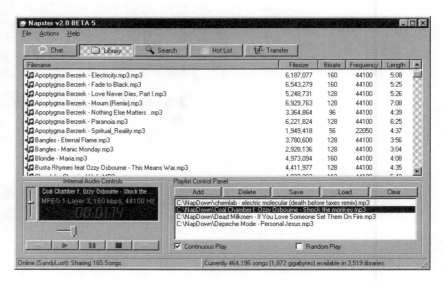

To delete a track from your library, right-click it and choose Delete (From Disk) from the context menu, then choose the Yes button in the resulting Delete File dialog box.

To refresh your library, right-click in it and choose Refresh Library from the context menu.

The lower-left corner of the Library page contains the controls for Napster's internal audio player: a volume control, a position slider, and the standard buttons—Play, Pause, Stop, Previous, and Next. If you chose to use your default MP3 player instead of Napster's internal audio player, clicking the Play button will launch (or switch to) your default player.

To play a song quickly, double-click it in the library. Otherwise, create and play a playlist as follows:

◆ To create a playlist, select tracks on the Library page and click the Add button.

◆ To play a playlist, select a track in the list box and click the Play button.

◆ To save a playlist, click the Save button in the Playlist Control Panel, specify the name and location for the playlist in the Save As dialog box, and click the Save button.

◆ To clear the current playlist from the Playlist Control Panel, click the Clear button. Doing this does not affect the saved version of the playlist.

◆ To load a playlist, click the Load button. Napster will display the Open dialog box. Navigate to and select the playlist you want to open, then click the Open button.

◆ To remove tracks from a playlist, select them in the Playlist Control Panel and click the Delete button.

Chatting on Napster

In addition to its file-sharing capabilities, Napster supports multiple chat channels that you can join and leave at will. The chat channels allow both public and private messaging.

NOTE Depending on the Napster server you're connected to, you may find that chat isn't a much-used feature. At this writing, it seems to be less popular on the general Napster servers than those on campuses.

To use the chat features, click the Chat button to display the Chat page, shown below.

Channel title   Chat area   User list

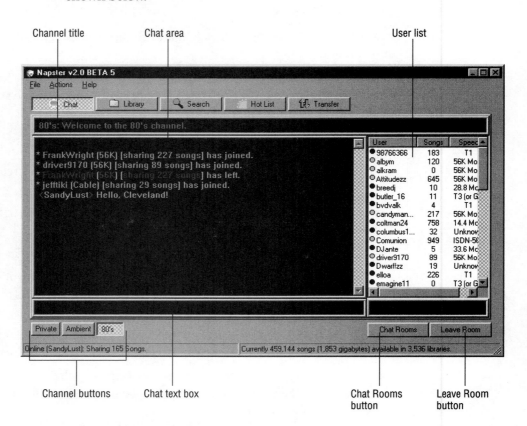

Channel buttons   Chat text box   Chat Rooms   Leave Room
                                                 button   button

You start off with a Private channel that is opened by default, and which you cannot close. The Private channel displays the Napster message of the day when you log on and also displays any private messages that are sent to you. (Private messages are also displayed on the current Chat page.)

To join another channel, click the Chat Rooms button. Napster will display the Channel List dialog box, shown next. Select the channel or channels you want to join (Shift-clicking and Ctrl-clicking work for multiple selections), then click the Join button to join them. You can join up to five channels at a time.

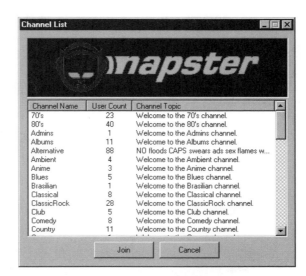

Each channel you join appears as a button across the bottom of the screen below the Chat text box. You can move from one chat channel to another by clicking the appropriate button, or you can move from one channel to the next (from left to right) by pressing Ctrl+X.

To view the information available about someone, right-click their entry in the user list and choose View Information from the context menu. Napster will display the Finger Information dialog box for the user, as shown below.

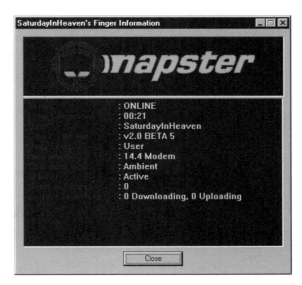

To send a private message to someone, right-click their entry in the user list and choose Private Message from the context menu. Napster will start the stub of a private message, entering **/tell** and the username in the Chat text box. Type the text of the message and press the Enter key to send it. Alternatively, just type **/tell <username>** and the message. For example, the following line sends a private message to BigBoy12:

```
/tell BigBoy12 You're really something.
```

A private message shows up preceded by *<username> tells you,* as in the last message in the illustration below.

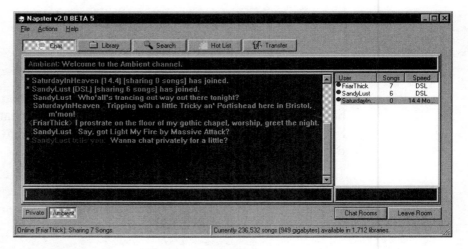

To ignore someone, right-click them in the user list and choose Ignore. Napster will display *Ignored user <username>'s channel and private messages* in the chat pane. The person being ignored receives no notification of the ignorance.

To unignore someone, right-click them in the user list and choose Unignore. Napster will display *Removed <username> from ignore list* in the chat pane.

To add someone to your hot list, right-click their entry in the user list and choose Add to Hot List from the context menu.

If you know that someone is online with the Napster server you're using, you can find out what channel (or channels) they're in by using the finger command in the Chat text box. For example, to find out which channel (or channels) the user Mustang999 is in, you could use the following command:

```
/finger Mustang999
```

If the user is online with this server, you'll see the Finger Information dialog box for the user; this dialog box includes the user's current channel or channels. If the user is not currently online with this server, Napster won't display the Finger Information dialog box, but instead will display the message *user <username> is not a known user* in your chat pane. (This message will not be visible to other participants in the chat room.)

NOTE Even if nothing interesting is happening in chat, use it to find out who's online and interested in the same types of music as you, the number of songs they're sharing, and the speed of their connection. Then check out interesting people by using the Hot List feature as described in the next section.

Getting Bleeped, Muzzled, and Killed

Napster aims to be a community, and as such, it has standards of etiquette. If you transgress against these standards, you may be punished by being "muzzled" or "killed."

The first item is the swear filter, which aims to bleep out the most common offensive words, substituting symbol characters. For example, if you send the message *Is your Labrador a bitch or a boy?*, it will get bleeped as *Is your Labrador a @!#^& or a boy?* or some similar mutation. You can turn the swear filter off in the Preferences dialog box (File ➢ Preferences).

If you get the message *You have been muzzled*, it means that a Napster administrator has gagged you. Napster chat is moderated (though not very consistently), and if you get spotted offending enough people, you'll probably be muzzled by a moderator. The moderator then gets to decide when to unmuzzle you.

Killing is the next stage of punishment after muzzling. When you get killed, you are disconnected from the Napster server.

Maintaining a Hot List

The Hot List page allows you to browse another user's library of music. Instead of searching by specific criteria, you can browse through all the MP3 files that a particular user is sharing. Doing so lets you find music that someone wants to share but that you don't know you want to search for.

NOTE At this writing, with the Napster pool of music split across many servers, the hot list is not as compelling a feature as it will become once Napster integrates all servers into a common pool. At this point, there's no guarantee that any person you add to your hot list in one session will log into the same Napster server as you the next session—so the hot list is primarily a tool for making the most of any given Napster session.

You create your own hot list by adding users to it at your discretion. To add a user to the hot list, choose Actions ➢ Add User to Hot List, enter the user's name in the Add User to Hot List dialog box (shown below), and click the OK button.

To browse via the hot list, click the Hot List button to display the Hot List page. The next illustration shows a hot list with two of the members online (in the Online pane) and three offline (in the Offline pane). Because of Napster's multiple servers, *offline* means "not online at this server" rather than "definitely offline at this time."

Online pane
Connection Speed Circles

Offline pane

To remove a user from the hot list, right-click their entry in the Online pane or the Offline pane and choose Delete User from the context menu. Napster will display the Remove User dialog box, shown below. Click the Yes button to complete the eviction.

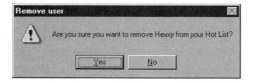

If you see the Napster Notification dialog box shown below, telling you that Napster is unable to transfer the file because both users are firewalled, you will need to find another host or change your configuration so that incoming TCP packets can get through the firewall to your computer.

79   Share Music with Napster

As The Jam said, "What you give is what you get"—and to keep your MP3 karma in balance, you should try to provide some MP3 tracks back to the community if you're big into downloading music via Napster. Remember that these tracks need to be legal—if you share the contents of even one CD with a hundred or so people without permission, you're committing a felony. (As you saw in the previous section, there are one hell of a lot of potential felons out there sharing pirated music via Napster, but being in legion company is no defense against the law.)

Before you start sharing tracks with Napster, make sure that you've chosen an appropriate number for simultaneous uploads per user in the Max Simultaneous Uploads (Per User) text box in the Preferences dialog box (File ➤ Preferences). For a modem connection, you'll probably want to limit each user to 1 or 2 uploads at a time; any more than this will deliver a lame data rate that will make the tracks take hours to transfer—and that's if only one user is downloading from your computer at a time. For a 64K ISDN connection, 2 or 3 is a reasonable number; 4 to 6 for a 128K ISDN line, a DSL, or a cable connection; and 10 to 50 for a T1, depending on whether you have the whole line to yourself (unlikely). If you have your own private T3, we'll let you experiment with suitable numbers on your own—we don't have a T3 to play with.

To share tracks via Napster, all you need to do is place the tracks in the folder or folders you designated for sharing during setup, then start Napster. (To check which folders you chose, or to change your shared folders, choose File ➤ Preferences to display the Preferences dialog box, then use the Shared Folders text box and the Add Folders button. Click the OK button when you're done.)

Once the tracks are in the folder, click the Library button to display the Library page, then right-click and choose Refresh Library from the context menu. Napster will rescan your shared folders and will display the Napster Notification dialog box shown below, telling you that it has loaded and shared the new files.

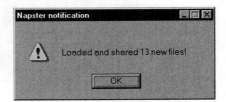

WARNING In theory, Napster shares only MP3 files in your designated directory, so it doesn't pose a security threat to your computer. Other Napster users can download the MP3 files you choose to share, but they cannot access any other files on your computer. But at this writing, Napster 2 beta 5 occasionally messes up and shares files in your download directory. The best way to prevent this from happening is to move the files out of your download directory to a holding directory once you've finished downloading them. The downside to doing this is that it prevents you from using Napster's library features.

Now anybody logged onto the same Napster server as you can access the files in the shared folder on your computer, either by turning them up in a search or by adding you to their hot list and explicitly scanning your shared files.

When someone is downloading a file from your computer, you'll see the entry appear in the Upload pane on the Transfer page, as shown in the illustration below, marked *Uploading*. If tracks are queued for upload from your computer, these do not appear in the Upload pane until they become active.

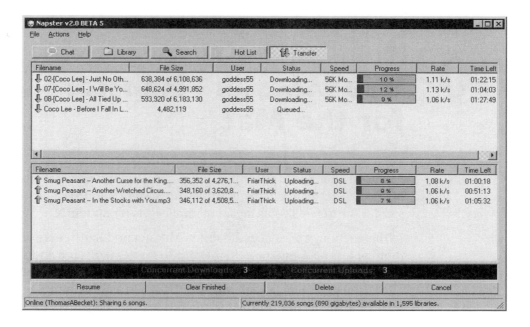

You can cancel a selected transfer by clicking the Cancel button (or by right-clicking the transfer and choosing Cancel Transfer from the context menu), or delete a selected transfer by clicking the Delete button (or by right-clicking it and choosing Delete/Abort Transfer from the context menu). In either case, the track will be listed as *Unavailable* to the would-be downloader.

If you disconnect from Napster (by choosing File ➢ Disconnect) or exit Napster while someone is downloading a track from your computer, the downloader will get a Transfer Error message for the track.

WARNING To exit Napster, use the File ➢ Exit command rather than clicking the Close button (the × button) in the window or using the control menu. Exit nukes your Napster session, while the Close button gets rid of the Napster window but leaves Napster running in the background, so people can continue downloading files that you're sharing. While Napster is running in the background, you'll see a Napster icon in your system tray. To restore Napster, right-click this icon and choose Restore from the context menu. To quit Napster, right-click the icon and choose Exit.

80 Use Macster—Napster for the Mac

At this writing, the Mac community is implementing several Mac clones of Napster. Macster and Rapster work with System 8 and System 9, while Napster for the MacOSX—as its name implies—is for System X.

In this section, we'll discuss Macster. Macster and Rapster are currently more or less neck and neck in the race to implement a full and satisfactory version of Napster on the Mac, but on the whole we've had fewer crashes and better experiences with Macster. That said, we encourage you to investigate Rapster as well: Both Macster and Rapster are getting very close to solid versions; both have strong features; and both are free. (What more encouragement could you ask for?)

Because the current version of Macster at this writing isn't final, we can't promise that what you'll find in this section will reflect the version of Macster that you download. In fact, because Macster Preview doesn't yet support uploading, we *can* promise you that the version you get will be different. Even so, the contents of this section should be enough to get you going with Macster.

Getting, Installing, and Configuring Macster

To get Macster, point your browser at `http://www.macster.com`. Navigate to the latest version of Macster and download it.

At this writing, the latest version is Macster 1 Preview 3.5. By the time you download Macster, there should be a later version available, so be warned that things may be different in the interface.

To get started with Macster, double-click the Macster item in the distribution folder. Macster will display the first Macster Setup Assistant dialog box, shown below.

To create a new account, make sure the Create New Account option button is selected, then click the Forward button (the button with the rightward-pointing arrow on it) to display the second Macster Setup Assistant dialog box, shown below.

Enter the login name and password you want, together with your e-mail address and your connection speed (if you know it). If you want Macster to save your password, make sure the Save Password check box is selected. If your computer connects to the Internet through a firewall (as many networked computers do), select the I Am behind a Firewall check box. Then click the Forward button. Macster will display the third and final Macster Setup Assistant, which provides you with a Create button to click to create the account.

Click that Create button. Macster will create your account with the server and will log you in. (If your name isn't unique, you'll need to try again.) If Setup crashes at this point, it probably means that your username wasn't unique. Delete the Macster Prefs file in the Preferences folder under your System folder, run Macster again, and try a different name.

Once you've successfully created a unique username and logged in, Macster will display the Macster panel, shown below, and the console window, which shows current messages.

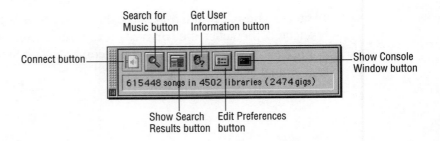

Before you start getting things done online, make sure the rest of your preferences are set up suitably, as described in the next section.

Setting Preferences in Macster

To set your preferences in Macster, click the Edit Preferences button on the Macster panel or choose Edit ➤ Preferences. Macster will display the Preferences dialog box, whose User Information page is shown below.

On the User Information page, change your e-mail address and connection speed if necessary, then click the Select Download Folder button to display the Choose a Download Folder dialog box, select the folder in which you want to store your downloaded music, and click the Open button.

Then click the Network Information button to display the Network Information page, which is shown below. Verify that your settings are suitable, and then click the Save button to save all the preferences you've changed.

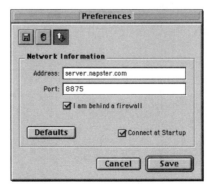

Finding and Downloading Music with Macster

To search for music with Macster:

1. Click the Search for Music button on the Macster panel, or choose Macster ➤ Search, to display the Music Search dialog box, shown below.

2. If you want to search for a particular artist or group, enter it in the Artist text box.

3. If you want to search for a particular track, enter it in the Song text box.

4. If you want a more manageable number of results than the 100 maximum that Napster servers currently deliver, drag the Results slider down to a suitable figure.

5. To specify a bitrate, frequency, or line speed, click the Show Extended Search button. Macster will display the hidden bottom section of the Music Search dialog box, shown below. Use the Bitrate, Frequency, and Line Speed drop-down lists to make your needs felt to Macster.

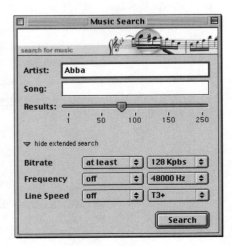

6. Click the Search button to set the search running. Macster will search the Napster server and will display the results in the Search Results window, as shown below. Here we've sorted the results by the Line Speed column, putting the fastest connections at the top of the list.

Name	Size	Bit Rate	Length	User	Line Speed	Ping
Abba – Dancing Queen.mp3	3.5 MB	128 Kbps	3:46	kristinabina	T1	18 ms
ABBA – Dancing Queen.mp3	3.5 MB	128 Kbps	3:46	vucheer	T1	9 ms
Abba -- Dancing Queen.mp3	3.5 MB	128 Kbps	3:45	nimh-cor	T1	timeout
ABBA – Dancing queen.mp3	3.5 MB	128 Kbps	3:45	Rusty777	T1	11 ms
ABBA – Dancing Queen.mp3	3.5 MB	128 Kbps	3:44	cedricqm	DSL	timeout
ABBA_Dancing Queen.mp3	3.5 MB	128 Kbps	3:45	zziks	Cable	8 ms
ABBA – Dancing Queen.mp3	5.3 MB	196 Kbps	3:43	n4ees	Cable	11 ms
Abba – Dancing Queen.mp3	3.5 MB	128 Kbps	3:44	dizzydevil	Cable	10 ms
ABBA – Dancing Queen.mp3	3.5 MB	128 Kbps	3:46	lagdawg	Cable	12 ms
ABBA – Dancing Queen.mp3	3.5 MB	128 Kbps	3:45	wizard01	Cable	73 ms
abba-dancing_queen.mp3	3.5 MB	128 Kbps	3:45	gnulab	Cable	33 ms
Abba--Dancing_Queen.mp3	3.5 MB	128 Kbps	3:45	Squalldog	Cable	21 ms
Abba– Dancing Queen.mp3	3.5 MB	128 Kbps	3:45	bethanncam	Cable	19 ms
ABBA – Dancing Queen.mp3	3.5 MB	128 Kbps	3:44	dobutt	Cable	19 ms
Dancing Queen– ABBA.mp3	3.5 MB	128 Kbps	3:46	greysolstice	Cable	12 ms
ABBA – Dancing Queen.mp3	3.4 MB	128 Kbps	3:42	baysameh	Cable	timeout
ABBA– Dancing Queen.mp3	1 MB	128 Kbps	1:04	napperal	Cable	timeout
ABBA-Dancing Queen.mp3	3.5 MB	128 Kbps	3:45	ooshlay	Cable	14 ms
{Abba} – Dancing_Queen.mp3	3.5 MB	128 Kbps	3:46	ECS88	128k ISDN	timeout
ABBA – Dancing Queen.mp3	3.5 MB	128 Kbps	3:45	MARNIEL	64k ISDN	12 ms
ABBA – Dancing Queen.mp3	3.5 MB	128 Kbps	3:45	badi18	64k ISDN	25 ms
Abba – Dancing Queen.mp3	3.5 MB	128 Kbps	3:45	TDolan	56k	58 ms
ABBA – Dancing Queen.MP3	3.5 MB	128 Kbps	3:45	MDemy	56k	34 ms
Dancing Queen – ABBA.mp3	3.5 MB	128 Kbps	3:46	boubpu	56k	26 ms
ABBA – Dancing Queen.mp3	3.5 MB	128 Kbps	3:45	MoNi_826	56k	50 ms
ABBA Gold – Dancing Queen.mp3	3.5 MB	128 Kbps	3:44	slavahim	56k	46 ms
Abba – Dancing Queen.mp3	3.5 MB	128 Kbps	3:47	jsantiago	56k	35 ms
ABBA -- Dancing Queen.mp3	3.5 MB	128 Kbps	3:46	rastan123	56k	timeout

Search Results — 55 items

To download a track, double-click it. Macster will display a dialog box listing the title of the track, the number of items remaining to be copied, and the time remaining, as shown below.

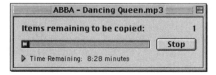

You can set multiple downloads running at once by double-clicking further tracks. Once you have multiple downloads running, you can use the Downloads menu to switch between them: It adds an entry for each track.

Getting User Information

To get information on a user, click the Get User Information button on the Macster panel or choose Macster ➤ Whois. In the User Information dialog box that Macster displays, enter in the Username text box the name of the user you're interested in, then click the Get Info button. The illustration below shows the type of information you're likely to see.

81   Use Napster on Linux

As you've seen already, Napster is one of the hottest programs on the net—so naturally it's being implemented on Linux as well. At this writing, there are multiple Linux versions of Napster being developed, including gnap, Gnapster, GNOME-Napster, and knapster. As you'd guess if you're into Linux/Unix naming conventions, the first three of these—Gnapster, gnap, and GNOME-Napster—are for the Gnome desktop, and the fourth (knapster) is for the KDE desktop.

Because of space limitations in this book, we had to pick one Napster implementation on Linux to cover. We chose Gnapster, which we'll discuss in the sections that follow.

Gnapster is a relatively full implementation of Napster for the Gnome desktop. It supports most of the "regular" Napster features, including searching for tracks, downloading and uploading them, and chatting with other users.

Gnapster doesn't support a hot list as such, but it lets you easily browse another user's files—which, as you'll see, can be more useful than a hot list. What's more, you can create and use multiple accounts on Gnapster.

At this writing, Gnapster does not show you the ping time or frequency when you search. Because most people rip music at CD quality—44.1kHz—this isn't usually a big issue. But not seeing the ping time to hosts means that you won't be able to tell which hosts are close and which are far—so you may get slower downloads than you'd like.

gnap is currently in what the developer terms "pre-alpha private release," with the annotation "Do not use it unless you are a developer. All it does is crash!"—so we won't discuss it here. If you're reading this in summer 2000 or later, you might want to look up gnap and see how it's doing. The current URL is `http://gnap.sourceforge.net`; if that link has gone south, look for a link from the Napster FAQ (currently `http://napster.cjb.net`).

GNOME-Napster, on the other hand, is well under way, and bears investigation at this writing. Knapster is currently in beta, but seems to be coming along nicely.

82 Get, Install, and Configure Gnapster

In this section, we'll run you through how to use Gnapster, one of the Gnome implementations of Napster. We'll expect you to have read through the section *76. Understand Napster* so that you know what Napster is and understand the legal issues involved in distributing MP3 files.

Here's how to get, install, and configure Gnapster:

1. Fire up your browser and head on over to `http://www.gotlinux.org/~jasta/Gnapster.html`.

2. Download the latest version of the software in either the source (if you feel like compiling the application, or need to compile it) or a suitable distribution package for the version of Linux you're using.

3. Install Gnapster by using the standard installation procedure for the version of Linux you're running.

4. Choose Settings ➤ Preferences to display the Gnapster Properties dialog box, whose User Information page is shown below.

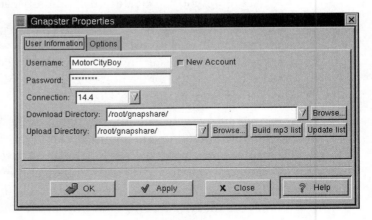

5. Enter the username you want in the Username text box, and your password in the Password text box. If this is a new account, select the New Account check box. If you're transferring an existing account to Gnapster, make sure this check box is cleared.

6. Select the connection speed you want to have listed in the Connection drop-down list. This setting doesn't affect the speed of your connection, just the speed at which it's listed. So if you want to be antisocial and avoid having people hitting your computer for downloads, you might choose a miserable speed such as 28.8K.

◆ First Corollary: It's a mistake to advertise a faster connection than you actually have because it will tend to draw attention.

◆ Second Corollary: If you want to lie low, it's a mistake to claim a 14.4K connection because very few people are using modems that lame any more—so people will think you're trying to hide a fast connection.

7. Enter your download directory in the Download Directory text box. You can either type it in or click the Browse button to display the Browse Download Directory dialog box, select the directory, and click the OK button.

8. Enter your upload directory (the directory you'll be sharing) in the Upload Directory text box. Again, you can type in the path or use the

Browse button and the resulting Browse Upload Directory dialog box to enter it.

9. Click the Build MP3 List button to make Gnapster create a list of the MP3 files in your upload directory. (You can click the Update List button later when you've added MP3 files to the directory.)

10. Click the Options tab to display the Options page of the dialog box, shown below.

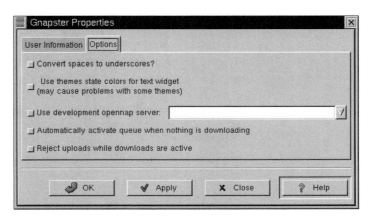

11. Select and clear the check boxes to choose Gnapster options to your taste:

Convert Spaces to Underscores? check box   This check box controls whether Gnapster changes spaces in filenames to underscores.

Use Themes State Colors for Text Widget check box   This check box governs whether Gnapster uses colors from your current theme to display text. As the listing in the dialog box notes, using this option may cause problems with some themes.

Use Development Opennap Server check box   This check box controls whether you log into the current default Napster server or into a server you specify in the text box.

Automatically Activate Queue When Nothing Is Downloading check box   This check box controls—well, it's self-explanatory. Chances are, you'll want to select this check box so that when the coast is clear, Gnapster can automatically start downloading items you've queued for download.

Reject Uploads While Downloads Are Active check box   This check box lets you decide whether you want to prevent uploads from happening while a download is running. Unless you're running a woefully lame computer with a fire-hose of connection, uploading and downloading at the same time should not be a problem.

12. Click the OK button to apply the choices you've made and close the Gnapster Properties dialog box.

13. Choose File ➤ Connect to connect to the Napster server.

If you see the Error dialog box shown below, you'll know that the username you created was already in use. Return to the Settings dialog box and choose another. (If you already have the username registered to you, chances are you've entered your password wrong.)

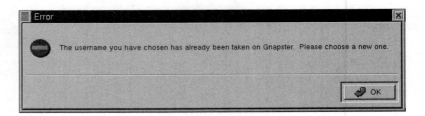

83 Find and Share Music with Gnapster

In this section, we'll show you how to use Gnapster to find and share music—and to chat with other people on the Napster servers you frequent.

As you can see in the next illustration, the Gnapster window contains five pages—Search, Download, Upload, Console, and Message of the Day—each identified by a tab at its top. To display a page, click its tab with the mouse. Alternatively, make sure the focus is on the tabs, then press the Tab key to highlight each tab in turn (from left to right), and then press the spacebar or the Enter key to display the page for the high-lighted tab.

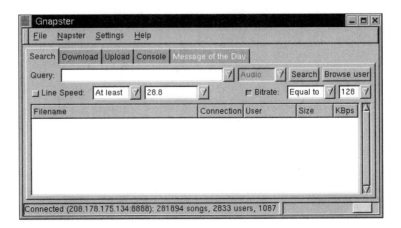

When there's something new for you to see on one of the pages, the text on its tab appears in white. The rest of the time, the tab text appears in black.

To connect to a server, choose File ➢ Connect. As you connect, you'll see the current status in the status bar. For example, as you log in, you might see a message such as this:

```
Connected (208.184.216.208:7777)…awaiting login reply…
```

To disconnect from your current server, choose File ➢ Disconnect. You may want to disconnect and connect again in order to be assigned to a Napster server that has material that's interesting to you.

If you've read through the Napster sections, you should find the names of the Search, Download, and Upload pages eminently clear. We'll look at these pages in detail a little later in this section.

The Console page displays textual information about what's happening in Gnapster. In the next illustration, you can see that we've requested a whole block of downloads from a number of different hosts, and the first of them has started sending the file.

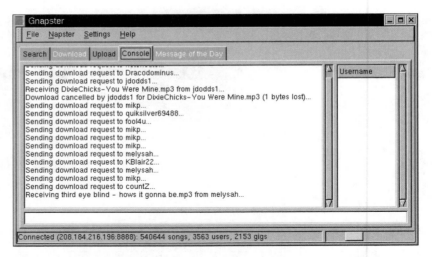

The Message of the Day page displays the message of the day from Napster. This isn't overly stimulating, so we won't show it here.

Searching for MP3 Files

Here's how to search for one or more MP3 files with Gnapster:

1. Click the Search tab to display the Search page. The illustration below shows the Search page after a successful search has been run.

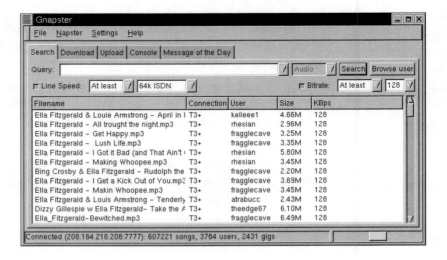

2. In the Query text box, enter the text that you want to search for—either the artist or the track name, or both. At this point, Napster does highly sentient matching, and it doesn't much matter in which order you enter the words. For example, *Ella Fitzgerald Making Whoopee*, *Fitzgerald Ella Whoopee Making*, and *Fitzgerald Making Ella Whoopee* (which has a certain naïf charm) will all return the track "Making Whoopee" by Ella Fitzgerald, assuming that someone currently online with this server is sharing that track.

3. If you want to make sure the host you access has a certain line speed, select the Line Speed check box, then choose At Least, Equal To, or At Best in the first Line Speed drop-down list and the speed in the second. For example, you might choose At Least in the first drop-down list and 64k ISDN in the second to specify that the connection be a 64kbps ISDN line or faster. (See the section *Finding a Track* in *78. Find Music with Napster* for a discussion of the pros and cons of specifying a line speed.)

4. If you want to specify a bitrate for the files you're seeking, select the Bitrate check box and use the first and second drop-down lists to specify the bitrate. For example, you might choose Equal To in the first drop-down list and 128 in the second drop-down list to restrict the search to tracks recorded at 128kbps.

5. Click the Search button to start the search running.

6. While the search is running, you'll see the indicator in the right-hand panel of the status bar moving to the left and right, and the word *Searching* will appear at the left-hand end of the status bar. If the search is successful, you'll then see the results displayed, as shown in the previous illustration.

NOTE If Gnapster is unable to find any tracks matching your query string, it returns nothing—the query string disappears, and the list box remains blank. (By comparison, Napster gives you the message *No matching files found!*, thus leaving you in no doubt.) If you're unsure that Gnapster even registered your query, you can check the Console page, where you should see a message saying *No search results found for* and your query string.

Once you've found a track you want, download it as described in the next section. Read on.

Downloading MP3 Files

With Gnapster, you can either download tracks immediately or queue them for download:

◆ To download a track, double-click it on the Search page, or right-click it and choose Download from the context menu. Gnapster will submit a download request to the host and, on getting a positive answer, will begin the download.

◆ To add a track to your queue, right-click it on the Search page and choose Add to Queue from the context menu. Gnapster will add the file to your queue, which appears in the lower pane on the Search page.

Once you've chosen to download or queue tracks, click the Download tab to display the Download page. The illustration below shows the Download page with three tracks being downloaded (very slowly) and a number more tracks in the queue.

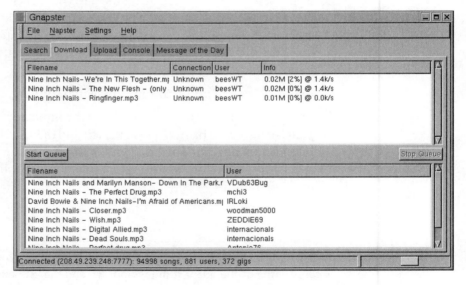

You can start your queued tracks downloading by clicking the Start Queue button, and stop them downloading by clicking the Stop Queue button. To remove a track from your queue, right-click its listing in the queue and choose Cancel Queue from the context menu.

To cancel a download, right-click it on the Download page and choose Cancel Download from the context menu. To delete a download, right-click it and choose Cancel and Remove File from the context menu.

Browsing a User's MP3 Files

One of the great things about Gnapster is that it makes it easy to thumb your way through all the MP3 files that a given user is sharing. At the moment, Gnapster's way of doing this is easier and more effective than Napster's hot list. The hot list is awkward because users are split across many Napster servers and may in any case not be online when you decide you need to see what they're offering.

Gnapster takes the approach of letting you identify a user who's online, then quickly check through the MP3 files they're sharing. You can only check out one user at a time, but it works well.

To browse a user's shared library of MP3 files, either select a user on the Search page and click the Browse User button, or right-click a user on the Search page or Download page and choose Browse User's MP3s from the context menu. You'll see a list of the user's shared MP3 files in the list box on the Search page, as shown below.

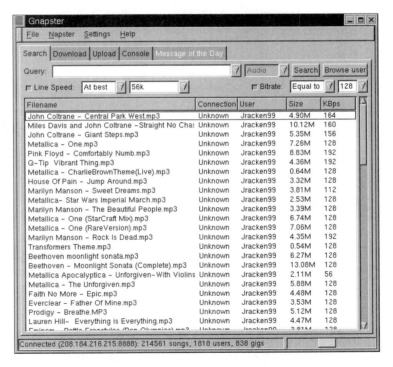

If you see something you like, you can download it or queue it as usual.

NOTE   If nothing happens when you try to browse a user's shared library, check the Console page. If you see the message *Error: Parameter is unparsable*, it means your request has gone off into never-never land. Try someone else.

Getting Information on a User

To get information on a user, right-click a listing featuring the user on the Search page and choose Whois User from the context menu. Then switch to the Console page to view the result. The illustration shown below provides an example of using the Whois command.

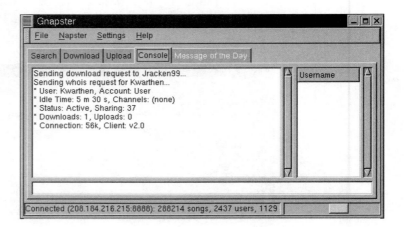

Sharing MP3 Files

To share MP3 files via Gnapster, place them in the upload directory you designated on the User Information page of the Gnapster Properties dialog box. (To change the directory, display this dialog box by choosing Settings ➤ Preferences.)

NOTE   Gnapster lets you quickly change the number of simultaneous uploads directly from the Upload page by selecting the Max Uploads check box and entering an appropriate number in the text box.

Once the MP3 files are in the shared folder, they're available to anybody who's logged into the same Napster server as you are. When someone starts to download a file from your computer, you'll see it appear in the list box on the Upload page, together with details of who is downloading it and the line speed they're using.

The illustration below shows the Upload page without any action taking place.

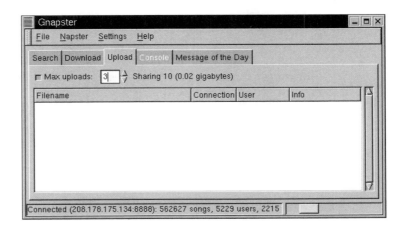

Chatting on Gnapster

Chat on Gnapster is somewhat primitive compared to chat on Napster—you can participate in only one channel at a time with Gnapster, compared with Napster's five channels, and the commands are all text—but what it offers gets the job done. Here are the commands you need to know:

- ◆ Use /join or /j to join a channel. For example, the following commands join the Alternative channel:

```
/join alternative
/j alternative
```

- ◆ Use /part to leave a channel. For example, the following command leaves the Alternative channel:

```
/part alternative
```

- ◆ Use /msg or /m to send a private message to a user. For example, the following command sends the message *Hello. Go away.* to the user LiveHerald:

```
/m LiveHerald Hello. Go away.
```

◆ Use /raw to send a message to everyone in the channel. For example, the following command sends the message *I love New York!* to everyone in the current channel:

```
/raw I love New York!
```

◆ Use /whois to display information about a user. For example, the following command displays information about the user voodoosweeney:

```
/whois voodoosweeney
```

A regular message shows up in the list box on the Console page preceded by the name of the user who sent it, enclosed in angle brackets. For example, a message from the user voodoosweeney would appear like this:

```
<voodoosweeney> Anyone got Metallica and SF Symphony?
```

A private message shows up in the list box on the Console page preceded by the name of the user who sent it, a slash, and privmsg, enclosed in angle brackets. For example, a private message from voodoosweeney would appear like this:

```
<voodoosweeney/privmsg> Wanna meet?
```

Exiting Gnapster

To exit Gnapster, choose File ➢ Exit or press Ctrl+Q.

Publish and SHOUTcast Your Music

So far in this book, you've been on the receiving end of the music—downloading it from Web sites or tuning into audio streams that people have chosen to blast your way. In this part of the book, we'll look at how you can turn the tables on the world by creating MP3 files of your own music or other audio and distributing the files via the Internet and Web.

As you've seen earlier in this book, the wired world offers three main possibilities for distributing music:

◆ Creating digital files of your music and putting them where people can get them—on your own Web site (if you have one) or on distribution sites. We'll look at how to get your music onto two of the leading sites—Riffage.com and MP3.com.

◆ Creating digital files and sending them to people via e-mail.

◆ Streaming audio over the Internet from a streaming server so that anybody who cares to can tune in to whatever you're playing. At this writing, the two leading audio-streaming servers are SHOUTcast and icecast. The SHOUTcast server software is free if you're using it for non-commercial purposes; for commercial use, you've got to pay after a 14-day trial period. The icecast server is free. Because we've had better experiences with SHOUTcast than with icecast, we'll focus on SHOUTcast in this part of the book, leaving you to investigate icecast on your own if you wish.

Before we get into the meat of this part, let's quickly revisit how you can break your bank account and land yourself in jail by screwing around with rights.

84 Careful with Those Rights, Eugene!

Earlier in the book, we touched on legal issues concerning ripping music from CDs or other media recorded by other people. You'll recall that some of the finer legal points there were a little vague or flexible—most people reckon you can legally rip CDs to MP3 files the way you can legally tape records (or CDs) on cassettes, and some people (typically those with money to lose from your doing so) say you can't. But even if you rip a ton of CDs and the local law enforcement agencies disagree drastically with your assessment of the copyright laws, it's unlikely that they'll kick down your door and drag you off if you're ripping the files for nothing more than your own personal use. (Yes, we said it's "unlikely," not "impossible." For all we know, you might be on the verge of becoming the sadly imprisoned poster child for the digital-audio generation—the Mumia of MP3, as it were.)

Distributing music tends to be a little more clear-cut. To distribute digital copies of any music, you need the rights to do so. If you created the music yourself and you haven't assigned the rights to anyone, you're most likely in the clear. If you created the music with other people, you need their permission to distribute it. And if you're signed to a record company, chances are that you distributing music without specific permission in writing will hack them off mightily—even if you made the music yourself in your own studio without the record company being involved in the slightest.

Bottom line: Before you distribute *any* MP3 files, make sure you have the rights to distribute them. Even if for some perverse reason you're drawn to the law, intellectual property's an area you really don't want to go spelunking in unless you have time and money to burn.

NOTE If you're thinking of signing with a record company, make sure that you retain the rights to distribute your music over the Internet like this. As a promotional tool for artists, MP3 is invaluable—but as we've seen, the record companies are still for the most part scared of how it could chew up their profit margins.

By distributing, we mean sending people the files of music or providing the files for download. If you're broadcasting music (or other audio), the rules are different, and somewhat more in your favor. Basically, you can broadcast, but you're going to have to pay for the privilege. Read on.

Until December 1, 1999, you could apply for a *statutory license* that cost a mere $20 and allowed you to broadcast to your heart's content. According to the RIAA's site, you can still go for one of these licenses—which probably means they're arguing about how much more you're going to have to pay. Check the RIAA site (http://www.riaa.com) for the latest information.

The alternative to getting a statutory license (which may no longer be available when you read this book) is to enter into licensing agreements with individual artists or record companies for the rights to broadcast their music. Unless your station's going to stick to promoting only a few artists, or perhaps just one record label, these licensing agreements will prove such a pain in the kiester that you'll run screaming to the RIAA and its cohorts.

The bit of legislation that sets up the hoops for you to jump through on Webcasting is the Digital Millennium Copyright Act, or DMCA for short. The DMCA was passed in October 1998 and implements copyright rules set by the World Intellectual Property Organization (WIPO to its friends).

If you're going to get heavy into Webcasting, you ought to read the U.S. Copyright Office Summary of the DMCA. Get a cup of caffeinated stimulant and browse on over to http://lcweb.loc.gov/copyright/legislation/dmca.pdf for a little light reading.

In case you can't be bothered to do that right now, below are the key points of the DMCA as it applies to Webcasting.

WARNING *Disclaimer:* We're paraphrasing here and reducing perhaps beyond the essentials. Also, we're not lawyers, though we do count some lawyers among our friends.

◆ Your ISP isn't responsible for any copyright infringements you perpetrate using their services—provided they're ready to give your contact information to copyright holders who demand it, and provided they actively try to prevent you from offending again. That means they'll rat you out to the first copyright holder who comes knocking, *and* they'll pull the plug on your Internet connection. Statistics are hard to come by, but anecdotal evidence suggests that many ISPs treat an accused subscriber as guilty as charged and drop their connection like a superheated potato. (Kafka would've approved—the Czechs are into hot potatoes big time.)

◆ You're allowed to make an *ephemeral recording* of music. An ephemeral recording is a copy of a recording "to facilitate performance"—for example, an MP3 file that you've created so that you don't need to use the CD. For the MP3 file to qualify as an ephemeral recording, it must be the only copy you have of the recording; you need to be the only person using that copy; you need to destroy the copy within six months unless you're keeping it as an archive; and you can only transmit the copy "in the Webcaster's local service area." The local service area requirement makes no sense, as everyone on the Internet can receive your broadcast; but the other three requirements are easy enough to comply with.

◆ You're allowed to Webcast sound recordings on the Internet, and you're obliged to identify the track, artist, and album, but you can't announce the details of your playlist in advance. What—that might make people actually listen to your Webcast? No—it's more that you can't tell people when you'll be playing a particular track because that makes what you're doing too close to providing a digital jukebox for it to be considered a bona fide Webcast.

N O T E SHOUTcast broadcasts artist and track information for you, so you don't need to announce tracks verbally to comply with the identification requirement.

◆ You have to take "steps" not to "induce copying," and you're not supposed to transmit bootlegs.

◆ There are a number of restrictions on what you can and can't play. For example, you can't play more than three tracks from any given album in a three-hour period, and you can't play more than two tracks from any given album consecutively. And if that's not enough, you can't play more than four tracks by any given artist or from any given box set within three hours, and you can't play more than three tracks by any given artist or from any given box set consecutively. (Got that? If not, read these two pages again four times within three consecutive hours.)

◆ If you loop a program, the loop needs to be more than three hours long. For a program to differ from another program, you need to make it substantially different—swapping out a couple of songs won't do the trick.

Okay, what about the paying bit? At this writing, exactly how much you'll have to pay isn't crystal clear. Typically, you'll need to get licenses from the following licensing agencies:

ASCAP   The American Society of Composers, Authors, and Publishers (http://www.ascap.com) bills itself as "since 1914 the leader in music licensing" and licenses the rights to "millions of songs created or owned by more than 80,000 of America's and hundreds of thousands of the world's best songwriters, composers, lyricists and publishers." ASCAP's lowest fee is $250 a year.

BMI   Broadcast Music, Inc. (http://www.bmi.com) claims to represent the public performance copyright interest of more than a quarter-million songwriters, composers, and music publishers, giving it a repertoire of more than three million musical works. (Reading between the lines, some of those folks must have only a work or two to their names…but nevermind, BMI's got 'em.) BMI's fees for Webcasting are $250 annually for a site with revenues up to $12,000; $375 annually for a site with revenues up to $18,500; and $500 annually for a site with revenues up to $25,000. (Someone should introduce BMI to the concept of buying in bulk and saving.) If your site pulls in more than $25,000 a year, you're looking at paying BMI a percentage: either 1.75 percent of total site revenues or 2.5 percent of music area revenues. (If your site makes this much money, get your bean-crunchers to work out which option is better for you.)

SESAC   SESAC, Inc. (http://www.sesac.com) describes itself modestly as the "second oldest and most innovative performing rights organization in the U.S." Innovation aside, SESAC seems to us to license the rights to fewer interesting artists than ASCAP and BMI. SESAC's lowest fee is $50 per six-month period.

85   Create MP3 Files of Your Own Music

If you have an ounce of musical talent in your body, you won't always want to be on the receiving end of the digital music revolution. If you've recorded anything (yes, *anything*) in any medium that's still playable, you can create

MP3 files of it and inflict them on the six billion other people in the world. (Note that we said *can*—you don't *have to* post your adolescent poems on the Web. In fact, we'd prefer that you don't. But technically, it's frighteningly feasible, as you'll know if you've read the remainder of this book.)

Once you're sure you have the rights needed to distribute content, create MP3 files of it. If your content is on CD (or DVD), you'll have no problem ripping it to MP3 files the same way as you rip anyone else's CD.

If your content is on a different medium, you'll need to pipe the audio into your computer and record it there. Typically, you'll want to record input as WAV files by using an application such as SoundForge XP or Cool Edit, and then convert them into MP3 files. (The Sound Recorder applet built into Windows can deliver okay music quality if your input and your sound card are up to the job, but it can record only up to 60 seconds at a time, making it near useless for recording normal-length tracks.)

WARNING When distributing your music, remember that the lack of security and copy protection that caused you to love MP3 as a consumer can work against you as an artist. If you're ready to embrace the world of open music, go ahead with MP3 files. But if you feel you need to secure the digitally available versions of your creations, you'll need to use another format, such as those we discussed in *1. Understand What MP3 Is and What It Does*.

86 Get Your MP3 Files onto Riffage.com and MP3.com

If you have rights to music and want to distribute it in MP3 format, consider getting it onto Riffage.com and MP3.com. The process for each site is simple but relatively volatile—the pages involved change frequently—so in this section we'll merely point out how to get started, leaving you to handle the details.

Before you start, arm yourself with the following:

◆ An image of your band. For Riffage.com, make the image 150 × 200 pixels (150 pixels wide by 200 pixels high); for MP3.com, make it 270 × 180 pixels, and save it in JPG or GIF format. For MP3.com, you'll also need the album or track picture you want to use. Trim this to 70 × 70 pixels. Use an image-editing program such as Paint (which ships with Windows) to trim the pictures to the right size.

◆ Your band name or artist name (the hardest decision, but one you should have taken a while ago).

◆ A description of your band; a list of members; any press reviews you want to post; a list of instruments played; and so on. (This is required, and you'll usually produce something better by creating it ahead of time and having a couple of other people read through it. If you doubt the wisdom of doing so, browse through a few band descriptions and cringe in horror at those that were clearly put together on the fly.)

◆ A short passage on the background and history of the band; a list of its top musical influences; a list of similar artists; and the URLs of any online reviews of your band. (All these are optional, but you'll probably want to enter them if you have them.)

◆ The band's main contact, together with address, and the name to which checks should be made out.

◆ The e-mail address you want to use for the band. Consider setting up a custom e-mail address for the band if you haven't already done so.

◆ A custom URL of 20 characters or fewer derived from the band name and consisting of only letters (uppercase and lowercase) and numbers.

◆ The MP3 files you want to post. Don't forget these—neither site will be much interested in you if you don't provide any music. (MP3.com will let you sign up, but nobody's going to pay any attention to you.) Have a description and credits for each MP3 file you plan to post.

Signing Up As an Artist on Riffage.com

To sign up as an artist on Riffage.com, click the Artist Sign In button on the navigation bar on the left-hand side of the Riffage.com home page. This takes you to the Artist Zone on Riffage.com, where you can click the Sign Up Now link to start the registration process.

Once you're safely registered, you can click the Login Here link on the Artist Zone page to log in as your artist persona (as opposed to your user persona) and manipulate your account—for example, updating your contact information or adding further tracks to your offerings.

Signing Up As an Artist on MP3.com

To sign up as an artist on MP3.com, follow the New Artist Sign Up link, which currently resides near the bottom of the MP3.com home page. Wade through the page of propaganda ("Earn CA$H – through our Payback for Playback promotion!") and click the Sign Me Up button at the bottom.

You then get to log in with your e-mail address but without a password, which gets you to the Creating New Master Admin Logon page, in which you create a password. MP3.com then sends you an e-mail for confirmation with a special URL to unlock your MP3.com Master Page. Click or double-click the URL's link (depending on the e-mail package you're using) to unlock the page, then click the Sign Up New Artist link in the Artist Management section of the resulting page to begin the signup procedure.

NOTE MP3.com automatically creates an instant-play version of any tracks you upload.

87 E-Mail Your MP3 Files to People

Instead of putting your MP3 files up on a public site for distribution, you may simply want to e-mail them to people directly. Ten to one you know how to send e-mail and attachments, so all we'll do in this section is point out is that, highly compressed as they are, MP3 files are still *several hun-dred times* more bulky than most e-mail messages. Their size can choke e-mail servers, not to mention tying up your Internet connection for uncom-fortably long times if you're using a modem to connect to your ISP.

As you can imagine, most ISPs don't like MP3 files much, and some will try to stop you from sending too large files at once. So you'll often want to chop up your MP3 files into several smaller bits so that they flow through the system more smoothly.

Alternatively, you can use a lower sampling rate and sampling precision when recording the MP3 file—but as you know, doing so may lower the quality of the resulting file below levels tolerable to the recipient.

If e-mailing MP3 files to people doesn't seem like a good idea, try the next option: Online drives. *Free* online drives. Read on.

88 Share Your Music via Online Drives

If you just want to share a few music files of your own with a few friends or members of your family, or if you want to shunt partial tracks or tenta-tive mixes from one band member to another, you won't want to expose the music to the wide world by putting it on Riffage.com or MP3.com. You could e-mail the files, but to get decent music quality, you need files of a size that aren't friendly to mail servers. And snail mail is so terribly 20th cen-tury—not to mention slow.

In cases like this, your best bet is to use one of the online-drive services that have been popping up over the last year or two like mushrooms in a well-dunged and well-watered field. Online-drive services you might want to try include FreeDrive and Visto. FreeDrive (`http://www.freedrive.com`) provides 50MB of space free; Visto (`http://www.visto.com`) provides 15MB of space for free for personal use and 25MB for each group that you create. With either service, you can pay for extra space for what they consider a nominal fee but which we consider CD money.

NOTE If you're a member of Yahoo!, you can store 10MB for free by using the Briefcase feature.

The good thing about using services such as FreeDrive, Visto, and their competitors is that you're not tied to using them for music. If you want to use them to share scanned photos of your grandmother's 1948 vacation from hell or video clips of your corgi savaging the neighbor's newspaper, there's nothing to stop you.

But if you *do* want to use your online storage space exclusively for music, you'll do best to go with a service that offers custom features. One example of such is myplay.com (`http://www.myplay.com`), which lets you upload audio recordings from your hard drive, CDs, or DVDs; store them online; and then play them from wherever you may happen to be. Best of all, myplay.com offers a huge amount of space—3GB—for free.

The catch—yes, Virginia, of course there's a catch—is that when you upload original content, myplay.com gets to use it. Here's the relevant language:

> *Any time you upload User Content that originates with you (such as original recordings made by you of your own performances), you grant myplay and its affiliates a royalty-free, perpetual, irrevocable, non-exclusive license and right (including any moral rights) to use that User Content in whole or in part, on the Service itself and in connection with the advertising and promotion of the Service, throughout the world in any form, media, or technology now known or later developed.*

We don't like the sound of this much—but if you can live with it, you may find myplay.com a valuable service.

89 Build a SHOUTcast Server and Get on the Air

Posting MP3 files on sites such as Riffage.com and MP3.com is all very well—but if you have the bandwidth, you can set up your own SHOUTcast server and stream music over the Internet 24/7. Anyone with an Internet connection and a SHOUTcast-capable client (such as Winamp, Sonique, or RadioSpy) can tune in and turn on until you drop out.

A SHOUTcast system consists of a SHOUTcast server that receives an audio stream from the Winamp player via a suitable DSP plug-in. In this section, we'll describe how to put together a SHOUTcast server. We'll assume that you have Winamp already installed and configured on your computer. If you don't, look back to *13. Get and Install Winamp.*

Before you plunge blindly into this section, think for a minute about the computer and connection you're going to use to bring your message to the masses.

Which Computer Will You Use?

To get broadcasting effectively with SHOUTcast, you need a computer that can devote continuous energy to delivering music. You may well want to set up SHOUTcast on a computer other than your main computer so that you can work (or play) while cranking out the tunes without worrying about interrupting your broadcast. That said, SHOUTcast doesn't hog memory or processor cycles. By most standards, and especially those of Microsoft applications, it's very modest in both regards— so it's more than possible to SHOUTcast from your one and only computer and still be able to do other things. But remember: Each time you install that new piece of demoware and have to reboot, your SHOUTcast server will be down for the count.

The operating system is less of a concern than the hardware: You can run a SHOUTcast server on Windows 95 or 98, Windows NT (Workstation or Server), Windows 2000 (Professional or Server), FreeBSD, BSDi, Linux, IRIX, Solaris, or AIX. (We'll show you an example using Windows 98 because it's probably the lowest common denominator.)

Getting Miked and Dangerous

Make sure you've got all the hardware you need. The specs for the computer are essentially those we set you up with in *2. Get the Right Hardware,* but if you want to put your voice on the air, you'll need to make sure that your soundcard is full-duplex, able to accept input and output it at the same time. Here at the dawn of the 21st century, a full-duplex sound card is pretty much a requirement for considering yourself alive—a half-duplex card is landfill waiting to happen.

Then you'll need to get a microphone that'll let you sound half-human to other people—that cheesy old headset mike in the back of your closet won't cut it. RadioShack will fix you up with something workable, but we'd suggest trying your local music store if you're looking for a higher-end mike. It's your choice between a headset mike and a stand-mounted one; chances are, the latter will make you feel more like a DJ than the former, and you'll be able to stagger off for a bathroom break without accidentally dragging the computer along.

For most soundcards, you'll need a mini-plug on the end of the mike's cable rather than a ¼-inch plug. Get an adapter if you need one.

Plug the mike's jack into the Mic input on your sound card, and then configure it as follows:

1. Pop the Volume Control window open by choosing Start ➢ Programs ➢ Accessories ➢ Entertainment ➢ Volume Control or right-clicking the Volume icon in your system tray and choosing Open Volume Controls from the context menu.

2. Choose Options ➢ Properties to display the Properties dialog box.

3. In the Show the Following Volume Controls list box, make sure the Microphone check box is selected. (Some sound cards call this check box Monitor rather than Microphone.) Click the OK button to close the Properties dialog box.

4. Clear the Mute check box for Microphone (or Monitor) and set the volume to a low level.

5. Choose Options ➢ Properties to display the Properties dialog box again. This time, select the Recording option button.

6. Make sure the Microphone check box is selected in the Show the Following Volume Controls list box, and click the OK button. You'll see the Recording Control window, an example of which is shown on the next page. Note that this window will look different depending on the configuration of your computer and the make of your sound card.

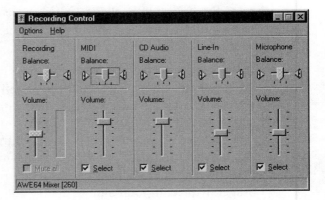

7. Make sure the Select check box for the microphone is selected.

8. Set the volume for the microphone to a sensible level—probably pretty low to start with.

9. Close the Recording Control window, or leave it open for the time being if you prefer to have quick access to it.

Is Your Connection Macho Enough?

To have people take you seriously, you'll need a halfway potent connection to the Internet. We touched on connections much earlier in the book, but at that time we were concerned with the speed with which they delivered information to you. Now the boot's on the other foot.

The bad news is that your trusty (or rusty) modem won't hack it for more than about one user at a time. Even the best 56K modem delivers only 33.6K upstream on the best of lines (that 56K—or rather 53K—is downstream only), and that low rate will mangle even ambient music beyond any hope of redemption if you try to broadcast (uh, maybe that should just be *cast*) any wider.

The minimum connection over which you'll be able to deliver to multiple listeners anything worth listening to is an ISDN connection running one channel full-bore—preferably two channels.

A DSL connection is typically preferable, but make sure that your upstream speed (from you to your ISP) is high enough—basic DSL connections may have only 128kbps upstream speeds, which will get you to fewer listeners than you have fingers. If you want to deliver quality audio to double-digit numbers of listeners, you'll need more bandwidth. To get it, you'll probably have to pay for it.

The same caveat goes for a cable modem: Many cable companies implement an *upload cap* that limits your upstream connection even when there's no bandwidth crunch on the wires you're using.

If you're unsure what you're getting, ask the cable company directly, and persist until you get a satisfactory answer. Some of them are reluctant to mention provocative words like "upload cap," preferring to say that they're ensuring 24/7 bandwidth availability to all subscribers and that their cable system is capable of 2Mbps (or whatever) upstream. (It is, but they're not giving you any more than your cap.) Translation: They're limiting your output to make sure that the loser next door can shunt something even worse onto the Internet day and night.

Before you ask the cable company how you're supposed to broadcast effectively with an upload cap in place, read your terms of service and make sure you know what you've agreed not to do. Often the basic home cable Internet package involves agreeing not to run a Web server. If you've signed an agreement like this, you'll need to claim that you need the speed for something legit like telecommuting.

....

N O T E   If your connection isn't up to snuff, consider Webcasting through a relay server. Check `http://www.shoutcast.com` for links to servers that provide this service. Some are free; some charge.

Making the Grand Collation

If you've got the computer and the connection, your next move is to download a ton of SHOUTcast software from `http://www.shoutcast.com`. Get the following:

- ◆ The latest version of SHOUTcast Server for the operating system you're using. For example, download the SHOUTcast Win32 Server if you're using Windows.

- ◆ The SHOUTcast DSP broadcasting tools. You'll find these on the CD at the back of the book in the `\Windows\SHOUTcast\` folder; alternatively, there are links to them from the SHOUTcast download page. They're wrapped up into a tiny self-extracting file and take only a few seconds to download. Note the filename on this; you'll have other files to deal with, and you don't want to get confused.

◆ The Microsoft NetShow Server tools. You don't want to run NetShow, but this package contains the *codecs* (coder/decoders) you need to compress the music you SHOUTcast. You'll find a link to these from the SHOUTcast download page as well, though you can get them from Microsoft if you prefer. The NetShow Server tools are a shade under 4MB, so they'll take a little while to download if you're using a modem.

◆ The SHOUTcast Live Input plug-in, also from the SHOUTcast download page. You need this plug-in to pipe microphone input into SHOUTcast. Even if your microphone is currently a twinkle in the eye of your next paycheck, download this plug-in—it's tiny and will take only a second or two to download.

◆ The NULL Output plug-in, also from the SHOUTcast download page. This lets you stream audio without it going through your sound card, so you can broadcast audio without playing it through your sound system. (With this plug-in, you can even broadcast from a computer that doesn't have a sound card—a cool way of reusing that 486 that's serving as a doorstop in the basement.) This plug-in is minuscule, too.

NOTE You can also download SHOUTcast commercials from the SHOUTcast download page.

Now that you've gathered all that software, you need to install it in the right order. Take the steps detailed in the following sections.

Unpacking and Installing the NetShow Tools

Run the nstools.exe file to unpack the NetShow Server tools. (Either double-click the file in Explorer or choose File ➢ Run to display the Run dialog box, use the Browse button and resulting Browse dialog box to locate the file, and click the OK button.)

NetShow will walk you through a mostly standard installation routine in which you get to ponder and accept a license agreement, choose the Complete Installation (the PowerPoint Add-Ins Only installation won't do you much good), and select a suitable directory for the tools files. If you get a NetShow Tools message box telling you that "The NetShow PowerPoint Add-Ins will not be installed as part of this setup. The functionality for these Add-Ins is integrated into the version of PowerPoint on this computer," just click the OK button, and it will go away.

Click the Finish button when NetShow says it's done. At this point you may have the eerie feeling that you don't really know what's going on, especially if you've just installed server tools onto Windows 95 or 98, a client platform. Beat those feelings down; the codecs have been installed, and all will be well in your MP3 world. If you check the bottom of your Start ➢ Programs menu, you'll see a NetShow Services group with several menu items. Your career as a DJ beckons.

Installing the Plug-Ins

Run the SHOUTcast DSP plug-in self-extracting file (double-click it in Explorer) and let it extract itself to your \Winamp\ folder, which it will auto-detect.

Unzip the SHOUTcast Live Input plug-in, and the NULL Output plug-in (if you chose to get it) to your \Winamp\Plugins\ folder. These two plug-ins are optional, but we think you'll find them useful. Even if you don't end up using them, installing them at this point is unlikely to do you any harm.

If you're feeling twitchy about what you're doing, fire up Winamp (if it's not already running) and choose Options ➢ Preferences from the main menu to display the Winamp Preferences dialog box. Check the Input, Output, and DSP/Effect Plug-ins categories to make sure that you've installed the plug-ins to the right place.

Installing and Configuring the SHOUTcast Server

Next, install and configure the SHOUTcast server.

Installation is easy. Unzip the SHOUTcast Server package into the folder in which you want it to live. (There's no installation routine to put the SHOUT-cast server in a suitable place for you, so choose wisely.)

Configuration is a pain in the anatomy. Double-click the `sc_serv.ini` initialization file in the `\gui\` subfolder of whatever folder you unzipped SHOUTcast to. Windows will open the file in Notepad (or your default text editor). The settings you need will vary depending on your situation, so read the information in the initialization file carefully. The settings we show below are typical for a Windows SHOUTcast server, but we're not promising they'll work for your computer.

LogFile Specifies the filename (and path, if used) under which to save the log file. For Windows systems, SHOUTcast Server uses the folder in which the server executable file is stored, which is usually a convenient location.

    LogFile=sc_serv.log

RealTime For Unix and Windows console (non-GUI) systems only; displays a status line updated every second when set to 1.

ScreenLog For Unix and Windows console systems only; controls whether SHOUTcast prints logging to the screen.

ShowLastSongs A value between 1 and 20 that specifies the number of tracks to list in the `/played.html` page. The default setting is 10; change it if you will.

    ShowLastSongs=20

HistoryLog Specifies a filename if you want to log the history of a number of listeners to a file; leave this variable blank if you don't want to create a file. For Windows systems, SHOUTcast uses the folder in which the server executable is stored, unless you specify a different path.

    HistoryLog=sc_hist.log

HistoryLogTime Specifies the number of seconds between entries created for the history log. The default setting is 30.

    HistoryLogTime=30

PortBase Specifies the TCP/IP port on the server to which listeners tune in to listen. SHOUTcast sends its audio stream to `PortBase+1`, so this port needs to be free, too. Try the default `PortBase` setting, 8000, unless you know you need to use a different port.

    PortBase=8000

SrcIP   Specifies the source IP (Internet protocol) address from which SHOUTcast should receive its source stream. The default setting, ANY, makes SHOUTcast accept a stream from any source. If your SHOUTcast server has multiple network cards, you can specify the IP address of the network card you want SHOUTcast to use. You can set SrcIP to 127.0.0.1 to prevent other computers from broadcasting via your SHOUTcast server.

```
SrcIP=ANY
```

DestIP   Specifies the IP address on which SHOUTcast should listen for clients and contact yp.shoutcast.com. Leave DestIP set to ANY to have SHOUTcast listen on any port; alternatively, specify the IP address if you have multiple network cards in the computer.

```
DestIP=ANY
```

Yport   Specifies the port that SHOUTcast should use for connecting to yp.shoutcast.com. Leave this setting set to 80 unless that doesn't work for you.

```
Yport=80
```

NameLookups   Set this variable to 1 to perform reverse DNS (domain name lookups) on people who connect to the server. You'll probably want to start with NameLookups set to its default 0 (zero).

```
NameLookups=0
```

RelayPort and RelayServer   You don't need to specify the RelayPort and RelayServer settings unless your SHOUTcast server is acting as a relay. Leave these lines commented out, with the semicolon at their beginning, or delete them entirely.

```
;RelayPort=8000
;RelayServer=
```

MaxUser   Specifies the maximum number of simultaneous users who can connect to your SHOUTcast server. The maximum setting is 1024 and the default setting is 32, but you'll want to lower this if your connection is slow upstream. Remember that users share the bandwidth, and that if your server is trying to deliver more bandwidth than is available, the music will skip. We've yet to meet anybody who likes skipping—this kind of skipping, that is.

```
MaxUser=8
```

Password   Specifies the password for changing the SHOUTcast stream. This password is your protection against someone hijacking your server, so make it good. The default `Password` is changeme, which you'll certainly want to change. Keep the standard password rules in mind: six characters absolute minimum; not a recognizable word in any language; including letters, numbers, and symbols. This password needs to be the same as the Winamp SHOUTcast DSP plug-in password, which we'll configure in a minute or two.

```
Password=1ndustr!@1N01SE
```

AdminPassword   Specifies an administrative password, an additional password that restricts plain old `Password` to controlling broadcasting, taking away its administration tasks (such as kicking off users or banning them). If you're the only person broadcasting on KILZ Rebel Radio, you won't need an `AdminPassword` because `Password` will serve all your needs, so leave the `AdminPassword` line in the file commented out with a semicolon (`;AdminPassword=adminpass`). But if you have an unruly staff, implement an `AdminPassword` by uncommenting the line and specifying the password (for example, `AdminPassword=I@mTheK!ng`).

AutoDumpUsers   Specifies whether SHOUTcast disconnects users automatically when its source stream disconnects. The default is 0 (zero)—do not automatically disconnect users. (See the entry about `BackupFile` a couple of blocks south of here.)

```
AutoDumpUsers=0
```

AutoDumpSourceTime   Specifies the number of seconds to wait before disconnecting an idle source stream. The default setting is 30; use 0 if you want SHOUTcast to wait indefinitely.

```
AutoDumpSourceTime=15
```

IntroFile   Specifies the MP3 file to stream to listeners when they connect, and before they get the live stream. Great for advertising. The intro file must have the same sample rate and channels as the live stream. The default setting is not to have an intro file.

```
IntroFile=c:\bc\Hello Cleveland.mp3
```

BackupFile   Specifies the MP3 file to stream to listeners if and when the source stream goes south. To use this feature, set `AutoDumpUsers` to 0 (zero). The backup file loops until the source stream is restored, so choose something either innocuous or extremely long (or both). As with the intro file, the backup file must have the same sample rate and channels as the live stream for it to kick in properly. The default setting is not to use a backup file.

```
BackupFile=c:\bc\Tedious Ambient Eno.mp3
```

TitleFormat   Specifies the title and format to send to the listener. Use %s to include the title of the current track. For example, Radio Free Cleveland: %s playing "Billy, Don't Be a Hero" will send the title **Radio Free Cleveland: Billy, Don't Be a Hero**. The default setting is not to send a title. Note that this feature doesn't work on relay servers.

```
TitleFormat=Radio Free Cleveland: %s
```

URLFormat   Specifies the URL and format to send to the listener. Again, use %s to include the title of the current track. The default setting is not to send an URL.

PublicServer   Specifies whether the server should be publicly available: Default (the default setting; publicly available), Always, or Never.

```
PublicServer=Default
```

MetaInterval   Specifies how many bytes to leave between sending metadata. The SHOUTcast documentation recommends leaving this setting at its default, 8192.

```
MetaInterval=8192
```

NOTE   In the SHOUTcast initialization file, you can also set options for logging SHOUTcast information in HTML files. Check the information in the initialization file on the CurrentLog, CurrentLogIn, CurrentLogOut, and CurrentTime variables for details.

Firing Up the SHOUTcast Server

Now fire up the SHOUTcast server by double-clicking the sc_serv.exe file in the \gui\ subfolder of the folder to which you unzipped it. SHOUTcast will read the initialization file and will display the Nullsoft SHOUTcast Server Monitor window shown below.

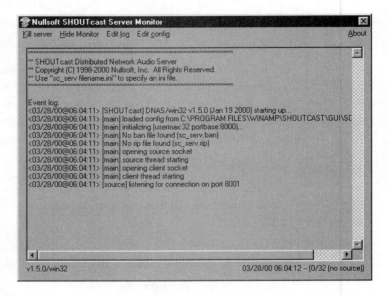

You'll see the last line in the illustration shows that SHOUTcast server is listening for a connection. Next, you have to give it one. Click the Hide Monitor button on the menu bar to hide the Nullsoft SHOUTcast Server Monitor window for the moment. (To get it back, click the SHOUTcast Server item in the system tray.)

Configuring Winamp to SHOUTcast

Configure Winamp's SHOUTcast plug-in so that it routes its output to the SHOUTcast server. Follow these steps:

1. Start Winamp if it's not running.

2. Press Ctrl+P, or choose Options ➤ Preferences, to display the Winamp Preferences dialog box.

3. In the left-hand panel, select the DSP/Effect item.

4. In the list box, select the SHOUTcast Source for Winamp plug-in to display the SHOUTcast Source dialog box, shown on the next page with settings chosen.

5. Click the upper Edit button to display the SHOUTcast Server Selection dialog box (shown below), and choose settings as follows:

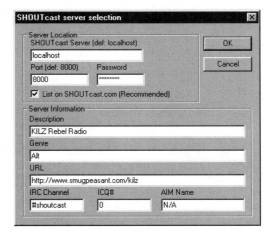

SHOUTcast Server   Leave the default setting of localhost if you're running the server on the same computer that you're configuring Winamp on. If the server's on a different computer, enter its IP address or hostname.

Port   Specify the port for listeners to use—the same port as the Port-Base variable in the SHOUTcast server initialization file. The default is 8000. Once you've specified the port, Winamp starts piping music to it, so you're on the air.

Password   Enter the password for the SHOUTcast server (the password you defined in the initialization file).

List on SHOUTcast.com   Select this check box if you want your server to appear in the index at yp.shoutcast.com and fill in the next three text boxes.

Description   Enter a short but descriptive name for the station.

Genre   Enter the genre for the station. Check with shoutcast.com and RadioSpy for the latest list of supported genres. You can enter a new genre of your own if you want, but chances are that people won't find it unless they're browsing all servers.

URL   Enter the URL for your station.

IRC Channel   Enter an IRC channel associated with the station.

ICQ#   If you have ICQ information, enter it here.

AIM Name   Enter any AIM name associated with the station.

6. Click the OK button to close the SHOUTcast Server Selection dialog box and return to the SHOUTcast Source dialog box.

7. Click the lower Edit button to display the Format Selection dialog box (shown below), and choose settings as follows:

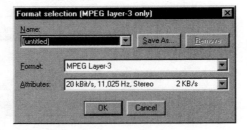

Format drop-down list   Make sure MPEG Layer-3 is selected.

Attributes drop-down list   Select an option that makes sense for the bandwidth you have, the number of users you're trying to serve, and what you're broadcasting. Typically, you'll want to broadcast in stereo at the highest rate your connection will support for your maximum number of users. Usually it's best to use one of the standard sample rates—11,025Hz, 22,050Hz, or 44,100Hz—rather than a nonstandard rate. (The plug-in will warn you if you choose a nonstandard rate.)

Save As button   If you want to save this format, click this button, enter a name in the Save As dialog box, and click the OK button. You'll then be able to choose this format by name from the Name drop-down list.

8. Click the OK button to close the Format Selection dialog box.

9. Click the Connect button to connect to your SHOUTcast server. You're on the air.

10. To change the title or URL being sent, clear the relevant Auto check box, enter the information you want, and click the Set button.

Now fire up RadioSpy and tune in to your station to make sure everything's working.

Adding Your Voice to the Airwaves

If you've got your mike plugged in and operational, you'll want to know how to get your voice on the air. You can do this in two ways: by adding voice input between tracks, and by adding voice input on top of the music that's playing. As you'd imagine, the former is easier, but the latter sounds ten times as professional, so you'll want to know how to do both.

Adding Voice Input between Tracks

To add voice input between tracks in your playlist, follow these steps:

1. Press Ctrl+L, or click the Add button and choose Add URL from the context menu of buttons, to display the Open Location dialog box.

2. Enter **linerec://** and click the Open button. The Playlist Editor will display *Line Recording* at that point in the playlist.

3. When the Line Recording item in the playlist comes up, take a deep but silent breath and speak your mind.

4. Click the next item in the playlist to start it playing.

Adding Voice Input on Top of the Music

To add voice input on top of the music, you need to run a second instance of Winamp and use it to pipe the voice in. Here's what to do:

1. Press Ctrl+P or choose Options ➢ Preferences from the main menu to display the Winamp Preferences dialog box.

2. Click the Options entry in the left-hand panel.

3. Select the Allow Multiple Instances check box.

4. Click the Close button to close the Winamp Preferences dialog box.

5. Start a second instance of Winamp.

6. Press Ctrl+L, or click the Add button and choose Add URL from the menu of buttons, to display the Open Location dialog box.

7. Enter **linerec://** and click the Open button. The Playlist Editor will display *Line Recording* at that point in the playlist.

8. Set a playlist going in the first instance of Winamp.

9. In the second instance, click the Play button for the Line Recording entry and speak into the mike.

10. Mute the mike when you're not on the air. It's amazing how easy it is to forget you're on the air and embarrass yourself in public.

Silencing Local Output

Here's how to broadcast without playing aloud on your own computer:

1. Press Ctrl+P or select Options ➢ Preferences from the main menu to display the Winamp Preferences dialog box.

2. Click the Output item in the left-hand panel.

3. Select the Nullsoft NULL Output Plug-In in the list box.

4. Click the Close button to close the Preferences dialog box.

5. Exit and restart Winamp.

To restore local playing, display the Preferences dialog box again and select your usual output plug-in, then exit and restart Winamp.

Bringing the Server Down

If you keep feeding your playlist, and your Internet connection stays up, you can keep broadcasting till the cows come home.

To bring your server down, follow these steps:

1. Display the Nullsoft SHOUTcast Server Monitor window by clicking the SHOUTcast Server icon in your system tray.

2. Click the Kill Server button. SHOUTcast will display the Shutdown SHOUTcast Server dialog box.

3. Click the Yes button. You're off the air.

MP3 Beyond the Computer

Love your computer? We bet you do. But there are times and places you really don't want to be taking it with you—like to the bathroom, to the health club, on a drive to Las Vegas, or to Club Med in Bermuda. (If you're taking your computer to places like this, we offer our sincerest condolences.) In this part of the book, we'll discuss the different options for listening to MP3 tracks when you're away from your computer.

You'll be glad to hear that, because of MP3's amazingly high profile, the possibilities are already extensive and new products are being announced or released almost every week.

As we see it, there are five categories of products that let you enjoy MP3 music without directly using a personal computer. These categories are somewhat fluid, in that some devices slop over from one category into another, but the categories are usable enough for roughly describing the different types of players you'll be considering for taking your usage of MP3 beyond your computer. The categories are as follows:

Ultraportable players   An ultraportable player is typically smaller than a packet of cigarettes and uses flash memory for storage. As you'd guess, ultraportables score on portability but suffer on storage capacity.

Portable players   A portable player is bigger and heavier than an ultraportable—perhaps the size of a medium-thick novel. This category is evolving more slowly than some of the other categories, but we feel safe enough in saying that portables outdo ultraportables on the storage front but suffer correspondingly in size.

Car players   Car players come in a variety of sizes and shapes, ranging from portable players that double doing car duty to players specifically designed to fit into the slot built into a car or into the last cubic foot in the trunk not occupied by the spare tire or the groceries.

Stereo components   Stereo components are MP3 players designed to fit into a home stereo system.

Computers that aren't PCs   Hand-held PCs, Palm-size PCs, Springboard modules for your Visor—there are a variety of portable computer-like objects that can also play MP3 files.

Here's what you'll know after reading this part:

◆ How to choose and use ultraportable and portable dedicated hardware MP3 players. We'll run you through the features of some of the players that are currently available: the Diamond Rio PMP500, the

Samsung Yepp, the Audiovox MP1000, the Pine Technologies D'music, the Sony VAIO Music Clip, the I-JAM, the i2Go eGo, and the HanGo Personal Jukebox. This isn't a comprehensive roundup—because of the number of players already in the field and the speed at which further players are being introduced, we can't reasonably try to cover all of them—but this coverage should help you in identifying a player that will meet your needs. We show you a picture of each of the players we cover, using the same medium-sized hand (one of Rhonda's) to give you an idea of scale.

◆ What kinds of Palm-size PCs can rock out, and how to persuade them to do so.

◆ How to play MP3 files on hand-held PCs such as the IBM WorkPad Z50.

◆ How to play MP3 files in your car.

◆ How to play MP3 files through your stereo system.

◆ What a stand-alone MP3 player is, and where you can get one.

We'll start by discussing what to look for in a portable MP3 player and what features you can't live without.

90 Choose the Right Portable MP3 Player for You

So you think you want a portable MP3 player? Read on. In this section, you'll learn how to decide whether you need a portable MP3 player, the capabilities of the leading MP3 players available today, and how to make an informed decision among them.

A Little Background

As you'll learn in this section (if you haven't already searched for portable MP3 players online), there are already several dozen portable MP3 players available, and new ones are being announced or introduced most every week. They vary widely in size, style, looks, capacity, and capabilities, not to mention price. And so far, none of them is a category killer—a product that blows away all the other products in its category.

There are several reasons for this:

◆ First, the market is fragmented. Because portable MP3 players can come in a variety of sizes and capacities, there's no one compelling size for manufacturers to concentrate on. Wuh? Okay, look: When Sony came out with the first cassette Walkman in the days the first gods of punk walked the earth, life was much easier. Then, music came on 12-inch LPs or on cassettes (CDs hadn't been invented yet); and LPs required a large player, while cassettes could be played on something much smaller. So (with 20/20 hindsight), the Walkman was a no-brainer—miniaturize the cassette player to wrap it around the cassette, and it becomes portable. But an MP3 player can be any size from matchbox up to briefcase.

◆ Second, the players are still too expensive to go mainstream. For a portable player to go *really* mainstream, it needs to sell for less than $100 and have decent features—say, 64MB memory minimum (128MB much better), USB connection, good headphones—the whole shebang. But even with memory prices having returned to around $1 per megabyte after that 1999 Taiwan earthquake we keep mentioning, a 64MB player is going to cost more like $200 at retail—too much to go mainstream. We'd say there's an opportunity here for an enterprising company that's prepared to lose a lot of money in the short term to lock up the market for the long term.

◆ Third, the players are not good enough to go mainstream. That's to say, many of them are well designed and well made, and they execute well enough the functions they're designed to perform—but none is so compelling in and of itself to make people pay above the odds for it. So right now, the players are competing with each other on price, features, advertising, and distribution.

◆ Fourth, for all but a few MP3 players, you need to have a computer. Computer ownership in United States and Canada households is tottering towards the 50-percent mark—but even that means that half the people in the continent will have no interest in portable MP3 players. Oops, you just lost half the market for your market-winning money-loser…

Do You Need a Hardware MP3 Player?

First, make sure that you *need* a hardware MP3 player. This step is easy, so it's embarrassing to get it wrong.

If you have a Palm-size PC that supports stereo such as the Cassiopeia E-100 or E-105, or a hand-held computer such as the HP Jornada 680, you can turn it into an MP3 player in just a few minutes. Many of the new Palm-size computers and a number of the hand-held computers have audio hardware built in, so you need only install software to make them into MP3 players.

If you have a Palm-size PC, check to make sure that its output jack supports stereo—some of them can manage only mono and will make your precious music sound like it's being played in a mortuary by someone with a tin ear.

With most Palm-size PCs, you'll need to add a CompactFlash card to supplement the computer's built-in memory and give you enough space to carry a decent amount of music.

The disadvantage of playing music on a Palm-size PC is that you'll usually be dealing with software-based controls rather than hardware-based controls. For example, to start the music playing, you'll tap on a Play icon rather than pressing a Play button. That means you'll need to look at the screen rather than working by touch, which implies that (unless you're a contortionist in training) you probably won't be able to keep your Palm-size PC in a belt-case or pocket—you'll need to pull it out to use it.

Minor details, you say—and perhaps you're right. But limitations like this put a severe dent into usability.

If you have a Handspring Visor, things are a little better. True, you'll have a grayscale screen rather than the fancy color screens that some of the Palm-size PCs boast, but you can get a Springboard module containing an MP3 player. (Actually, strike that "can get" and make it "will soon be able to get"—though Innogear announced its MiniJam Springboard module in September 1999, and Diamond Multimedia's RioPort announced a Digital Audio Player Springboard the same month, neither is available at this writing… and Visor owners are beginning to champ through the bit.) These players have hardware buttons, so they're easy to use.

We'll look at how to play MP3 files on Palm-size PCs in *100. Play MP3 Files on a Palm-Size PC*. In the meantime, we'll assume you've established that you do need a hardware MP3 player.

What Features Do You Need?

So you *do* need a portable hardware MP3 player? Okay. Next, assess what features you need on your MP3 player. The list is short but important.

Basic Controls: Pause, Fast Forward, and Rewind

One thing that may sound too obvious to even consider is to check that the portable MP3 player you choose provides the basic playing functionality you need, especially pause, fast forward, and rewind. Here, MP3 players differ from most CD players and cassette players.

First, the pause functionality on many portable MP3 players is somewhat impaired, at least in comparison with what people typically expect in a Pause button. When you press the Pause button, you want play to stop, and you want to be able to resume from that point. But on some portable MP3 players, pressing the Pause button pauses play for about 15 seconds, but after that the player registers a Stop instruction and turns itself off. This is good in that you want to save the battery power, but bad in that most of the players that do this do not save your place in the track; instead, they make you start back at either the beginning of that track or (much worse) at the beginning of your playlist.

Second, most players totally lack fast-forward and rewind capabilities within a track, so you can't move quickly through a track to find the section you want to hear. All the players we've seen have Previous Track and Next Track buttons, so you can jump to the previous track or to the next track with no problem. In some players, pressing the Previous Track button while playing a track takes you to the beginning of that track rather than to the beginning of the previous track.

How Much Storage Do You Need?

The key feature of hardware MP3 players is to make sure that it has enough storage. Remember that a minute of near–CD-quality audio takes up about a megabyte of storage. So if you want to be able to tote an hour of music around with you, you'll need at least 64MB of memory. If you want two hours, or three…okay, you can do the math.

NOTE   As mentioned earlier in this book, if you're interested in spoken audio, you'll be able to get away with a lower quality (and lower compression rate) than for music. 64MB of memory on a hardware MP3 player will contain a good two to three hours' worth of spoken audio—enough for even severe commutes or tedious lectures.

At this writing, the leading ultraportable players come with 64MB of memory on board; most have an expansion slot that can hold another 16MB or 32MB, giving a total of 80MB or 96MB. That's enough to keep most people entertained for a while, but not enough for that category killer we're eager to see. We'd like to see an ultraportable with 128MB on board and an expansion slot that can hold another 64MB or 128MB—maybe even 256MB for audiophiles with fat wallets.

The upgrade cards are expensive—about $50 for 16MB and $90 for 32MB at this writing. (Prices may go down, but they can't go down soon enough for music fans.) They're tiny—about the size of your big toenail after you've chewed it down. And they're even more delicate than your significant other's ego. So they're really portable, but they're a pain to carry around and handle. Even if you can afford a bunch of them, you usually won't want to carry them around with you and swap them back and forth. Instead, you'll want to get the biggest one your player supports, slide it in, and leave it there permanently. If you arrange your music libraries effectively, you can group tracks in hour-long clumps (for a 64MB machine) and quickly upload a new "mood," CD, or artist's greatest hits.

One other thing to keep in mind: Because each MP3 track is an integrated unit, the whole of the track needs to fit in the available memory—you can't wedge 4MB of a 5MB track into the last 4MB free on a player the way you could cram four minutes of a five-minute track onto the end of a cassette. Either you have enough space to fit the whole track on the player or none of it goes on. This means that you'll usually have up to a couple of megabytes free when you've loaded a player "full." And if the player's memory is split into internal and external, those usually act as two separate areas—you can't break an MP3 file across them. So you'll almost always end up with some empty space in each area.

Bottom line: When buying an ultraportable MP3 player, get as much on-board memory as you can. You won't regret paying more for the memory-heavy models.

Portable players are a better bet than ultraportables when it comes to storage—but you'll still be paying top dollar for the space. The eGo has one or two CompactFlash slots, which can hold either CompactFlash cards or IBM Microdrives, giving you up to 680MB of storage for a cost somewhere north of $1000 (that's including the Microdrives). The HanGo Personal Jukebox contains a 4.8GB hard drive and costs $799.

One portable player that offers less expensive storage is the Sharp MiniDisc player MD-MT15. By using special cabling and software to connect to your PC, this MiniDisc player lets you record MP3 files onto MiniDiscs. The drawback is that recording to the MiniDisc happens in real time—to get an hour's worth of music onto a MiniDisc, it'll take you an hour.

Do You Need to Be Able to Record?

Some MP3 hardware players include microphones and the ability to record audio (either as MP3 files or in other audio file formats), usually for making voice notes or practicing dictation. Others don't. If you need to record, this feature may be a deal-breaker when you're choosing a player. Most of these microphones are designed for recording voice rather than music, so if you try to bootleg a concert with one of them, you'll wish you hadn't bothered.

For good effects when recording music via a microphone, make sure the MP3 device supports stereo recording and provides a microphone input, not just a cheesy built-in microphone.

Do You Need a Tuner in It?

If you need a tuner in your MP3 player, you'll be able to narrow down your choices still further. Relatively few of the MP3 players have built-in tuners; those that do advertise them prominently.

Size and Ease of Use

Next, consider size and ease of use. This part is easy enough.

All the ultraportables are much smaller than Walkmans and Discmans, while some of the portables are a little bigger than a Walkman, though a little differently proportioned.

Because many MP3 players are so small, those of you with larger hands may actually prefer the larger players or those that offer larger buttons for controlling play. For example, most people find the pinkie-nail–sized buttons on the Rio easier to use than the tiny buttons on the top of the MPMan or the match-head–sized buttons on the side of the Yepp—though when you're working by touch, even the larger buttons are easy enough to get wrong.

Most players have a Hold button or Lock button that disables the controls. Use the Hold button or Lock button with the player switched off to make sure it doesn't get turned on accidentally in your pocket. Use it with the unit running to make sure you don't bump the player when jogging, working out, or packing your butt into a crowded subway train.

Line-Out Jack

If you're seriously into MP3, you may want to be able to plug your MP3 player directly into your stereo system or into an input jack on your car. If so, look for a line-out jack in addition to the headphone jack. The line-out jack provides output at a standard level, allowing you to control the volume more effectively through the stereo system or car stereo rather than having to control it first at the MP3 player.

In many cases this isn't a big deal, but the output on some headphone jacks can be high enough to damage the inputs on a receiver that's geared to the more moderate output of a line-out jack. If you end up using the headphone jack, wind the volume down to just a fraction above the minimum before making the connection.

Battery Types and Battery Life

Next, what kind of batteries does the player use—removable batteries or a built-in rechargeable battery? Will it make a difference to you? And what kind of battery life will you get from the player?

As long as a built-in rechargeable battery is powerful enough to provide decent battery life, it's typically a good solution. What constitutes decent battery life will depend on your needs, but it'll probably be on the order of 6 to 12 hours a day. You can then recharge the battery while you're asleep—but bear in mind that the recharging will typically involve a hefty AC adapter that you'll need to schlep around with you.

If you need to be able to use the player for extended periods away from a battery charger, you may prefer removable batteries: Once you've burned through one set, you can pop in the next set and keep rocking. And of course these removable batteries can be rechargeable batteries—for example, rechargeable AA or AAA batteries—though there's a downside to rechargeables too. The main disadvantage of rechargeable batteries is that they never deliver their full voltage. Even when they're in theory fully charged, they deliver much less than a disposable battery does at the start of its life. For example, a disposable AA battery gives its rated 1.5 volts at the start of its life, whereas a rechargeable AA battery typically starts with more like

1.2 volts. A secondary disadvantage is that their battery life is usually much shorter than that of quality disposable alkaline batteries.

Battery life on the ultraportables and portables we've used has ranged from magnificent to miserable. For example, the Rio 500 delivers 8 to 12 hours on a single AA battery, and the Yepp gives us around 8 hours on two AAA batteries. But the eGo, with its monster capacity (two CompactFlash cards, either or both of which can be IBM Microdrives, which hold 340MB apiece), is correspondingly savage on batteries, chewing up and spitting out a pair of Duracell Ultra AA batteries in less than an hour and a half. (To be fair, we should mention that the eGo is designed primarily for use in the car with an adapter cable.) The HanGo Personal Jukebox comes with a lithium-ion battery that provides 8 to 10 hours—and which you can replace with another battery if necessary, giving you great flexibility.

For a player that you'll use in the car or attached to your stereo system, make sure that you can get a lighter-socket cable or an AC cable so that you can plug it in and forget about the batteries.

How Will You Carry It?

If you'll want to wear the player on a belt, make sure that it comes with a belt clip or a case that offers a belt clip. A surprising number of players don't come with a belt clip or a belt-friendly case: The MPMan F10 and the D'music come with drawstring pouches that are decorative but essentially useless—they'll keep the player and its headphones together in your pocket, but you have to take the player out to access the controls. The I-JAM comes with a cute case with a strong belt clip—and the case provides easy access to the controls. And while the Rio PMP300 (the original Rio) has a sturdy and removable belt clip, the Rio PMP500 (the latest and greatest Rio at this writing) comes with a case that clips determinedly to your belt but that prevents you from easily accessing any of the controls other than the On/Off/Hold switch. The Yepp, on the other hand, doesn't look nearly as good as the Rio, and the Nex looks decidedly clunky, but each comes with a belt clip that beats the Rio's case into a cocked hat. (You see what we meant about there not being a category killer yet?)

The Sony VAIO Music Clip comes with a neck strap and a shirt-pocket clip. This clip is feeble and barely holds the VAIO Music Clip in place even when you're stationary.

The eGo (which is primarily designed for the car) also comes with a belt clip, albeit one so poorly located that you have to loosen and swivel the belt clip in order to change the batteries on the player. (And as we mentioned in the previous section, you'll be needing to change the batteries frequently if you're using the eGo as a portable player.)

At this writing, about the coolest MP3 player to have is the soon-to-be-released Wrist Audio Player from Casio, which is basically a watch on steroids with the capacity to hold less MP3 music than you probably want. (The current model maxes out at 30 minutes of music.) The Wrist Audio Player looks satisfyingly unique, but we wonder how you'll avoid snarling the headphone cord on things as you boogie down the street playing windmill air guitar *à la* Pete Townshend.

Operating System Support

Which operating system will you be using with the portable MP3 player? If you answered Windows 98 or Windows 95 (or the upcoming Windows Millennium—Windows Me for short) you're in luck—most MP3 players come with software for Windows 95/98 and nothing else. If you want to use another PC operating system, you'll have to download some third-party software and expend a little more effort configuring it.

If you want to use the Mac, you'll need to make sure that your portable comes with a USB connection because a parallel port won't be an option with the Mac. Now that more USB devices are being released, using them with the Mac is less of a problem—but make sure that the player comes with Mac software (or that you can download Mac software that will work with it).

Does the Software Want to Manage Your Life?

The software that comes with the MP3 players we've used varies widely in its scope, capabilities, and ambitions. If possible, find out approximately what the software attempts to do and make sure that this meshes with your needs.

The most basic software lets you download MP3 files to the player, rearrange them, and delete them to make space for further tracks. (For copyright reasons, the software that comes with most players does not let you upload MP3 files from the player to your computer, though some software and players let you upload other files, such as audio files you've recorded on the player. You can fool some such software by changing the file extension on the MP3 files—but then the player probably won't play them.) The software doesn't care where you keep your MP3 files—it lets you deal with such questions—and doesn't try to start ripping any audio CD that gets within kissing distance of your computer. We like this approach because the software is easy to use and isn't constantly imposing itself on you.

The more "advanced" software wants to manage your life for you. Before you can put any tracks on the player, you need to tell the software about them so that it can manage them into a library. Then (depending on the software) you may have to build a playlist before exporting the tracks to the PC. And if you put an audio CD in your computer, the software will start trying to rip it, probably without consulting you.

We don't like this approach much. We can see the advantages, but unless the software is exceptionally well designed, it tends to be harder to use. Your mileage *will* vary here.

Look for Equalization Controls

If you want the music you play on your portable player to sound good, make sure the player has adequate equalization controls. Equalization has been a weakness of portable MP3 players, but manufacturers are now starting to include it.

As you'd imagine, equalization isn't the easiest thing to implement on portable players. First, you need a little more hardware and software, which makes the player more expensive. Second, the lack of real estate on the players makes it tricky to build satisfactory hardware controls on the player. For an effective graphical equalizer, you'd want six to ten mechanical sliders, and there's essentially nowhere to put them. You'd also want to be able to lock the sliders against accidental movement when the player gets bumped or put in a pocket. Tricky.

Most of the ultraportables and portables offer a number of DSP settings, some of them more successful than others. Others let you set the treble and bass to your own liking.

Listen to It

If the suggestions in the preceding sections haven't helped you decide which MP3 player to get, the final test should be your ears. Listen to the players you're evaluating for as long as possible. Play with those equalization and volume controls. Jog around the store with the player if you can do so without attracting undue attention or store detectives.

If you can, listen to the same types of music that you're planning to listen to in the long term. For example, if your musical taste encompasses everything from Bach to Britney Spears to Metallica, listen to examples of each extreme of the range of music when evaluating the player. Don't listen to evaluation tracks that contain different types of music. To give an obvious example, it's a mistake to use classical music to evaluate a player that you'll use for reggae. (Unless, of course, your idea of "classical" music is Bob Marley's "Jammin'" or "Buffalo Soldier.") If you're evaluating a player that uses removable media—CompactFlash cards, say—you might even be able to take in some music of your own to listen to (though in doing so you might run the risk of being suspected of shoplifting). Otherwise, even MP3-savvy stores will give you an earful of Pavarotti or Julio Iglesias, which will help you not one iota in evaluating whether the player can handle the all-out attack of Marilyn Manson.

91 Use the Diamond Rio

The Diamond Rio PMP300 was the pioneering dedicated hardware MP3 player in the U.S. market. (The MPMan F10 claims to have been available before the Rio on the international scene, but the Rio was the first to make it big in the U.S.) As a result, it grabbed most of the initial market share for hardware MP3 players.

In November 1998, the imminent release of the Rio provoked a lawsuit by the Recording Industry Association of America (RIAA). To address the RIAA's concerns that the Rio would contribute to piracy of music via MP3 files, Diamond added a Serial Copyright Management System—SCMS, if you like abbreviations—to the player. Undaunted, the RIAA sued Diamond Multimedia to prevent the release of the Rio. But the judge denied the motion, and the Rio was released, to the delight of MP3 fans. Diamond later followed up with a Special Edition of the PMP300, and more recently released the PMP500.

The Rio PMP500, shown below, costs about $275 street, has 64MB RAM and takes a 16MB or 32MB memory card, and comes with a USB cable, a pair of Koss ear-clip supra-aural headphones, and a carrying case. The ear-clip headphones are an interesting choice. People tend to find them comfortable provided they're not wearing glasses (or shades) at the same time—because the headphone clip goes over the ear, it's right where the earpiece of your glasses wants to go. The clips hold the ear buds steady under modest movement, but if you jog with them, you'll find the buds flapping away from your ears, giving an annoying wowing effect to the music.

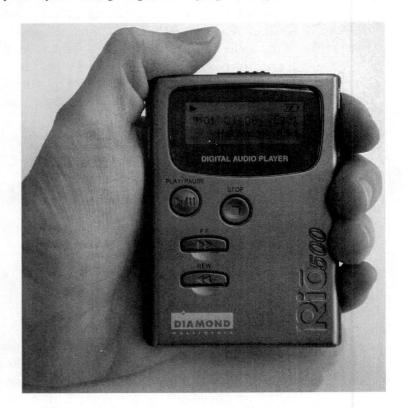

The carrying case is truly strange and (to us, at least) a great disappointment. Where the original Rio came with a sturdy integrated belt clip that left all its controls accessible, the Rio PMP500 comes with a bizarre leather-and-lace pouch horribly reminiscent of those specialty catalogs you never really looked at before throwing them away. The back of the case is stiff black leather and has a ferocious belt clip built in; no way is this sucker going to come off your belt unless you're pulling about 15gs upside down or you wipe out on your street-luge. The bottom of the case is flexible leatherette, and the front and sides are wide-mesh string. An elastic loop at the top slips over the belt clip to prevent the Rio from exiting vertically. The problem with the case is that it denies you access to most of the buttons you'll need for controlling play on the Rio—and it looks peculiar at best.

The Rio PMP500 is quick and easy to install. You plug in the USB cable and turn the Rio on, and any USB-enabled version of Windows (such as Windows 95 OSR2 or Windows 98) will recognize it.

Windows will start the Add New Hardware Wizard, which will invite you to search for new drivers for the *Rio500*. Decline this kindly offer by clicking the Cancel button, and then slip the RioPort CD into your CD drive. If the Autorun feature doesn't respond, open an Explorer window and double-click the Autorun application (`Autorun.exe`) at the root of the CD to start the installation routine. The rest of the installation routine is straightforward and includes designating a music folder for your music.

One thing to note here: The File Monitor dialog box, shown below, offers to monitor the music files you create. Audio Monitor makes it easy to keep track of your MP3 files. However, you may dislike the Big-Brother implications of its peering over your virtual shoulder the whole time and so choose to turn it off.

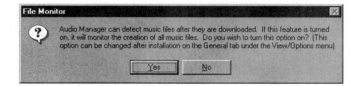

NOTE To turn File Monitor on and off, choose View ➢ Options to display the Options dialog box. Click the General tab to display the General page. Then select or clear the Add Song to Database When Song File Is Downloaded check box.

When Setup ends, you'll need to let it restart your computer or restart it yourself manually. You can then start the RioPort Audio Manager by double-clicking the icon it installed on your Desktop. You'll see the Empty Database dialog box, shown below.

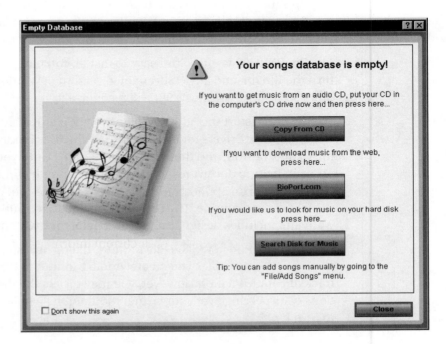

Because RioPort Audio Manager is one of the type of applications that insists on knowing about every track you want to download to your player, you may want to click the Search Disk for Music button now to have RioPort Audio Manager round up your music. If you do, you'll see the Progress dialog box shown below as it works.

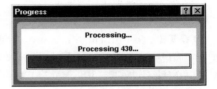

After that, you'll see the Review New Songs dialog box, shown next.

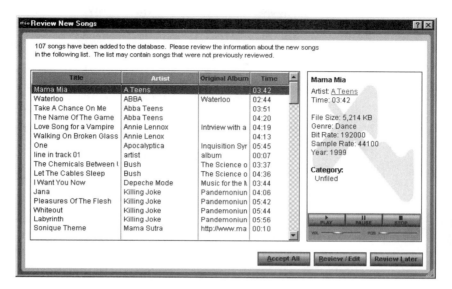

Nope, you're not done yet. You can accept all the tracks as listed, importing them into the database with their current information, by clicking the Accept All button. Or you can click the Review Later button to postpone the chore of checking the information for each track. Or you can select a track and click the Review/Edit button to display the Edit Song dialog box, shown below, check and fix the info, and then click the Save/Close button.

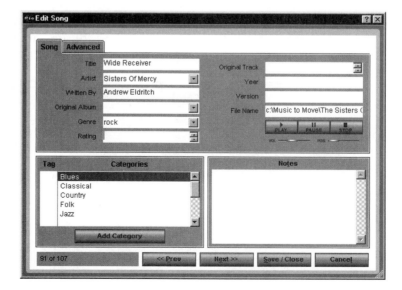

After that, you finally get to see the RioPort Audio Manager itself. As you can see in the illustration below, the RioPort Audio Manager has four pages (Playlist, Copy from CD, Devices, and RioPort.com), which you access by clicking the buttons across the top of the window. The illustration shows the Devices window.

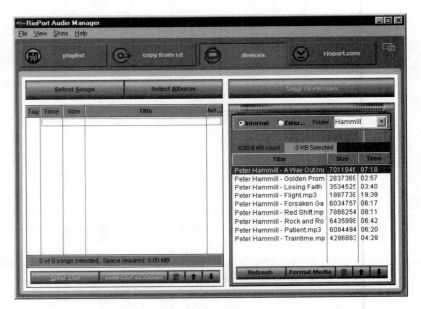

From here, you can load tracks onto the player by clicking the Select Songs button and working in the Select Songs dialog box, shown below, or whole albums, by clicking the Select Albums button and working in the Select Albums dialog box.

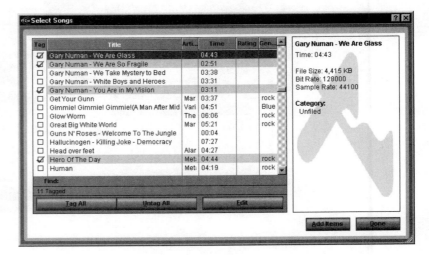

You see what we mean about some software wanting to manage your life for you? Once you've made your selection, you then have to create a folder on the portable before you can copy files to it. If not, you'll get this helpful message.

To remove tracks from the Rio, fire up the Rio Manager and display the internal or external memory as appropriate. Shift+click or Ctrl+click to select the tracks, then click the Delete button and choose the Yes button in the confirmation dialog box.

92   Use the Pine D'Music

The D'music from Pine Technologies is an ultraportable player that comes in a variety of translucent cases. The illustration on the next page shows the D'music. As you can see, there's a smallish LCD that displays part of the track name; a good-sized rocker control on the front providing quick access to Play/Pause, Previous Track, Next Track, and Stop buttons; and four buttons—Menu, Sel, Mode, and Eq—for accessing modes, functions, and the graphical equalizer.

The D'music has 32MB of memory on board and one expansion slot that can hold a memory card of up to 32MB, giving you a maximum capacity of 64MB. It attaches to the PC via the parallel port, works with Windows 95, Windows 98, and Windows NT 4, and comes with shareware versions of MusicMatch Jukebox 4 (now outdated) and AudioCatalyst along with its basic but effective software, D'music MP3 Manager. The D'music costs about $175 street.

The D'music has a five-position DSP, which offers Flat, Pop, Classic, Jazz, and Ex-Bass (extra-bass) settings. It has a built-in microphone, so you can record with it. The microphone is designed for voice recording; the quality is fine for taking notes, but it's a mistake to try to record music with it. You can upload the voice files you record to your PC and listen to them there if the fancy takes you.

Disappointingly for a portable player, the D'music comes with one of the most wretched carrying cases imaginable—a drawstring bag intended (presumably) for carrying in a purse or pocket when the player is not in use. The D'music has no belt clip, neck strap, or other carrying arrangement that would let you use the player while carrying it. It has a Hold button, so you can set it playing (or off) and drop it in your pocket without any danger of the buttons getting pushed unintentionally.

WARNING In order to work, the D'music needs a parallel port set to ECP mode. If you have an older computer, make sure that your parallel port is ECP-capable; if not, you'll need to upgrade it. If you have a newer computer with an ECP-capable parallel port but you can't get the D'music MP3 Manager software to communicate with the D'music, make sure that the port is set to ECP mode. Usually, you'll have to make this change in the BIOS settings for the computer.

Before installing the D'music software, you need to install the D'music voice driver. The process is simple, but (as usual) you have to reboot your computer. You can then install the D'music MP3 Manager software, which (for once) doesn't require a reboot.

The first time you fire up D'music MP3 Manager, you'll see the LPT Setup dialog box, shown below, in which you select the parallel port on which you installed the D'music. Unless you have multiple parallel ports, chances are that this will be LPT1. (If that proves to be incorrect, choose Player ➤ Comm Option to display the LPT Setup dialog box again and try one of the other ports.)

The D'music MP3 Manager, shown on the next page, is pleasantly simple. Unlike more sophisticated software, it makes no attempt to manage all of your music into one interface. Instead, you use the left-hand Explorer pane to navigate to the folder containing the files you want to copy to the D'music. You then select the files in the upper-right pane and drag them to the lower-right pane. The Memory readout in the status bar shows the total amount of memory, how much you've used, and how much is still available. But the D'music MP3 Manager is a little too simple: There's no readout totaling the size of the files you select for transfer, and you'll need to do the math on your own to see if you've selected even approximately the right number of megabytes of music for the player.

As we mentioned, the D'music's memory is divided into internal memory and an external flash card. To toggle the D'music MP3 Manager between the two, you click the Memory button and the M.Card button on the toolbar (or choose Player ➤ Memory or Player ➤ Memory Card if you prefer to use the menus).

As you transfer files, the D'music MP3 Manager displays the Downloading dialog box shown below. As you can see, this dialog box also is a little primitive: The figures aren't comma-separated into thousands and millions, making them hard to parse, and there's no warning that we've chosen more music (about 69MB, in the Total Length readout) than will fit into the player's internal memory. The D'music also truncates the names of tracks in the D'music pane to 30 characters—a passing annoyance.

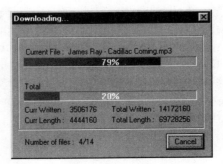

When the D'music hits the memory wall, it displays a warning message box. You'll need to check the lower-right pane to see which MP3 files were transferred and which weren't.

For copyright-protection reasons, the D'music won't let you transfer music files from the D'music to your computer, but you can transfer other files without problem. This means that you can use the D'music as a sort of portable storage device: You can copy a file to the D'music, then transfer it to another computer. Bear in mind that you'll need the D'music MP3 Manager software installed on each computer to do so, and you'll need to take the cable with you—so this isn't exactly a convenient solution. But if you occasionally need to transfer large files from A to B or to carry a backup of crucial files, the D'music can provide an effective solution.

93 Use the Audiovox

The Audiovox MP1000 (about $150 street) is a pleasantly shaped ultraportable player that fits neatly into the hand (as shown in the photograph at the top of the next page), connects to the PC via a parallel cable, and comes with a carrying case that has a good belt clip *and* lets you manipulate the controls. The MP1000 has 32MB RAM on board and an expansion slot that can take another 32MB. (The forthcoming MP2000 and MP3000 models will have 64MB on board.) It has Treble and Bass settings from 1 to 20, Contrast from 1 to 10, a Wide setting (On or Off), and an Intro mode that plays the first ten seconds of each track.

The MP1000's MPDJ software uses a standardized installation routine remarkable only for requiring you to enter a company name (very strange for a consumer-targeted product).

MPDJ provides a simple four-pane interface with an Explorer-style tree on the upper left, an information pane on the lower left, a file-selection pane on the upper right, and a player pane on the lower right. The player pane has one page for the player's onboard memory and one for the memory card, so that you can access each quickly. To transfer files to the MP1000, you select them in the file-selection pane and drag them to the player pane. The illustration at the bottom of the next page shows MPDJ transferring files.

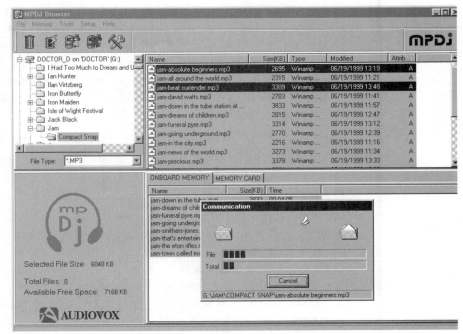

The MPDJ software includes a simple but effective player (shown below) and a minimalist encoder whimsically shaped like a whistle. The encoder lets you either extract and rip from CD to MP3 in one step or perform the steps separately, but it has no CDDB connectivity, so you'll have to supply track information yourself via the Tag feature. Compared to, say, Music-Match Jukebox or RealJukebox Plus, the encoder is Spartan indeed—but the price is right, which may convince you to try it.

94   Use the I-JAM

The I-JAM, from I-JAM Multi Media LLC and shown on the next page, is an attractive but irregular-shaped player that looks like a cross between a portable telephone and ET. It comes in colors from hard-hat yellow through purple; runs on AAA batteries; features a built-in FM radio and ten-position treble and bass controls; and uses removable memory cards the size of a stamp.

At this writing, the I-JAM comes with two 16MB cards, which are disappointingly small and which you'll need to augment with one or more higher-capacity cards if you want sustained listening. (Because the I-JAM holds only one card at a time, you'll do better with one high-capacity card than two or more low-capacity ones.) Its six front buttons are small and a little complicated to use (for example, some actions require holding down a button for several seconds to reach a different mode). The I-JAM costs about $225 street.

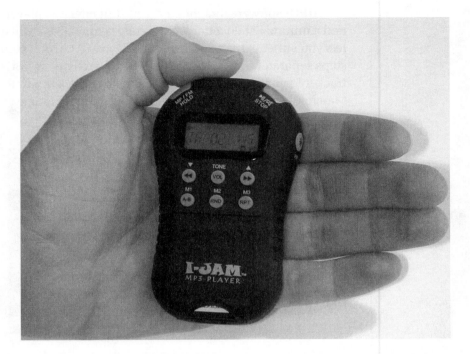

The I-JAM doesn't connect directly to the PC, instead using a Multi-Media Card Reader unit called the JAM-Station that plugs into your PS/2 keyboard port (for power) and your parallel port (for data). You use the card reader to stuff a memory card with audio, then plug it into the I-JAM.

The I-JAM comes with its own JAM-Station software, a group of applications for connecting to and managing the JAM-Station card reader, and MusicMatch Jukebox version 4.

Once you've wrestled the PS/2 and parallel ports into place and plugged your keyboard and printer (or other parallel-port peripheral) into the pass-throughs, installation is straightforward. You get to choose whether to install just the JAM-Station or MusicMatch Jukebox as well; if you choose both, it installs MusicMatch Jukebox first.

NOTE When installing JAM-Station, make sure you select an appropriate directory in the Destination Location dialog box—by default, the program tries to install itself in a directory called SCMMICRO off the root rather than under your Program Files folder.

When installation is complete, you'll see the MMC Reader Drive Identification message box, shown below, telling you which drive represents the JAM-Station.

Once you've clicked the Finish button in the Setup Complete dialog box (and closed the readme file if you chose to view it), agreeing to restart your computer, you may see a Warning message box such as the one shown below, asking you to close myriad applications before restarting your computer. If some of the names don't look familiar, that's because these are background processes that run automatically under Windows. Close any applications that are available to you by Alt+Tabbing, then click the OK button. The Setup program should be able to close most of these automatically; failing that, you'll need to restart your computer manually.

After the restart, you'll see the SAFEINST.EXE dialog box, shown below, telling you that JAM-Station is about to detect your parallel port chipset. Click the OK button and cross your fingers. If all goes well, you won't get another message box, but you'll simply be able to access a card inserted in the JAM-Station by using the drive letter previously indicated.

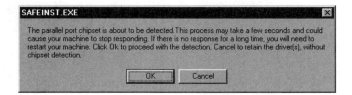

You can then format a Multi-Media Card by running the MMC Prep program installed as part of the JAM-Station software, and you can transfer MP3 files to the card by using Windows Explorer or another file-management program.

95 Use the Sharp MD-MT15(S) MiniDisc Player and Voquette MiniDisc NetLink

The Sharp MD-MT15(S) MiniDisc player (about $225 street) and Voquette MiniDisc NetLink form perhaps the most unusual and awkward MP3 solution we cover in this book. This combination solves the problem of getting MP3 files onto MiniDiscs, which provide both listening convenience and inexpensive and virtually unlimited storage—but this solution is unlikely to be of much interest to anyone who isn't already hooked on MiniDiscs.

The Sharp MD-MT15(S) is essentially an enhanced portable MiniDisc player and is a little shorter and squatter than a pack of cigarettes (see the illustration below).

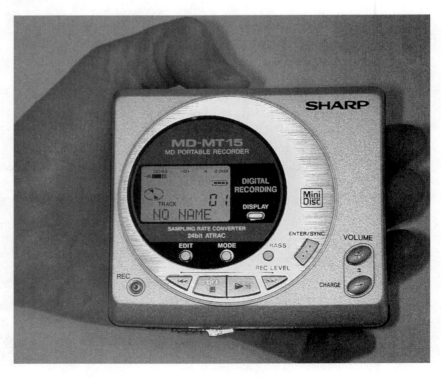

It uses standard MiniDisc media that provide 74 minutes of storage for audio files—about the same as a CD. Each MiniDisc costs a few bucks, is highly portable, and (in its case) is resilient enough for everyday wear and tear, so MiniDiscs are an easy way to carry a small collection of music around with you. Better yet, if you have a cassette adapter or direct line into your car stereo, the MiniDisc player can be a great solution for tunes on the road.

One problem with recording MP3 files to MiniDisc is that you're doing literally that—recording them, not downloading them. So the recording is real time: To get an hour of music on a MiniDisc, it'll take you an hour. If you go for the MiniDisc and Voquette MiniDisc NetLink solution, you'll probably want to build a collection of MiniDiscs rather than recording music to a MiniDisc temporarily, the way you download music to an ultraportable MP3 player.

To get MP3 files onto the MiniDiscs, you need to use the Voquette MiniDisc NetLink hardware and software. As you can see in the photograph of the Voquette MiniDisc NetLink hardware below, it's a fair-sized piece of cabling. At the PC's end, it plugs into your parallel port and into a PS/2 keyboard port. (Don't worry—it doesn't mess with your keyboard. This is just its way of getting the power it needs without dragging along a clunky DC adapter.)

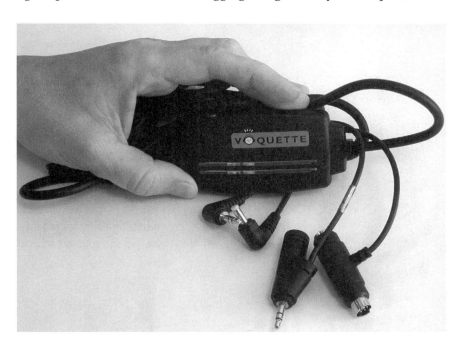

In order to get full functionality on the Voquette software, you have to register it online, providing your name and a valid e-mail address.

Once the Voquette MiniDisc NetLink is safely connected, you install the Voquette software following a relatively standardized installation routine. The main thing to note is the Start Voquette dialog box, which offers you the option to start Voquette every time Windows starts or to start it manually. If you think you'll be using Voquette frequently, the former may be a good choice.

The Voquette Setup Wizard then walks you through setting up the Voquette software: selecting the recording device you're using (shown below), scheduling automatic recording from the Internet (which you probably won't want to do), having Voquette automatically read your e-mail (likewise), specifying and testing your Internet connection, and (yawn) restarting your computer.

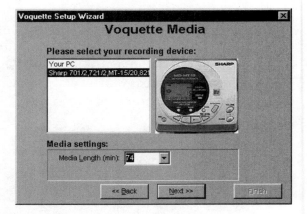

Once your PC is back up, start the Voquette software if you chose not to have it start automatically. You'll see the Voquette Basket, shown below, on top of your Desktop (and on top of any running application), and a Voquette icon will appear in the system tray. You can then drag MP3 files and drop them in the Voquette Basket, which will open and close to indicate that it has received the item or items. You can also drag and drop music files and streams from online sources once you've registered Voquette.

Once you've gotten your Voquette Basket into shape, you can record any or all of the tracks to the MiniDisc. The illustration below shows Voquette recording away happily.

When you've finished recording, you can play the tracks on the MiniDisc as usual.

96 Use the HanGo Personal Jukebox

When we first heard about the HanGo Personal Jukebox, we were skeptical as to how usable it could be. Sure, putting a hard drive into a portable MP3 player solved the storage problem well enough, and it'd be way cool to have the best part of 5GB of MP3 files to carry—but would it be stable enough for use as a portable player? Wouldn't it skip? And wouldn't it be far too big? And if it was a USB device (it is), why didn't it work with the Mac?

When the Personal Jukebox arrived, we were blown away. It *is* on the big side—it's 6" × 3" × 1", or a bit longer and narrower than most Walkmans—but HanGo has used the size well, providing large and well-spaced buttons and a nice big LCD screen that makes navigating its contents very easy. If you've used a smaller player, you might not want to go jogging with the Personal Jukebox on your belt—but for lower-impact use, it's great. (We've used it for walking, cycling, and working out, and had no problem with it.) The Personal Jukebox includes a leather belt case with a clear window for the screen and cutouts for the buttons, and a pair of supra-aural Koss headphones that we found comfortable and admirably clear.

The Personal Jukebox shown in the photograph below is the model we evaluated; it has a different skin from most of the models you'll find in the marketplace, but everything else is the same.

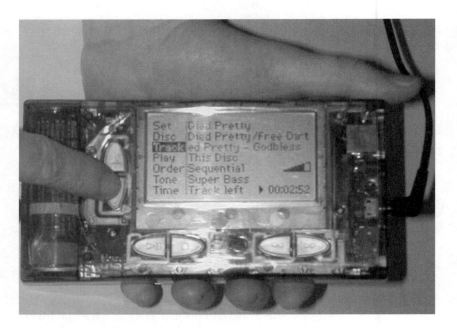

The Personal Jukebox uses a rechargeable battery that claims a ten-hour life and that in our testing delivered between six and eight hours. Plug it in every night, and you shouldn't have a problem rocking through the days. This battery is hefty—it's about the thickness of a man's forefinger—because it needs to power the hard drive around which the Personal Jukebox is built.

What's not to like about the Personal Jukebox? For us, just two things: the price—$799 at this writing—and the fact that it doesn't work with the Mac. You may also find it a little weird to hear the hard drive and the heads in the player moving (this sounds just like the hard drive noises your computer makes)—and to *feel* the movement when you're holding the player in your hands.

If we're *really* picking nits, we'd like to see a bigger hard drive so that we can store even more music. Given that desktop hard drives are now barreling into the 40 to 50GB range, and portable hard drives of 25GB are becoming common, we expect HanGo to release a new version of the Personal Jukebox with a much larger hard drive in the not-too-distant future. We can hardly wait… Oh, *and* we'd like to see the whole device made smaller—though we realize that this demand is anything but reasonable.

The Personal Jukebox comes with a straightforward software package called Jukebox Manager that you use to copy tracks to the Personal Jukebox and manage the tracks on it. We found Jukebox Manager easy to use and much less aggressive than many other packages in the Year-2000 generation of MP3-related software. Many packages seem to feel the need to organize you and your music collection to within an inch of your lives, and using them is like dealing with a bureaucracy that combines the best features of the DMV with the worst features of the U.S. Patent and Trademark Office.

The Personal Jukebox uses a USB connection to communicate with the PC (and, as we mentioned, it's best to have a PC rather than a Mac). As with many USB devices, you need to install the software before connecting the device, so that Windows doesn't get too confused. Jukebox Manager installs smoothly using a regular installation routine—a Welcome dialog box, selecting a program folder and Start menu group, and so on—that we won't show you here. Once you've got Jukebox Manager installed, you connect the Personal Jukebox unit, and Windows auto-detects the driver.

The first time you fire up Jukebox Manager (which you can do automatically from the end of the installation routine), you'll see the message *No Selected Jukebox*—it hasn't yet identified the Personal Jukebox unit.

To identify the Personal Jukebox unit, choose Jukebox ➢ Select Jukebox. Jukebox Manager will display the Select Personal Jukebox dialog box, shown below. Select the appropriate jukebox—chances are, you'll have only one choice—and click the OK button.

Jukebox Manager will then display the contents of the Personal Jukebox (nothing, if you've just bought it). The illustration below shows Jukebox Manager with a good helping of music installed.

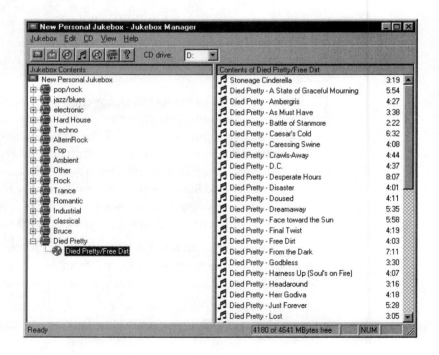

Jukebox Manager organizes your music into containers called collections, sets, discs, and tracks. Each of the terms stays within easy commuting distance of its conventional meaning:

Collection   A *collection* is a group of sets. Typically, you'll have one collection on your Personal Jukebox at a time.

Set   A *set* is a subset of a collection and contains discs. Usually, you'd use a set to organize music into different categories, such as Brutal Christian Metal, Saturday Ambient Trance, or Springsteen Acoustic Live.

Disc   A *disc* is a subset of a set and contains tracks. Normally, you'll use a disc to organize tracks into the virtual equivalent of an album or CD.

Track   A *track* is a track in the sense used for CDs—a self-standing item of music, be it a song or a sonata.

You can add tracks to the Personal Jukebox in either of two ways—by ripping them from a CD using functionality built into Jukebox Manager, or by adding previously ripped tracks stored on a drive accessible by Jukebox Manager.

To rip tracks, choose Jukebox ≻ Capture CD Audio. Jukebox Manager will display the Select Tracks to Capture dialog box, shown below. You can then click the Titles button to query the CDDB database for the CD and track titles, then select the tracks you want to rip and click the OK button to start the ripping process.

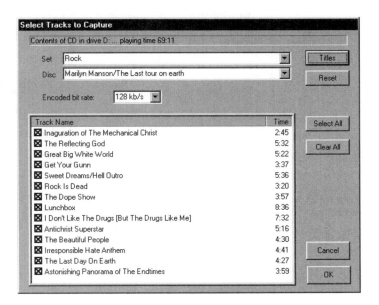

Jukebox Manager will capture the audio directly to the Personal Jukebox. The illustration below shows the Audio Capture Progress dialog box, which you'll see as Jukebox Manager rips the CD.

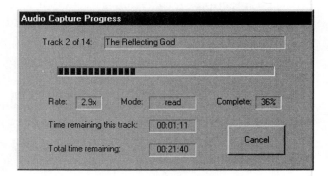

The Personal Jukebox uses a USB connection, but because of its phenomenal capacity, filling it with tracks can be a long process. That said, you're unlikely to need to *fill* it with tracks in a hurry, unless you buy it and immediately go on a vacation. More likely, you'll add to it a bunch of tracks at a time, weed out the ones not worth keeping, and gradually build the collection that you want to carry around with you.

As a rough data point, we found it took about 21 minutes to load 222MB of files onto the Personal Jukebox—roughly 10MB a minute, a decent speed, though not as exciting as if the Personal Jukebox used a Fast Ethernet connection. The illustration below shows a music transfer in progress.

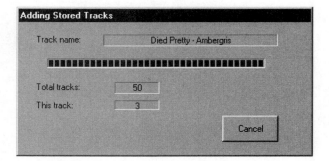

97

Use the Sony VAIO Music Clip

In this section, we'll walk you through the highlights and lowlights of the Sony VAIO Music Clip (about $299 street), an innovatively designed player that represents a belated first entry by Sony into the MP3 hardware-player market. Lowlights? Yes—despite looking wickedly cool and delivering good-sounding music, the VAIO Music Clip proves to be poorly designed and awkward to use. What's more, it's saddled with software that seems to have come from the seventh level of Hell. (Actually, a better title for this section would be "*Don't* Use the Sony VAIO Music Clip.")

You can find the VAIO Music Clip at many retail outlets, both physical and online. If you're having difficulty finding it, try Sony Xtras Direct (`http://xtrasdirect.sel.sony.com/`).

The VAIO Music Clip (shown above) is about the size of your average fat highlighter pen, and without its one AA battery weighs little more than such a pen. It has 64MB RAM, but 3.2MB of that is used for its operating system, leaving you with 60.8MB for music; it has no expansion slot, which shouldn't be surprising given how small it is. It comes with a pair of lightweight earbud headphones—the kind with a headband—and Sony's OpenMG Jukebox software, which runs on Windows 98. It has a three-position DSP: Jazz, Pop, and Rock. It includes an Auto Volume Limiter System (AVLS) to prevent you from hammering your ears too hard. And it connects to your PC via an admirably compact USB cable.

Looks great, doesn't it? So what's not to like? Well, here's a quick laundry list:

◆ You can't use standard MP3 files on it: To get audio onto the VAIO Music Clip, you need to convert it to either the OpenMG MP3 format (which most other players shun like the plague) or the ATRAC3 format. Conversion is slow and tedious, and wastes space on your hard drive (unless you delete your MP3 files, which we're betting you won't want to do). And ATRAC3 files and OpenMG MP3 files are locked to the computer on which you recorded or converted them—you can check them out to a portable player, play them there, and check them back in, but you cannot move them to another computer and then play them. If you try, you'll run into messages such as the one shown below. (We think it's the song's integrity that OpenMG Jukebox is doubting, not our integrity, but we're not willing to bet.)

N O T E ATRAC3 files recorded at the 105kbps bitrate are about 80 percent the size of MP3 files recorded at 128kbps and sound as if they have the same quality. OpenMG MP3 files are about 1 percent larger than 128kbps MP3 files and sound the same.

◆ The controls are small and fiddly. Because the player is so small, you have to use a Shift mode to access some of the features.

◆ The AVLS setting seems too high for hearing safety—at least, to our ears. Even when AVLS is on, the VAIO Music Clip delivers far higher sound levels than other AVLS-limited equipment (CD players and cassette players) we've used. Be careful if you use this feature.

◆ The regular DSP setting sounds fine, the Jazz DSP setting is pleasant, and the Pop DSP setting is crisp and just about right—but the Rock DSP setting is a muddy, bass-heavy disaster.

◆ The shirt-pocket clip is too weak to be much use. The neck strap is a better carrying option—but you're not going to be exercising with this player unless you jerry-rig a more secure carrying arrangement.

◆ The software is confusing, and some of the English is atrocious. The illustration below shows a small example of what you'll have to interpret.

◆ In order to download music from the Internet directly and use it with the VAIO Music Clip, you need to register your VAIO Music Clip download and install the Electronic Music Distribution (EMD) software. The registration form is only slightly less intrusive than a census Long Form and includes *required* fields such as the manufacturer of your computer. Optional questions quiz you on your age, occupation, income, and the number of MP3 files you download from the Internet. The form claims that "with your permission" it will allow "Sony and its affiliates to bring special offers to you"—but it gives you no way to opt out from this generous offer. And at this writing—*months* after the release of the VAIO Music Clip—the EMD software was not available, crippling a significant part of the VAIO Music Clip's functionality.

Installing the VAIO Music Clip

Before you plug in the VAIO Music Clip, you need to install OpenMG Jukebox. The Setup routine quickly gives you notice of Sony's attitude: After the initial Welcome screen, you get hit with an Input of CD Key dialog box for a 20-digit code. (Earth to Sony: We doubt anybody is going to want to rip off copies of this software.) Get this right, and you get to choose the destination location for the folder and "contents," and program folder. The "contents" is where music will be stored, so you may want to specify a different location from the default \Sony\OpenMG Jukebox\Packages\. Make sure there's plenty of space on the drive—this is where all your music will be stored, and OpenMG Jukebox will be viciously unhappy if you try to move it.

Setup will then install a stack of software and will prompt you to add OpenMG Jukebox Startup to your system tray. If you use your VAIO Music Clip aggressively, this may be a good idea.

It will then prompt you to set up OpenMG Recorder to be launched when you insert a CD. We don't think this is a good idea unless you're planning to rip your entire collection of CDs.

At the end of the installation, you'll need to restart your computer. Unlike most civilized software, this Setup program doesn't give you an option of restarting later. If you're running other software that you need to close, use Alt+Tab to switch to it and close it down before clicking the Finish button in the Setup Complete dialog box.

Once you've restarted your computer and logged in, connect the VAIO Music Clip to its USB cable, and you'll be in business.

Using the VAIO Music Clip

In order to get any music into the VAIO Music Clip, you have to get it into the ATRAC3 format or Sony's OpenMG MP3 format. If you haven't ripped your CDs yet, you can rip them directly to the ATRAC3 format using OpenMG Recorder. The first illustration on the next page shows OpenMG Recorder ripping away. In our testing, it managed better than real-time ripping, but trailed fast rippers such as MusicMatch Jukebox by a considerable margin.

WARNING Ripping with OpenMG Recorder takes an inordinate amount of processing power. Sony lists system requirements of a Pentium MMX 233 and 64MB RAM but recommends a Pentium II 400 or better. They're not kidding, either. One of our test machines, a Celeron-433 with 128MB RAM, was unable to play back audio without dropouts and interruptions while ripping with OpenMG Recorder.

If you already have MP3 files, you can convert them to ATRAC3 or OpenMG MP3 format by using Sony's included software. Be warned that the conversion process is slow. The illustration below shows what you'll see when you're converting a batch of files.

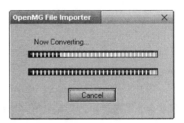

As you can see, there's no way to know which file is currently being converted, so unless you go spelunking in the folder you designated for "contents," you'll have no way of knowing how many files are left to convert. The top bar here shows the total progress, and the lower bar shows the progress on the current track—though it would sure be nice if the dialog box told you so. And get this—OpenMG Jukebox puts each converted file *into its own folder* along with its licensing information.

Clunkiness aside, OpenMG Jukebox is beset by awkward and confusing terminology. To get the tracks to the VAIO Music Clip, you choose Portable

Player ➤ Execute (*execute?*) or click the Start button. You *check out* a music file in order to put it onto the VAIO Music Clip. To get a file off the VAIO Music Clip again, you check it in again. Yes, you've got it—the metaphor is a library, and you have to return each copy of a file that you check out. OpenMG Jukebox implements the SDMI (Secure Digital Music Initiative) specification, which by default lets you have four copies of a track. Once you've put one copy of a track on the VAIO Music Clip, you then have three copies left in the library; when you check the track back in, you have four copies again.

OpenMG lets you create items called My Selects, which approximate to what other players and jukeboxes call playlists.

To be fair to the SDMI and OpenMG Jukebox, this system is workable enough for many people, and it undoubtedly helps protect the copyright holder's intellectual property. But compared to the free-and-easy world of MP3, OpenMG Jukebox feels like a straitjacket strapped down tight. Having to convert every track from MP3 to a secure format makes the VAIO Music Clip a hard sell indeed to the average North American consumer.

One piece of good news here: RealNetworks is integrating the ATRAC3 sound compression format and the OpenMG copyright-protection technology into RealJukebox, so you'll be able to use RealJukebox to transfer music from your computer onto the VAIO Music Clip and the Memory Stick Walkman, Sony's second entry in the portable-player stakes.

98 Use the Samsung Yepp

The Yepp, shown on the next page, is an ultraportable from Samsung that has a sleek, regularly shaped metallic case. You can get a 32MB Yepp, which is barely worth having, and a 64MB Yepp, which is a serious contender in the ultraportable-player arena and costs about $220 street. Each Yepp contains an expansion slot that can hold a memory card of up to 32MB, giving you 64MB total on the base model and 96MB on the advanced model.

The Yepp ships with its own software, named Yepp Explorer, and a custom version of RealJukebox that provides 128kbps encoding (in other words, better than the free version of RealJukebox, which can manage only 96kbps).

The Yepp ships with a parallel-port cable, but you can also get a USB cable. As usual, using the parallel port is slower than using USB, but it means that you can use the Yepp with older computers that do not have USB jacks.

Unlike many of its competitors, the Yepp supports recording via a built-in microphone. The mike and recording quality are suitable for voice notes but not for music. The Yepp has a seven-position DSP that gives you a good range of choices for different types of music, though the 3D settings tend to produce a muffled effect through headphones.

The Yepp software installs smoothly (with the usual restart) and is functional, but its interface is rough and clearly designed by someone for whom English was a second or subsequent language. Still, everything is understandable. The Yepp Explorer is on the minimalist side, providing none of the music-library functions of software such as the RioPort Audio Manager: Instead, you simply drag files to the Yepp Explorer and drop them there. We got on well with the Yepp Explorer because it let us manage our music effectively without forcing us to create the mother of all databases.

The illustration below shows the Yepp Explorer with its flash memory (in the left pane) stuffed to the gills, with a mere 17K left, and three tracks in the Yepp card external memory (in the right pane).

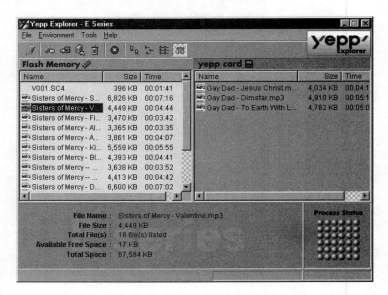

To arrange the tracks you drag to the Yepp into a playlist, choose File ➢ Play Order and work in the Play List dialog box, shown below.

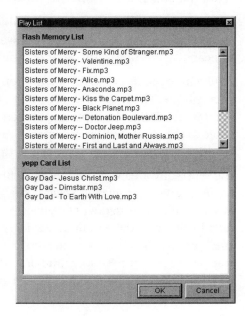

99 Use the i2Go eGo

The eGo from i2Go.com is a crossover player: It hovers on the borderline between ultraportable and portable both in size and in capacity, and it's designed for use both as a portable player and as a car player.

As you can see in the photograph below, the eGo is a handful. It takes two AA batteries, can hold one or two CompactFlash cards (either or both of which can be IBM Microdrives), and has an internal speaker. It connects to a Windows 95 or 98 PC via a hefty USB cable that's included in the package. Because the eGo uses CompactFlash cards, you can also load it by using a CompactFlash reader (attached to a desktop PC or a laptop) or a PC Card CompactFlash adapter.

Each of the eGo's two CompactFlash sockets can hold any size of Compact-Flash card. For example, a brace of 96MB cards gives you 192MB of memory, enough for more than three hours of music. Each Microdrive holds 340MB, so if you get two Microdrives, you'll have 680MB available—enough for about 11 hours of music.

The eGo comes with a full kit for car use, including a dashboard mount, a car power adapter, and a cassette adapter for directing output from the eGo into your car stereo.

As we mentioned earlier, the eGo eats AA batteries like nobody's business, getting only about 90 minutes out of a pair of heavy-duty batteries such as Duracell Ultras. Because of this ravenous consumption, you'll probably want to use rechargeable batteries if you use the eGo as a portable player—but be warned that with most rechargeables, you'll be looking at around an hour of battery life. Be further warned that if you use one or two Microdrives in the eGo, you'll need to run the player from an AC adapter or a car adapter—it is possible to run the Microdrives on battery power, but because running them on low batteries can damage the Microdrives, it's a really bad idea.

NOTE Unlike most other players, the eGo lets you copy or move music files from the player's storage onto your computer.

The eGo comes with MusicMatch Jukebox and the mp3Agent MP3-management software, together with a voice driver and voices for converting e-mail to audio files and storing them on the eGo for playback. Installation of mp3Agent is straightforward but (guess what) requires a reboot of your PC. You'll need to manually identify the USB driver on the CD when Windows announces that it has found an unidentified device.

After the reboot, the mp3Agent Configuration Wizard walks you through setting up your PC to communicate with the eGo via USB or a Compact-Flash adapter, selecting a music directory, creating a local playlist, setting up mp3Agent to send and receive e-mail, and connecting to playlists you've created at i2Go.com.

You'll then see mp3Agent. As you can see in the illustration on the next page, mp3Agent provides a two-pane interface: The left-hand pane contains trees for the Browser, Programs and Content, Portable Players (here, just the i2Go eGo), and My Computer, and the right-hand pane displays the contents of the current selection. In the illustration, the Audio folder on the eGo is selected. The status-bar readout shows how much space on the eGo is occupied and how much is free. (In this case, the eGo has a single 96MB CompactFlash card.)

To upload files to the eGo, you select them in the right-hand pane and drag them to the Audio folder on the eGo. You'll see the mp3Agent Tasks dialog box by default as the files are uploaded.

100 Play MP3 Files on a Palm-Size PC

In this section, we'll discuss briefly how you can play MP3 files on a Palm-size PC.

If you're considering a Palm-size PC and want to play MP3 files on it, keep these two key things in mind:

◆ First, make sure that it has full audio capabilities, including stereo playback. (Some Palm-size PCs do not support stereo.)

◆ Second, make sure it has plenty of storage space. Because MP3 files are typically a few megs each and Palm-size PCs are typically light on memory (8, 16, or 32MB for both applications and storage), you'll usually want a Palm-size PC with a CompactFlash slot. Apart from capacity, the key advantage of a CompactFlash card is speed: You can quickly transfer information (read: a boatload of MP3 files) to it from your PC by using a CompactFlash reader or a PC Card adapter, then slot it into the Palm-size PC and play them from there. This beats transferring MP3 files via the docking cable, which can take half an hour or more to transfer a single track.

Using the Windows Media Player for Palm-Size PCs

Your best bet for playing MP3 files on a Palm-size PC is to use the Windows Media Player for Palm-size PCs.

Download the Windows Media Player for Palm-size PCs from `http://www.microsoft.com/windows/mediaplayer/en/download/WinPortPlay.asp`. If you're not already registered with Microsoft, you'll need to do so, but after that, the download is free. At this writing, there are three different versions of the Windows Media Player for Palm-size PCs available—one for the Cassiopeia E-100 or E-105, one for the Compaq Aero 1500 and 2100, and one for the Hewlett Packard Jornada 430se—so make sure you get the right one.

NOTE You can also download skins for the Windows Media Player for Palm-size PCs from the same site.

After downloading it, run the executable file. It will run you through a CE installation routine involving making sure your player is connected, accepting an end-user license agreement, and agreeing to the default application install directory (or choosing a different directory). After devoting a small chunk of your life to watching the progress indicator crawl along the Installing Applications dialog box as Windows forces the application down the serial cable, you'll see the Application Downloading Complete dialog box, instructing you to see if your Palm-size PC needs any further attention. Do so, and you should be ready to rock.

Other Options for Playing Music on Palm-Size PCs

If for some reason you choose not to use the Windows Media Player for Palm-size PCs, here are a couple of other possibilities for playing music on a Palm-size PC:

Hum   Hum for CE from UtopiaSoft (http://www.utopiasoft.com) lets you play actual MP3 files on a Palm-size PC. Hum provides an easy-to-use interface and supports skins. In May 2000, UtopiaSoft started giving Hum away free—good news for everyone except those who'd paid $19.95 for it earlier.

Mobile Audio Player   Some Palm-size PCs, including the Cassiopeia E-100 and E-105, come with Mobile Audio Player, a Windows CE application for playing music in the WMA (Windows Media Architecture) format. Mobile Audio Player isn't wonderful, because you have to convert the MP3 files to WMA format, but it does work. Here's the short version:

1. Dock your Palm-size PC so that it establishes a connection to the computer. (If you need to establish a connection manually, do so.)

2. On your PC, launch the Mobile Audio Player Manager application. (By default, it's installed to the Windows Media group on the Start menu.)

3. In the left-hand list box, navigate to and select the file you want to transfer.

4. In the right-hand list box, select the folder on the Palm-size PC that will receive the track. Mobile Audio Player suggests using the My Documents folder.

5. Click the → button to convert the file to WMA format and transfer it. This typically takes several times as long as the playing time of the file.

6. On the Palm-size PC, you can then play the tracks by launching the Mobile Audio Player (Start ➢ Programs ➢ Mobile Audio Player) and using its play controls.

101 Play MP3 Files on a Hand-Held PC

Another quick section, this one discusses how to play MP3 files on a hand-held PC.

As you'll recall if you don't have one, a hand-held PC isn't a Palm-size PC but rather a small computer that has a keyboard and runs Windows CE. Some of the more successful hand-held PCs have been the IBM WorkPad Z50 and the HP Jornada hand-helds (in case you're confused, IBM and HP also use the WorkPad and Jornada names for their Palm-size PCs).

Hand-held PCs have been going out of fashion in the last few months as of this writing, which is both bad news and good news for their fans: The bad news is that hand-held PCs aren't going to be very important in the future of computing; the good news is that right now you can pick one up for a song. If you do, make sure it has either a good amount of onboard memory or a CompactFlash socket that you can use for MP3 files. You'll usually do better with CompactFlash, because you can load it with music far more quickly than you can get the music to the hand-held's onboard memory using the serial cable.

Your best bet for playing MP3 files on a hand-held PC is to get Hum from UtopiaSoft. (As we mentioned in the previous section, Hum is now free.) Read the Hardware Compatibility List at UtopiaSoft's Web site first to make sure that your hand-held is up to the job, and be warned that some hand-helds can manage only mono rather than stereo.

Here's what to do:

1. Download the latest version of Hum from UtopiaSoft's Web site (http://www.utopiasoft.com).

2. Unzip the distribution file to a holding location of your choice.

3. Double-click the Setup.exe file to run the Setup routine.

4. Read the readme file that Setup displays, then click the Next button in the UtopiaSoft Hum Setup dialog box.

5. Agree to the end user license agreement.

6. In the Installing Applications dialog box, accept the default application install directory (or specify a different directory if you prefer).

7. Twiddle your thumbs and toes vigorously while Hum is installed.

8. When the Application Downloading Complete dialog box instructs you to check *your mobile device screen to see if additional steps are necessary to complete this installation*, do so. Chances are, you'll find your hand-held resting quietly.

9. Choose Start ➤ Programs ➤ UtopiaSoft Hum to launch Hum, and it'll start walking you through the creation of a new playlist.

102 Play MP3 Files in Your Car

Once you're heavily into MP3, you'll want to be able to play MP3 files wherever you go. The good news is that there are already a number of ways to play MP3 audio in your car; the bad news is that most of them will set you back some serious bucks.

In this section, we'll examine two main ways of playing MP3 audio in your car, discussing their advantages and disadvantages.

Connecting Your Portable Player to Your Car Stereo

The first way of adding MP3 to your car, and the least expensive, is to connect your portable player to your existing car stereo. The advantages of doing so are that the cost can be minimal, the sound quality high, and the task trivial. The disadvantages are that the task can be Herculean, the sound quality horrible, and the amount of music you can take disappointing.

In other words, it all depends.

The first thing it depends on is your car stereo. Some car stereos have an auxiliary input into which you can slap a signal from a portable player. This input might be a miniplug socket on the front face of the car stereo, but it's more likely to be a pair of wires with RCA jacks protruding from the back of the player (or a socket into which such wires would go). So you'll have to go hunting for it, and if professionals installed the stereo for you, they probably bundled up and hid the extra wire, so you may have to dig it out. If you find this wire, you'll probably need an adapter for it, which means a trip to your local car stereo outlet (or RadioShack) for some high-quality connectors. You'll then most likely need to enable the auxiliary input on the stereo and switch to it, and you'll be in business.

If your stereo doesn't have an auxiliary input, but it has a cassette player, your best bet is to use a cassette adapter. Some portable players, such as the i2Go eGo and some RCA Lyra packages, come with cassette adapters included in the package. If yours didn't, you should be able to buy one easily enough either at retail or online. Once you've got that, plug it into the player and the stereo, flip any switches necessary, and you're away.

If your stereo doesn't have a cassette player either, you may be able to patch your portable into your existing wiring by using an RF modulator. Unless you're an electronics wiz, you probably should let your car stereo dealership handle this task.

The second thing it depends on is (obviously enough) your portable player. If you're planning to use the player in the car, make sure that it has enough memory for your needs; that it can use a car adapter for power if it's at all heavy on the batteries; and that it produces a sound signal of a quality high enough for your car stereo.

Getting an In-Dash Player or In-Car Jukebox

The other way of adding MP3 to your car is to get a custom in-dash player or in-car jukebox. An in-dash player fits into the car-stereo slot in the dashboard of the car, while an in-car jukebox usually lives in the trunk and feeds into a dashboard unit that acts as a controller, in an arrangement similar to that used by in-car CD jukeboxes (also known as *CD changers*).

Both these options are for the serious MP3 fan because they involve a serious chunk of dough (think several hundred to a thousand dollars).

An in-dash player also means getting rid of your car's current CD player or cassette deck (or having one of the two dangling loosely or strapped to the dash with duct tape).

The advantage of the in-dash player is clear—it doesn't take up extra space. The advantage of the jukebox is that the amount of space available for the main unit is limited by the size of the trunk rather than the size of the dash slot, so (in most cars) you can include a much larger player.

Most of the jukeboxes currently available or in development range in size from a shoebox to a VCR and have one or more hard drives inside. Most of the in-dash players use a hard drive or two, though some are CD drives that can read both regular audio CDs and data CDs containing MP3 or other audio files. (If you remember that a CD can hold about 11 hours of MP3 files at 128K, these CD drives should sound pretty good to you.)

At this writing, there are about two dozen competing products in this category, most of them from small companies who, though selling energetically over the Web and developing their products fast enough to give larger companies indigestion, have yet to make a major impact. Given that the picture will certainly have changed by the time you read this, we won't attempt to round up the current players. Instead, we'll point you to a good source of information on car players: http://www.mp3car.com. And in the next section we'll examine one in-car player that has more or less broken free of the pack—the empeg car.

If you're in the market for an in-dash or in-car player, these are the main considerations:

Price   Basically, whichever in-car player you're looking at, the price will sting like grated ginger on road-rash. We can't help you much with that except to advise you to shop around as much as possible.

Size   An in-dash player is going to look much more attractive than a jukebox if you've got a small trunk and aren't prepared to sacrifice your luggage for your listening.

Medium   CD or hard drive—or another medium such as Zip drive? Decide what's going to work best for you.

Data Transfer   How will you get the files onto the player? If the player has a non-removable hard drive and is permanently installed in your car, you're probably looking at running an Ethernet network connection out to the street, testing the length limitations of USB cables, or hauling your computer out to the garage. (Hint: Ethernet's the best solution here, as it can go up to 328 feet under typical conditions, and good Category 5 cable is strong enough to snare a few skateboarders without interrupting data transfer.)

103 Use the empeg car

The empeg car, from the UK company Empeg Ltd. (`http://www.empeg.com`), is one of the longest-lived and leading in-dash MP3 players for the car. We evaluated an empeg car Mark 1 player for this book; the empeg car Mark 2, due in for June 2000, wasn't available in time, but promises a number of significant improvements, of which we'll mention a couple in this section.

In a nutshell, the empeg car is a player built around one or two hard drives and an FM tuner crammed into a car-stereo case and is designed to fit into the car-stereo slot in your dashboard. The empeg car Mark 1, shown in the photograph below, has a somewhat stark and functional faceplate and boasts only a choice of display colors (blue, amber, or green). The Mark 2 will have a much more stylish faceplate and an additional color choice—red.

The empeg car comes in a variety of capacities offering up to 36GB of storage; as you'd expect, the larger the capacity, the higher the cost, but (as usual) we recommend getting the most storage you can afford. As you'll see in a minute, it's easy enough to add music to and remove music from the empeg car. But if you're anything like us, you'll want to gradually build a library of all the music you might ever possibly want to listen to in your car, and just keep it on your empeg car—that way, you'll never be without the tracks you need.

The empeg car is powered by penguins: It runs Linux on a 220MHz Strong-ARM processor and 8MB RAM. In case you're slavering for specifics, it uses a custom in-car DSP and has a five-band equalizer for each of the four output channels. (Enough details? No? If you're still slavering, check out the tech pages at `http://www.empeg.com` for all the minutiae we haven't mentioned.)

The Mark 1 has four buttons on its faceplate that you can use to navigate its menus from short range, plus a remote control that gives you many more buttons and more range—good for both backseat music drivers and for using the empeg car with your home stereo. The Mark 1's menu system and controls are a little clumsy—you have to drill down through a menu or two in order to perform almost any action—and the unit suffers from not having an easily accessible volume control. (We understand that the Mark 2's faceplate will provide more direct access to primary functions such as volume and track navigation.)

We mentioned home stereo a moment ago: The empeg car is designed to play a dual role. It comes with a removable chassis, so that you can yank it quickly from the dashboard of your car and carry it inside to connect it to your PC or your stereo. For non-car use, the empeg car uses a standard power cable and a DC adapter, so you can plug it in anywhere.

By connecting it to your PC, you can load and unload music from the empeg car; by connecting it to your stereo, you can use the empeg car as a stereo component. Chances are, it won't match your stereo components for size, but the Mark 1's discreet dark faceplate and colored display makes a stylish enough addition to many a system.

The empeg car connects to your PC via either a serial cable or a USB cable. If you have any choice in the matter, go with the USB cable because file transfer will be up to an order of magnitude faster with it than with the serial cable. Note that you'll need to keep the serial cable in case you want to upgrade the software on the empeg car unit with a later release—for this task, the USB cable is of no use.

The empeg car uses custom software punningly named *emplode* that installs easily on Windows 95 or 98 using a standard InstallShield installation routine involving nothing more challenging than entering the player's serial number (which you should find on top of the unit). As usual with USB-connected hardware, you do best to install the software before connecting the unit via USB—if you connect the hardware first, Windows starts demanding a driver information file for the unknown device it has just encountered.

Once you've installed emplode and plugged in the empeg car, you're ready to start transferring files. emplode, shown in the next illustration, provides a simple interface that lets you easily manage the contents of the empeg car.

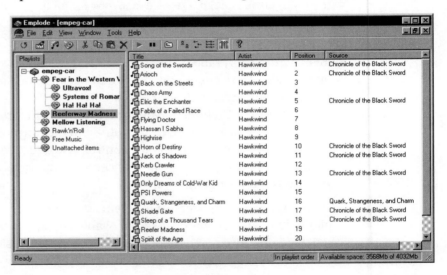

You can add tunes and playlists to the empeg car. (A *tune* is essentially the same thing as a track or a song.) You can also nest one playlist within another or keep all of your playlists at the empeg-car root of the tree.

Once you've arranged tunes and playlists to your heart's content in emplode, synchronize the changes to the empeg car unit by issuing a Synchronize command. Depending on how much music you're transferring to the empeg car, synchronization can take anything from a few minutes to a few hours. During synchronization, emplode displays the Synchronising dialog box, shown on the next page, to tell you what's happening. In the Operation group box, you can see the operation that's being performed—*Uploading to unit*—and the track (item) being processed (*Dateline*).

NOTE You can't download files off the empeg car, though you can of course delete them.

When you've finished loading the empeg car, power it down, detach it from your PC and from its power source, and take it out to your car. Then get your motor runnin' and head out on the highway…

104 Choose an MP3 Home Stereo Component

Portable players and car players are well and good, but if you rely on MP3 to fulfill all or most of your music needs, you'll probably want to get an MP3 player with greater capacity that you can plug directly into your home stereo and leave there. (The alternative is to connect your PC to your stereo system, which we'll discuss in the next section.)

At this writing, the field of home-stereo components is either disappointingly thin or just starting to grow encouragingly, depending on whether you think the glass is half-empty, half-full, or filled with the wrong liquid. Several companies are racing to bring products to market, but unfortunately, there have been several delays in the race.

At this writing, the top contenders are the AudioReQuest from ReQuest, Inc. (http://www.request.com) and the SongBank from Lydstrom (http://www.lydstrom.com). Both are due to be released shortly.

The AudioReQuest is a stereo component–like CD player with a built-in 17GB hard drive. At 128K, that'll hold 320 hours of music—enough to keep you running for a solid month or so. You can rip from the CD directly to the hard drive, or you can copy existing files to the AudioReQuest.

The AudioReQuest has a built-in LCD display but also can interface with your television if you want to get a bigger picture of what's on it, if you want to use its custom GUI, or if you want visualizations to enhance your appreciation of the music.

The AudioReQuest comes with a remote control, but you can also add a keyboard, either through the AT keyboard port or through one of the USB ports. The AudioReQuest can connect to your PC via its parallel port, via USB, or via its built-in Ethernet port, so you shouldn't have any problem getting music onto it.

Details are a little scarce about the SongBank, but it too is a stereo component–like CD player with a built-in hard drive capable of holding something like 7,000 songs.

105 Connect Your PC to Your Stereo System

If you have a good component stereo system, you'll probably want to connect your PC to it so that you can play MP3 tracks through the stereo and record MP3 files from your cassettes and LPs. If your hi-fi system has a receiver (or separate amplifier) with a graphical equalizer, you can make good any shortcomings—real or perceived—in the equalization your MP3 player delivers.

Connecting your PC to your stereo system is a little more difficult than getting the right cable and plugging it into the right sockets at either end. We'll take each step from the top.

Typically, you'll need a quality cable with a ⅛-inch stereo mini-plug for your computer's end and two RCA plugs on the receiver's end. Check your equipment before you go to buy a cable because some high-end sound cards offer different outputs, and some receivers boast a ⅛-inch stereo input jack for connecting personal electronics such as portable CD players. Make sure the ⅛-inch mini-plug is stereo—it's easy to get a mono one by mistake, and it'll sound horrible. If this discussion sends you rooting through the back of your closet for old cables, a stereo mini-plug has two black plastic rings around its prong, while a mono mini-plug has only one. If you want to use your PC to record MP3 files from your cassette deck or record player, you'll need a second cable of the same sort.

Plug the mini-plug into the line-out socket on your sound card—not the speaker socket, because that has amplification built in. Then plug the RCA plugs into a free pair of input jacks on the amplifier. If your receiver has auxiliary jacks (typically labeled AUX or AUX1 and AUX2), those are a good bet. These days, the input most likely to be free on your amplifier is the one you mustn't connect your PC to—the Phono input, which is built to be more sensitive than the other inputs so that it may interface with the feeble output of a record player. Even if the sound card doesn't smoke the Phono input on first contact, the sound will be grotesquely distorted—worse than Korn feeding back on an overdriven boombox dancing in a metal trashcan in a boiler factory.

Check the connections and make sure the input selection button on the receiver is set to the input jacks to which you connected the cable from the PC. Then set the volume on both your MP3 player and your receiver way low and start an MP3 track playing on the PC. Turn the volume up a little at a time at each end until you reach a good volume—or the police arrive.

Once that's working, you can set up a connection to carry sound from your stereo to your sound card. You'll want to do this if you need to make MP3 files from your band's old cassettes. Grab another cable with the same specs as the first, and slide the RCA plugs onto a set of output jacks on the receiver. Plug the mini-plug into the line-in jack on your computer's sound card (*not* the microphone jack). Choose the right output channel on the receiver, and test the connection to make sure the stereo is delivering sound to the PC and that the sound is clean and undistorted.

Top 11 MP3 Troubleshooting Tips

In this part, we present our Top 11 tips for troubleshooting MP3. These tips cover both hardware and software, concentrating on the types of problems that most people ask for help on.

Sad to say, there are far more things that can go wrong with your MP3 setup than we can cover in this section. We suggest you use this section as a starting point for troubleshooting problems you run into when ripping, playing, and downloading MP3 files. Remember that we can't see what your problem is, and you may have invented a problem that nobody else has experienced.

106 I Can't Rip Digitally

If your MP3 ripper won't rip *anything* digitally, your CD drive may not be able to hack it, or the drivers may not be up to par. Some experts say as many as a third of the CD drives out there aren't up to digital recording. The good news is that these are mostly older drives, not ones you might buy down at your local Three Guys and a Goat PCs nowadays; the bad news is that Three Guys (or the Goat) might have installed one of these impotent drives for you a couple of years back.

Here's what to do:

Get new ASPI drivers   Doing so may not fix the problem, but it's worth a try first because this will typically be the cheapest solution.

Get a second opinion   Try a different ripper. Some rippers are much better than others at tolerating older drives. For example, we have an old 8× drive that wobbles badly enough to make the computer's case vibrate loudly when it runs a CD it doesn't like. MusicMatch Jukebox records fine from this drive, while another jukebox (one we chose not to cover in this book) affects to believe it doesn't exist.

Record in analog mode   It'll be slower and the results will almost always not sound as good, but it will get you started and rocking until you're ready for the final solution, which is the next item.

Get a new CD drive   Before you buy the drive, troll the Web for recommendations. Read MP3 sites and newsgroups for picks and pans. Then get something good that'll last you a year or two.

If your MP3 ripper won't rip *a particular track* digitally, the CD may be scratched or may be suffering from *bit-rot* (loss of digital data). Test for scratches first: Try cleaning the CD with a soft cloth and see if that improves things. If it improves them a bit but not quite enough, or if you have a stack of CDs in a similar semi-trashed condition, you may want to invest in a CD-buffer, which cleans the CD more gently and effectively than most people can manage by hand.

If cleaning the CD has no apparent effect, try ripping it on another computer (if you can get your hands on one). If even that doesn't work, you may have to give up on that particular track.

107 My Computer Rips but Sucks

Here's what to do if your computer meets all the specifications to run a ripper but sucks big rocks when you try to make it do so:

Avoid running your computer low on memory Generally speaking, during a long computing session, any computer running Windows leaks memory and system resources the way your '69 Duster leaks oil. If your computer seems to be running out of resources, close Windows down and restart the computer. Doing so should maximize the amount of memory and system resources the computer has available. If everything's still miserable, consider adding RAM to bring your computer up to a decent amount—64MB minimum, 128MB better, and more if you have the slots free and the cash burning a hole in your shorts.

Shut all other windows to minimize overhead To minimize the overhead on your computer, shut any windows you don't absolutely need running at this particular point. (That means all windows except the ripper.) If you can catch any background processes that are running, nail them too. A great example is the Microsoft Office Find Fast indexing utility, which runs when it thinks your computer isn't busy, judging by the amount of keyboard and mouse activity that's been happening. On a slow computer, Find Fast can royally screw up ripping.

Stop running other processor-intensive applications Don't run any other processor-intensive applications when you're ripping CDs. Because most MP3 rippers need large amounts of processing power to compress and encode MP3 files successfully, any other application that's trying to hog the processor will cause problems. (If you don't know what's processor intensive and what isn't, avoid running any other application when ripping and see what happens.)

NOTE Operating systems with preemptive multitasking (such as Windows 2000, NT, and Linux) can handle multiple demanding applications successfully: When an application is trying to hog the processor, they drop the hammer on it lightly until it desists. Windows 95 and Windows 98 use some preemptive multitasking, but older applications still run in a cooperative multitasking mode, which means they can grab more than their due share of processor cycles (and, if ambitious, can crash the whole computer). The Macintosh also suffers from a cooperative multitasking model. If you're having problems ripping CDs on an adequately powered Mac, try avoiding running other applications and tasks at the same time.

Defragment the drive If your hard drive is fragmented, any file of any size will be spread about in different areas of it, and any program that creates or opens files has to do a lot more work assembling the different pieces of the file. Try defragging the drive to improve performance. For Windows 95/98, use the built-in defragmenter (Start ➢ Programs ➢ Accessories ➢ System Tools ➢ Disk Defragmenter); for Windows NT or Windows 2000, use Diskeeper from Software Shelf International Inc. (http://www.softwareshelf.com).

If it's a laptop, give up We're overstating this a bit, but if you have a powerful laptop that won't rip worth squat, you may have to give up on ripping with it. As you'd imagine, the CD drives on laptops are significantly different from the CD drives on desktop computers. In layman's terms, they're built to withstand much more punishment and to come out smiling. Because of the compromises involved in making sure the drive can withstand somersaults in your carry-on luggage as you race through Stapleton against a tide of what passes for humanity, sometimes the smile may be somewhat crooked. Laptop CD drives typically deliver a much lower data rate than desktop CD drives, and you may not be able to get a decent data rate or recording sound from a laptop CD drive. The other factor is that laptops tend to have small, proprietary (and often cheap) sound chip sets that deliver lower quality than the much larger and more complex sound boards that you can insert in a desktop computer—and you haven't a hope in hell of upgrading them.

108 My Computer Rips Fine, but the Tracks Sound Lousy

So your computer rips fine—without any clicking, popping, or stuttering—but the music in the resulting tracks sounds, uh, disappointing? Look at these four possible solutions first:

Fix your MP3 player   First, make sure there's nothing obviously wrong with your MP3 player. For example, if you've wound up or down the pitch on a player that supports pitch changing, it'll sound fast or slow. If you've applied some bizarre equalization unintentionally, that'll change the sound too. If you've applied a special effect (for example, by using a Winamp audio plug-in), that too could make the tracks sound peculiar.

Increase the bitrate   If you record at radio quality, the tracks will sound as bad as music on the radio. Use a bitrate of 128kbps for most music— more if your ripper supports it, your ears demand it, and you have the hard disk space. Usually there'll be no point in going above 192kbps unless you have storage to burn.

Get a better encoder   The quality of the encoder you're using affects the quality of the tracks produced. Fraunhofer's encoder is well regarded (as it should be—you'll remember Fraunhofer put together the MP3 format) and is used by rippers such as MusicMatch Jukebox. If you're using Bill's Best Freebie Ripper based on the UltraDog encoder and are disappointed by the results, see if using a different encoder helps.

Get a better sound card   Have you got a decent sound card, or are you making do with one that doesn't have enough voices to do the music justice? Unless you're using a laptop, you can easily upgrade the sound card.

Get better speakers   Are your speakers good enough? There's no sense in ruining good music by playing it through $10 speakers. Get a solid subwoofer set as discussed in *2. Get the Right Hardware*.

109 No—They Sound *Really* Lousy

If MP3 files you've downloaded sound totally screwed up, they may have gotten mangled in the download process. Either try downloading them again (if you have a fast connection) or try using a utility such as Uncook 95 or Detox to clean the garbage out of them, as discussed in *72. Uncook Cooked Files with Uncook 95*.

110 The Tracks Go Snap, Crackle, and Pop

If you're getting a lot of clicks and pops on your MP3 files, you should be able to improve things in one or more of the following ways.

If the tracks you're complaining about are ones that you've ripped yourself, try ripping them again. Set the recording rate lower to minimize the number of read errors; in extreme cases, you may want to rip at less than playing speed to get good results.

If you have any choice in the matter, rip on a good sound card rather than a card that's merely okay or actively lousy. (As we mentioned before, if you have only a laptop, you may not have much choice in sound cards. With a desktop, you should be on more solid ground.)

If your ripper offers error correction, turn it on. You'll recall that error correction slows down recording speeds on most CD drives known to mankind—but if you're getting poor results, you should be glad to take the extra time in ripping. For example, in MusicMatch Jukebox, choose Options ➤ Settings to display the Settings dialog box, click the Recorder tab to display the Recorder page, select the Digital option button and the Error Correction check box in the CD Recording Mode group box, and click the OK button.

111 The Graphical Equalizer on My Player/Ripper Doesn't Work

You'll hate us for pointing this out, but you've probably forgotten to turn the graphical equalizer on. If you're using Winamp or MusicMatch Jukebox, click that tiny On button so that it shows a light-green light. If you're using Sonique, select the Equalizer Enabled check box on the Audio Enhancement screen. You get the idea.

112 I Can't Get Any Sound out of My Speakers

Assuming you've made sure that your sound card and software are configured correctly, you're probably looking at a minor hardware problem if your speakers won't produce any sound. So try these:

Fix the cabling   The #1 hardware problem in this area is that you've screwed up the cabling in some way. It's all too easy to do, but it should be even easier to fix. Make sure the cables are plugged securely into the right jacks—move the computer if necessary so that you can see those tiny letters engraved on the sound card between the jacks. If the volume is unacceptably low and you can't adjust the sound from the computer, chances are you've plugged the cable into the line-out socket rather than the speaker socket.

Power on   If you're using a powered speaker set, make sure it's plugged in and switched on. If you're playing music through your stereo, make sure the right source is selected and that you're not monitoring the tape input by accident.

Volume up   You do have your computer outputting some volume, don't you? You haven't muted it accidentally? Just checking…

113 CDDB Doesn't Work

If you're online, you'll want to use CDDB to help you rip and enjoy digital music. If you're having problems using CDDB, try the following:

Use a different CDDB server   If your CDDB server appears unresponsive, it may be swamped or sleeping. Try another CDDB server and see if things improve.

Use a different protocol   If your CDDB connection times out, try connecting via a different protocol—switch from TCP/IP to HTTP (or vice versa).

A proxy upon your house   Are you using a proxy server to access the Internet? Some versions of MusicMatch Jukebox and other programs are not able to access CDDB successfully through a proxy server. Check for an update to the product; try using an HTTP server; or try a direct (non-proxy) connection.

114 MP3 Plays When I Want to Download and Save It

If clicking the link to download an MP3 track from a Web site (such as MP3.com) and saving it to disk in Internet Explorer causes the track to start streaming instead, try right-clicking the link and choosing Save Target As from the context menu.

115 The Wrong MP3 Player Starts When I Open an MP3 File

If the wrong MP3 player—say, Winamp instead of Sonique—starts up when you double-click an MP3 file to open it, the player that appears has probably stolen the association for the MP3 file type in the Windows Registry. Go back to *65. Choose a Default MP3 Player under Windows* for instructions on how to assign and reassign file associations.

116 Downloading Files Is So Slooooow!

Yeah. Ain't life rough? But seriously—we went over all this at the beginning of the book. Here's the short version:

◆ If you can get a cable connection or a digital subscriber line (DSL), get it.

◆ If not, get an ISDN line (integrated services digital network).

◆ If you can't even get ISDN, see if you can afford satellite service.

◆ Failing that, tweak your Internet connection and/or get dual modems.

INDEX

Note to the Reader: Throughout this index **boldfaced** page numbers indicate primary discussions of a topic. *Italicized* page numbers indicate illustrations.

Here's the brief version of the CD is stuffed with MP3 tools and music. (See the file on the CD for details.)

More Than 150 MP3 Tracks

Nearly ten hours of high-quality music—everything from soothing electronica to cutting-edge metal.

MP3 Players

- ◆ Winamp (Windows)
- ◆ Sonique (Windows)
- ◆ MACAST (Macintosh)
- ◆ SoundApp (Macintosh)

MP3 Ripper/Jukebox Software

- ◆ MusicMatch Jukebox 5
- ◆ RealJukebox

SHOUTcast Broadcasting Software

- ◆ SHOUTcast DSP plug-in for Winamp